Bottom Line's

Best-Ever Kitchen Secrets

Joan Wilen and Lydia Wilen

Bottom Line
Books
www.BottomLineSecrets.com

Table of Contents

Foreword.. vii

Introduction viii

About the Authors..................................x

A Word from the Authors...........................x

Chapter 1 • The Best-Ever Kitchen Secrets

Safety...1
   Fire 1
   Distilled White Vinegar 2
   Food Handling 2
   Plastic Wrap in the Microwave......................2

Cleaning Basics 3
   Make-It-Yourself Scouring Powder 3
   Dish Detergent Mixture 3
   Dish Detergent Substitute 3
   Steel Wool Tips 3
   Deodorize and Disinfect Sponges....................3
   Rubber Gloves 4
   Wrap It Up..4

Appliances..4
   Cleaning a Can Opener 4
   Cleaning a Blender 5
   Cleaning a Toaster 5
   Cleaning a Drip Coffee Maker 5
   Cleaning a Coffee Grinder/Mill 5
   Cleaning a Waffle Iron..................................6
   Cleaning a Hand Mixer/Electric
      Mixer 6
   Cleaning a Food Processor 6
   Cleaning a Microwave Oven...........................6
   Cleaning a Stove or Range 7
   Cleaning a Refrigerator.................................8

Optimizing Refrigerator Efficiency 9
Cleaning and Defrosting A Freezer...............10
Optimizing Freezer Efficiency.......................10
Cleaning a Dishwasher 11
Cleaning a Garbage Disposal........................12

Pots & Pans...12
   Removing Stuck-on and
      Almost-Burned Food..............................12
   Cleaning Burned Pots/Pans 13
   Caring for Aluminum Pots 13
   Caring for Stainless Steel Pots 13
   Caring for Cast-Iron Cookware 13
   Caring for Clay Cookware 14

Glass & Crystal 14
   Caring for Glassware 14
   Caring for "The Good Crystal".....................15
   Cleaning Crystal Vases 15

China 16
   Cleaning Stains 16

CorningWare 16
   Cleaning CorningWare 17

Everything *and* the Kitchen Sink......................17
   Cleaning a Porcelain Sink............................17
   Unclogging a Sink Drain..............................17
   Preventing Clogged Drains...........................17
   Removing Jar Labels and Glue......................18
   Jar Opening Made Easy 18
   Make Life Easier for the Chief
      Bottle Washer 18
   Starchy Protection.......................................19
   Washing Wood Salad Bowls 19
   Stacking Cookware 19
   Cleaning a Garbage Can 19

Taking Care of Kitchen Knives......................19
Taking Care of Scissors......................20
Caring for a Cutting Board or
    Butcher's Block 20
Caring for All Types of Countertops............21
Cleaning a Grater......................21
Cleaning a Thermos......................22
What's That Smell?......................22
Removing Stains from a Plastic
    Container......................22
Cleaning a Highchair Tray......................22

Products **23**

Chapter 2 • The Best-Ever Food Secrets

Food A to Z **25**

Chapter 3 • Magical Recipes 69

Chapter 4 • Easy Holiday & Party Plans

Invitations **79**

Place Cards......................**80**

Napkins & Napkin Rings......................**81**

Table Decorations **81**
    Fruit-Flavored Fun......................81
    A Festive Touch......................82
    Centerpiece Enhanced 82
    Tablecloth Substitute......................82
    Glass Dinnerware Extraordinaire......................82

Candles **83**
    Lighten Up with Carbs 83
    Relighting a Candle......................83
    Drip Prevention......................83
    Candle Holders 83
    Candle Holder Alternatives 83
    Votive Candles 84
    Candle Cleaner 84
    Candle Storage......................84

Alcohol & Other Beverages **84**
    Wine 84
    Ice Cubes 86
    Other Beverages 00

Picnics **89**

Theme Gatherings......................**89**

Guest Treatment......................**90**
    Putting a Guest at Ease......................90
    Getting Rid of Dinner Guests 90
    Welcome a Sleepover Guest 90

Taking Pictures **90**
    Set Up Your Shot 90
    Positioning the Camera......................90
    Souvenir Photos 91

Holidays **91**
    New Year's 91
    St. Valentine's Day......................92
    Easter......................93
    Independence Day (4th of July) 94
    Halloween 95
    Thanksgiving Day......................96
    Chanukah......................99
    Christmas 101
    Kwanzaa 103

Products **106**

Chapter 5 • Our Favorite Folk Remedies

Conditions A to Z......................**108**

Products **147**

Chapter 6 • Head-to-Toe Magic

Skin Care for Your Body **149**
    Bumps Remover 149
    Soften Dry Elbows 149
    All-Natural Underarm Deodorant 150
    Prevent Body Odor......................150
    Temporary Varicose Vein Treatment 150

Skin Care for Your Face **150**
    Firming Facial......................150
    Skin Beautifying Mask 151
    Cleansing Mask......................151
    Unclog Pores......................151
    Face and Neck Toner......................151
    Oily Skin Balancer 151
    Exfoliation Scrub 151
    Make Pimples Disappear 151
    Combating Age Spots and Freckles......................152
    Skin Slougher for Dry, Chapped Lips......................152

Makeup......................**152**
    Lipstick 152
    Do-It-Yourself Lip Gloss 152
    Prevent Eye Shadow Buildup 153
    Eyeliner Protection......................153
    Keep Eyelashes Curled Longer 153
    Babyish Makeup Removers......................153
    Makeup Touchups......................153
    Eyebrow Taming 153

Hair **154**
   Hair Color and Dye 154
   Redhead and Brunette Luster 154
   Solutions for Chlorine-Damaged Hair 155
   Dry Shampoo 155
   Hair Volumizers 155
   Hair Thickener 155
   Freeze Frizz 155
   A Nutty Way to Care for Hair.............155
   Shine On..156
   Combat Oily Hair 156
   Soften and Moisturize Dry Hair 156
   Herbal Dandruff Remover.................156
   Combat an Itchy Scalp 157
   Homemade Conditioners 157
   Restore Bounce and Highlights 157
   An End to Split Ends..........................157
   All-Natural Styling Gel 157
   Get Big Bouncy Curls........................157
   Avoid Too-Short Bangs 157
   Hairspray 157
   Get Rid of Sticky Buildup 158
   Removing Gum 158
   Tear-free Tots 158
   Hairbrush and Comb Cleaner............158
   Prevent Blow-dryer Burnout 159
   Improvised Diffuser 159
   Curling Iron Cleaner 159

Teeth..**159**
   Remove Stains Between the Teeth 159
   Prevent Teeth Stains..........................159
   Good to the Last Drop 159
   Quick Toothpaste Substitute..............159
   Simple Cleaners for Dentures or a
      Retainer 159

Bad Breath.. **160**
   Homemade Mouthwash 160
   Tea for Sweet Breath.........................160
   Odor Buster 160

Hands **160**
   Reverse Roughness and Dryness 160
   Soften and Exfoliate 160
   Cracked Skin Healer 161
   Pain-Easing Solution 161
   Cleaning Grimy Hands 161
   Odor Remover 161

Nails **161**
   Speedy Grower and Strengthener 161
   Brighten and Strengthen 161
   Yellow Stain Remover 162
   Shine Up Those Nails........................162
   Ridge Remover 162

Nail Polish and Manicures...........................162
   Emergency Nail File Substitutes................163

Feet...**163**
   Eliminate Foot Odor 163
   Fix Up Your Hot, Tired Feet 163
   Flaky Skin Scrub................................164
   Treating Blisters 164

Shaving..**164**
   Shaving Cream Substitutes 165
   Aftershave Substitutes 165
   Shave Legs Less Often.......................165
   Prevent Razor Rust............................165
   Prevent After-Waxing Redness 165

Perfume & Cologne **165**
   Shelf Life of Scents...........................166
   Is It for You? 166
   Increase Staying Power 166
   Tone Down Fragrance 166

Jewelry **166**
   Watch Scratch Remover 166
   Safe Way to Clean Pearls 167
   Safe Way to Clean Diamonds.............167
   Remove a Ring Without the Sting 168
   Untangling a Chain 168
   Storing Jewelry 168
   Easy Bracelet Fastening 168
   Temporary Replacement for
      Pierced Earrings 169
   Costume Jewelry 169

Eyeglasses **169**
   Cheers to Your Specs! 169
   Fog Prevention 169
   Fast Fix for Scratches........................169
   Temporary Screw Replacement....................170

Clothing **170**
   Clothing Storage................................170
   Hide Cellulite 171
   Swimsuit Shopping Made Kinder 171
   Zippers 171
   Pantyhose 171
   Lingerie Camouflage.........................171
   Create Cleavage 171

Footwear..**172**
   Keep Shoes On 172
   Put on Boots 172

Handbags...**172**
   Perk Up a Straw Bag 173
   Nonslip Shoulder Strap Solution 173
   Pen Holder for Your Purse 173

Products **174**

Index **175**

Foreword

Smarter. Cheaper. Better. Safer. There's no question that this is how you want to run your life and household. The question is...how?

How can you save time and money on those everyday chores—cleaning, cooking, repairing, maintaining, storing, shopping, grooming, entertaining...living? How can you easily ensure a healthier and nontoxic environment for yourself, your family and your pets—using common household products instead of costly or dangerous commercial products? What are the simple shortcuts and penny-pinching procedures that make quick work of all the necessary jobs around the house...so that you can get more from your rare moments of leisure time?

That's what our readers want to know, so the editors at Bottom Line Books turned to Joan Wilen and Lydia Wilen to research those questions—and countless others. The Wilen Sisters have a knack for finding solutions, consulting the best experts and presenting information in a personal and engaging style.

In their books, the Wilen Sisters offer smart solutions, tips and techniques that use everyday items to make housework hassles disappear—from stubborn stains to annoying insects. You'll get tricks-of-the-trade tips for sleight-of-hand efficiency in the kitchen, laundry room and workshop. You'll discover the wizardry of potent potions made from inexpensive and readily available products that will improve and maintain your furniture, your possessions and even your person.

Each chapter brims with sage advice and uncommon wisdom—and the Wilen Sisters' breezy wit. Whether it's cleaning the carpet or maintaining your car...repairing furniture or growing a garden...preventing disease or preparing dinner...the Wilens suggest a better way—in fact, they offer more than 2,000 of them—to help you cut time, costs and aggravation in virtually everything you need to do around the house.

But rest assured, these remedies are not hocus-pocus. The techniques suggested by the Wilen Sisters have been approved by leading experts who recognized their ingenuity and impact. These helpful hints have worked for them, and we know they will work for you!

The Editors of Bottom Line Books ■

Introduction

When people learn that we're sisters AND writing partners, they often wonder, "How can you possibly work together?" Our answer is that it's a blessing to have a sister (or brother), and we feel that it's a double blessing to be able to work with a sibling. Siblings are together for life, they share memories and a point of view...and they trust each other completely.

After the how-can-you-work-with-your-sibling question, people then ask where we find the information that we share with our readers. It would be fun to say that, like our folk remedies, our household hints have been passed down through many generations of our family. Fun, yes—but true, no. Because of the amazing advances in technology and the invention of time-saving appliances, many of the helpful suggestions that our grandmothers—and even our mother—had to share no longer apply in this day and age.

The true answer is that our information comes from *research*. We've been investigating folk remedies, household hints and environmentally safe cleaning alternatives as well as grooming, cooking, entertaining and space-saving tips for more than two decades. We gather these ideas from the people we meet, from people who contact us, from the Internet and from other published sources.

But make no mistake—gathering information is just the beginning of the process. We know that all of the great things we discover need to be tested and evaluated. So, in addition to ourselves, we ask our family, friends (and our friends' families) as well as our neighbors to be our testers. We also talk to medical doctors, naturopaths, herbalists, chefs, chemists, cleaning experts—you name a specialty, and we've found an expert. We rely on these people to confirm or deny our research, so that we can share the best (and most accurate) information with our readers.

We also make the recipes, mix the formulas and buy LOTS of baking soda and distilled white vinegar, two products that we think are miraculous and endlessly useful. Sometimes our experiments fail...popular or odd-sounding hints may not work as well as some of the more sensible, simple solutions. We're equally happy to help you avoid the remedies that *don't* work as we are to bring you the best. So, we won't suggest that you polish your furniture with SPAM anytime soon!

You may (and we hope you will) find a few surprising suggestions in our books. Be assured that whenever you see something that seems unusual, we feel that it's also wonderful…and useful. We investigate and track down the sources of information whenever we can. For example—a reputable Internet site stated that a very famous daytime soap opera star uses sardines to lighten the dark circles under her eyes. We contacted the star's manager, and when she stopped laughing, she told us that the information was positively untrue. This star has her own cosmetics line—and it has never included sardines!

We prefer to stay away from harsh chemicals like bleach and ammonia, and instead opt for other harmless, lung-friendly, ecologically sound household helpers. Of course, you can always take comedian Joan Rivers' playful advice and just not clean…she said that when you have guests, just put out drop cloths and say you are having the place painted.

Many chapters contain some product ideas from reputable companies. We want you to know that there was absolutely NO advertising or payment for those items to be included in our book. The folks at Bottom Line Books would never permit that! We chose these products simply because we felt they would make your life easier, healthier or just more fun.

We won't be insulted if you don't read our books from cover to cover. In fact, they are designed to be used as reference guides to help you with specific needs and projects. But we do hope that you will enjoy reading them and will discover new ways to use familiar products to manage your everyday tasks.

We're happy to be able to share all of this good stuff with you, hoping it will work like magic. If you have your very own helpful shortcuts and efficient ways of doing chores in and around the house, we'd love to hear from you.

—Joan Wilen & Lydia Wilen ■

About the Authors

The Wilen Sisters—Joan and Lydia—are energetic and enthusiastic health investigators. In a career that's spanned two decades, they have uncovered thousands of amazing "cures from the cupboard," which they share through their best-selling books, dozens of magazine articles and with appearances on numerous national television programs, including NBC's *Today Show* and *CBS This Morning.*

While their passion and search for natural folk remedies continues, they have now broadened their expertise to include household hints. Their wonderful, wide-ranging collection of ways to make your home cleaner, neater and nicer would make their mama proud. ■

A Word from the Authors

We'd like to extend a BIG THANKS to our family and friends for sharing their helpful hints...giving their loving support...and for tasting and testing many of our special remedies.

Our most grateful thanks to Marty Edelston, the master magician who turned an idea into Boardroom Inc.—the publishing empire that includes Bottom Line Books and other publications.

How lucky we are to be Bottom Line authors, working with people like publisher Marjory Abrams, marketing maven Brian Kurtz, chief editor Karen Daly (who waved her magic wand to start this project) and editor Amy Linkov (who cast her magic spell on every page).

And to the entire talented, creative and caring Boardroom team—we sincerely thank you for making us proud of our book. ■

The Best-Ever Kitchen Secrets

No room in the house declares "home, sweet home" more than the kitchen. It is the place where the food that sustains you and your family is stored, prepared and/or served. The kitchen is usually a warm, cozy room—and it always seems to be the busiest spot during a good party.

We hope the suggestions in this section help to keep your "kitchen, sweet kitchen" safe and clean, as well as providing ways for you to treat your appliances and dishes with the best care possible.

SAFETY

We don't want to frighten you with statistics concerning accidents that occur in the kitchen. But take our word for it—the numbers are high, the details are gruesome and (sadly) many disasters could have been controlled to minimize harm and damage...or even completely avoided. In many cases, all it would have taken was an ounce of prevention or some basic emergency-procedure information.

Please read through the following safety advice and take action now to prevent kitchen accidents—before you need to, but can't.

Fire

Every home should have a fire extinguisher on each level. It's important to know exactly where it is and how to use it! As soon as you bring a fire extinguisher into your home, go over all of the instructions with everyone who lives there. Have each person, including you, review the instructions thoroughly.

Then place 1 of the extinguishers in or near the kitchen—it should be in an easily accessible place. It's also a good idea to review the instructions each time you change the battery in your smoke detectors.

Statistics and our reasoning powers tell us that more fires start in the kitchen than any other room. *For safety's sake…*

◆ **NEVER** put out a grease fire with water. It will cause the grease to splatter, and the fire to spread quickly.

◆ **DO NOT** put a smoke alarm above the stove or kitchen sink. It will go off every time steam comes out of a pot or the hot-water faucet. You may get so annoyed with the

1

false alarms that you disable the detector. Then, when you *really* do need it, it may not be working. The best spot for the smoke detector is right outside the kitchen.

◆ **DO NOT** douse flames in a pot or pan with water. Water will make the fire grow bigger. Instead, put a cover on the pot or pan, which will cut off the oxygen supply and smother out the fire.

◆ **DO NOT** keep a toaster under a shelf or kitchen cabinet. A little spark could pop up and ignite the wood above it.

◆ **DO** check the batteries every month, and change them twice a year—the easiest way to remember is to do it when you change the clocks to and from Daylight Saving Time (if applicable in your area).

Distilled White Vinegar

As you may have noticed by now, we think distilled white vinegar is a great cleaning and disinfecting solution. *There are, however, a few cautions that need to be addressed…*

◆ **NEVER** combine white vinegar with ammonia or bleach of any kind (neither of these is ever recommended in this book). This combination creates a toxic gas, which can be harmful.

◆ **NEVER** use white vinegar on your teeth. It dissolves calcium.

◆ **DO NOT** use white vinegar on or around glued joints of furniture. It will dissolve most glues.

◆ **DO NOT** leave white vinegar on a metal surface. It may pit it.

◆ **DO NOT** sniff white vinegar, especially if you are sensitive to acidic fumes.

◆ **DO** clean up white vinegar with plain water. Vinegar is soluble in water, so if you get it on something, simply rinse it off with water (or neutralize it with baking soda), then clean up everything with a damp cloth.

Food Handling

How much time do you spend washing your hands before you handle food? Go through the motions of your typical hand-washing session, and you might be surprised at how quickly you do it. Maybe 4 seconds?

To be sure your hands are bacteria-free, the recommended amount of wash-up time is 20 to 30 seconds using warm, soapy water (and plain soap is often a better choice than the antibacterial type). If you sing the "Happy Birthday" song or recite your A-B-C's while washing up, your hands will spend the right amount of time getting clean. And don't rush through it! Finish the job by wiping your hands with a clean piece of paper towel.

Plastic Wrap in the Microwave

◆ Make sure the plastic wrap you use in the oven is labeled "microwave-safe." It's important that the plastic wrap does not come into direct contact with the food that you're cooking in the microwave—chemicals from the plastic can leach into your food.

◆ After zapping a plastic-wrapped dish, remove the plastic wrap and try to stay out of harm's way—fold back the plastic from the corner that's farthest away from you.

By doing this, you will avoid getting burned by the poof of scalding-hot steam that bursts out of the dish.

CLEANING BASICS

 Don't you just hate it when you run out of a cleaning product—especially when you get that overwhelming urge to clean? We hope that doesn't happen to you, but if it does, there are suggestions in this section for several make-it-yourself substitutes.

And while you're here, there's helpful information on using some of the tools of the trade—sponges, steel wool, rubber gloves, our beloved baking soda and more. So don't let us keep you. Get to it!

Make-It-Yourself Scouring Powder

In a covered container, mix 1 cup of baking soda, 1 cup of borax powder (available at supermarkets and drugstores) and ¾ cup of table salt. Make it easy to use by keeping a portion of the mixture in a large salt shaker. Sprinkle some on whatever surface you need to scour, like sinks and bathtubs.

> **CAUTION:** Make sure you label the salt shaker clearly so that nobody mistakes the mixture for regular table salt! And be sure to keep the shaker in a cupboard along with your other cleaning supplies—out of the reach of children and pets. Borax can be dangerous if ingested.

Dish Detergent Mixture

In a plastic squeeze bottle, combine 1 part liquid dish detergent with 1 part distilled white vinegar and 3 parts water. Shake it a few times before using. The detergent cuts the grease, the white vinegar disinfects and helps clean, and the water acts as detergent-extender…making it last longer.

Dish Detergent Substitute

If you have a sinkful of dirty dishes and no dish detergent, use shampoo (make sure it's the non-conditioning kind) to clean them. If you have oily hair and use shampoo specifically formulated for it, all the better. It will cut right through the oily pots and pans and greasy dishes.

Steel Wool Tips

◆ After using a steel-wood pad, if there's still some scrub left in it, place it in a little plastic bag and store it in the freezer. It will stay rust-free. When you're ready to use it again, put it under warm water and it will thaw in a few seconds.

◆ To avoid getting metal splinters, wear rubber gloves when you use steel wool. If you don't have them, you can protect your fingers by cupping the steel-wool pad in the rind of a lemon, orange or grapefruit.

Deodorize and Disinfect Sponges

We don't mean to gross you out, but it's important to know that the average kitchen sponge contains more germs than the average toilet seat. The good news is that it's easy to disinfect the sponge.

◆ Each time you run your dishwasher, toss the sponge on the top rack and let it go along for the ride.

◆ Rinse the sponge and zap it (while it's still wet) in the microwave for 1 minute. (Be sure there aren't any metal fibers in the sponge.)

◆ Soak the sponge overnight in a solution of 1 cup of hot water, ½ cup of distilled white vinegar and 3 tablespoons of table salt. In the morning, rinse the sponge and use as usual.

Rubber Gloves

◆ If you're having a hard time taking off rubber gloves, hold your hands under cold water—they'll glide right off.

◆ Next time, before you put on the gloves, sprinkle a bit of baking soda or talcum powder on your hands or into the gloves.

◆ If a glove has sprung a leak and your fingers are wet after using it, throw the gloves away and put on a new pair.

If your fingers are wet because water seeped into the gloves while you were wearing them, thoroughly dry the outside. Then, take each glove off by grabbing onto the cuff and pulling it over the fingers, turning the glove inside out. Let them air dry.

When you're ready to wear them again, turn them right side out—and don't forget to sprinkle your hands or the gloves with a little baking soda or talcum powder.

Wrap It Up

◆ If plastic wrap gets unmanageable because of the way it sticks to itself, keep the box in the freezer. Cold plastic wrap will behave the way you want it to.

◆ If you have a hard time finding the beginning of the plastic wrap roll, take a piece of tape (any kind), and dab at the roll until it picks up the loose edge.

◆ If plastic wrap doesn't stick to the bowl or dish you're wrapping, dampen the outer edge of the bowl or dish, and then put the plastic wrap on.

◆ When aluminum foil touches acidic foods—tomatoes, onions, lemons—a chemical reaction takes place that can affect the taste of the food. Also, foil may rust when it comes in contact with salty foods. So, if you think a food is acidic or salty, use plastic wrap on it instead of foil.

A Freshness Test for Baking Soda

If not for baking soda, this book would be a pamphlet. In order for baking soda to perform to the peak of perfection, it must be FRESH.

To test the powers of your baking soda, pour ¼ cup of distilled white vinegar in a little bowl, then add 1 tablespoon of baking soda. If it fizzes, it's fresh enough to use.

If there is no reaction when the baking soda combines with the vinegar, forget it. Just pour the contents of the box down the drain. Stale or not, it's always good for the drain.

APPLIANCES

 Yes, kitchen appliances—such as the toaster, microwave, blender, bread machine, mixer, juicer, food processor, can opener and coffee grinder—make life easier, but you still have to clean and maintain them…once you find room for them in your kitchen. Read through these suggestions, and they may make the job less formidable and the appliances more efficient.

CAUTION: When you're using any small kitchen appliance, pull the plug from the electrical outlet when you're done. It rarely happens, but if an electrical component malfunctions (or there is a power surge in your house) while an appliance is plugged in, it can burst into flames.

Cleaning a Can Opener

When it comes to cleaning, the single most overlooked item in the kitchen seems to be the can opener—electric or manual. Each time you use it, food particles are left behind. We're talking breeding grounds for germs here.

Wash your can opener with dish detergent after every use (if it's electric, be sure to unplug it first). If there's any dried-on food, clean it with a toothbrush or fuzzy pipe cleaner. As an added non-bacteria-spreading precaution, always wash (not just wipe) off the top of the can you're about to open.

 Easier Can Opening

If your can opener doesn't operate as smoothly as it should, run a piece of waxed paper through it a couple of times.

Cleaning a Blender

Let your blender clean itself...sort of. Once your blender is ready to be washed, fill it ⅓ of the way with just-boiled water. Add a few drops of liquid dish detergent and, when the water cools, toss in a couple of ice cubes. Put on the lid securely and blend for about 15 seconds on *high*. Then rinse and dry.

Cleaning a Toaster

If your toaster has a bottom door, open it and get rid of the crumbs. Then turn the toaster upside down over the sink and shake it. To get at any remaining crumbs, use a small food brush, or a compressed-air spray (available at art and computer stores. The spray is also good for getting the dust out of keyboards).

 CAUTION: It might be common sense, but it needs to be said—before you clean a toaster, be sure to unplug it.

Cleaning Melted Plastic Off the Toaster

◆ If plastic wrap or the plastic bag from a loaf of bread gets melted on your toaster, here's what to do—first, wait for the toaster to cool. Then sprinkle baking soda on a damp cloth and rub off the plastic.

◆ Apply petroleum jelly on the melted plastic, and toast a piece of bread so that the toaster heats up. Then, rub off the plastic with a paper towel or cloth. Be careful not to burn your fingers.

◆ If the plastic seems stuck on for good, try nail-polish remover when the toaster is cool. It should take it off. The problem is, it may take the finish off as well. Test a tiny spot before you use it.

Cleaning a Drip Coffee Maker

Once a month—or whenever mineral deposits clog the coffeepot (you'll know because it will take longer than usual to prepare the coffee)—fill the water reservoir with equal parts of distilled white vinegar and water, and run it through the brew cycle. Then, using just plain water, rinse it out with another cycle.

Cleaning a Coffee Grinder/Mill

◆ Bitterness buildup from coffee residue will be scoured away when you run 1 cup of uncooked white rice through the grinder once a month. The grains of rice also help sharpen the blades.

◆ If you always use the grinder for coffee, and you occasionally use it for spices, be sure to clean out every morsel of spice before you go back to coffee. Do it by grinding 2 or 3 pieces of plain wheat bread.

Taste the last piece of ground bread to make sure there is no trace of the spice.

Cleaning a Waffle Iron

Nobody wants to clean the mess made by a waffle iron that won't let go of the waffles. To bring your waffle iron back to its *nonstick* condition, place 2 pieces of waxed paper where the batter goes, and let it heat up. Keep an eye on it, and as soon as the waxed paper turns dark brown, remove it. Your waffle iron should be good as new. Make yourself a waffle coming-out party!

Cleaning a Hand Mixer/ Electric Mixer

Make cleanup easier by spritzing the beaters with cooking spray before using them.

 NOTE: The only time you shouldn't spray the beaters with cooking spray is when you want to beat egg whites—the spray will prevent the egg whites from stiffening.

Cleaning a Food Processor

Once the food is in the work bowl, waiting to be processed, cover the bowl with a piece of plastic wrap. Then place the lid on top, and you're ready to go. Once the machine does its thing, take off the lid (which has remained clean), and throw away the splattered-on plastic wrap.

You still have to clean the bowl and the blades, but you won't have to bother digging out any food particles from the lid.

Cleaning a Microwave Oven

◆ In a microwave-safe glass bowl, squeeze in the juice of 1 lemon and add 1 cup of water. Place it in the middle of the microwave, and zap it on *high* for 1 minute. Let the bowl stay in the oven, with the door closed, for about 10 minutes. Then all the caked-on gunk will be loose and easy to wipe off. And the kitchen will have a great, citrusy scent.

◆ Clean and sanitize your microwave with a mixture of 1 part baking soda to 7 parts water in a microwave-safe glass bowl. Put the bowl in the oven, and set it on *high* for 2 minutes. Notice that the liquid turns to steam and coats the interior of the oven.

◆ When it's finished, carefully remove the bowl, and wipe down the oven with a clean cloth or paper towels.

◆ If there's a dry, caked-on spill inside your microwave, cover it with a wet washcloth, then set it on *medium* for 20 seconds. Wait until the cloth cools before handling it, and then wipe up the loosened mess.

 Prevent Spills in the Microwave

If you're zapping something that may leave a messy splatter—such as vegetable soup or lasagna—put a paper plate or a piece of waxed paper under the dish to catch the splashes. Instead of having to clean the microwave, just throw away the paper plate or the paper.

You can also cover the open food container with a paper plate, coffee filter, or a piece of waxed paper or paper towel, which will help prevent the food from splattering.

Deodorize Your Microwave

Toss the peel of a lemon in a microwave-safe glass bowl, along with 1 cup of water, and zap it for about 30 seconds. (*See* "Cleaning a Microwave Oven" on this page, using the juice of the lemon instead of the peel.)

Microwave Facts

Microwave ovens were invented in 1946. A year later, the first commercial microwaves were sold. They were 5½ feet tall and weighed over 750 pounds. Each unit cost $5,000.

That's some mighty expensive popcorn!

Cleaning a Stove or Range

First, make sure the oven is off and cool inside. Then, use a wet sponge or wet cloth to wipe the inside of the oven. Next, before the oven surfaces dry, quickly sprinkle on baking soda. Leave it this way overnight. In the morning, wipe off the baking soda, along with the grease and grime.

Cleaning Spills Inside the Oven Or on the Stovetop

◆ If it's a *wet* spill (such as sauce, stew or gravy) …as soon as the food is out of the oven, carefully cover it with table salt. Remember—the oven will still be hot, so proceed with caution…and an oven mitt.

◆ If it's a *dry* spill (such as flour, sugar or ground coffee)…wet it with water and sprinkle on enough baking soda to cover it. Once the oven or stovetop is cool to the touch, you can scrape or scour off the spilled mess.

 CAUTION: Keep any type of oven cleaner away from the heating elements. Even baking soda can cause corrosion, which will result in a short-out.

Exterior Cleaner for a Gas or Electric Range

One guess as to what to use—you're right if you said baking soda. Sprinkle some on a damp sponge or cloth, then rub the outside of your range, rinse and dry.

Eliminate Oven-Cleaner Smells

If you are still using a store-bought, air- and lung-polluting aerosol oven cleaner, you can at least prevent the awful smell and smoke that happens when you turn on the oven.

Wet a sponge with distilled white vinegar, and wipe inside the entire oven with it. The vinegar neutralizes the lingering residual effects of the strong and irritating alkali from the commercial oven cleaner. It will also help prevent grease buildup.

Cleaning Burner Drip Plates and Burner Grates

Yes, that's what those removable, metal things on which you cook are called! To clean them, you will need a large pot that's *not* aluminum—glass or stainless steel will do. Put 1 quart of water in the pot, along with 1 tablespoon of baking soda. Put in the stainless steel or enamel burner drip plates and/or the cast-iron burner grates, and boil them for 5 minutes. Then remove them from the pot and let them cool. When each is cool enough to handle, rinse and wipe dry.

Unclogging Clogged Burner Holes

When spilled, caked-on food clogs the burner holes of your gas range, use a small, fuzzy pipe cleaner (available at art-supply stores) to clear the clogs. It's the perfect size for the job.

Cleaning an Oven Fan Filter

If you have an oven fan, chances are you have a greasy fan filter. It's easy to clean. Just take it out (that may be the hardest part), put it on the upper rack of your dishwasher, and let it go through a full wash cycle. (You may want to wash it by itself if it's really greasy.)

 NOTE: Pay close attention when you remove the filter from the fan, so you can reverse the procedure and put it back correctly once it's clean.

Cleaning a Broiler Pan

While the broiler pan is still hot, carefully sprinkle on some powdered laundry detergent —enough to cover the burned-on food. On top of that, place a wet paper towel. Leave everything for about 15 minutes. Then you should be able to scrape off the food easily.

Cleaning an Oven Rack

◆ Run very hot water in the bathtub—enough to completely cover the oven racks. Add ⅓ cup of liquid dish detergent and 1 cup of distilled white vinegar. Let the racks soak in the tub for at least 1 hour. Then scrub if necessary, rinse and wipe dry.

   If some stubborn caked-on crud refuses to come off, you can carefully scrape it away with a knife.

◆ If you want to save yourself the job of having to clean a dirty bathtub, then put the racks in a heavy-duty plastic bag with the water, detergent and vinegar. Fill the bathtub with hot water and soak the bagged racks in the bathtub for 1 hour.

 Pretreatment for a Grill Rack

Spray the grid or rack with nonstick cooking spray before you heat the grill. It will keep food from sticking—which makes cooking easier and cleanup quicker.

Cleaning a Grill Rack

If there are lots of baked-on food and burned grease, take a sheet of heavy-duty aluminum foil and wrap it around the cooking grid (rack) —shiny-side down. Put it back on the grill, and turn up the heat for 12 minutes (give or take 1 or 2 minutes). Let the rack cool down, and when the foil is cool enough to handle, take it off the grill. The encrusted food should fall right off the rack.

 Foiled Again!

If the food doesn't come right off, crinkle a piece of aluminum foil into a ball and use it to clean the grill as you would use steel wool.

   You can also do this if there's only a little bit of caked-on gunk on the rack.

Cleaning a Refrigerator

◆ To get your refrigerator clean and shiny inside and out, use (what else?) baking soda on a damp sponge or cloth.

◆ You can also wipe down the exterior surfaces of the fridge with a solution made from 1 part distilled white vinegar to 5 parts water—this will make everything extra-shiny.

 Butter Up Your Fridge

Want to clean behind the refrigerator? If you want to move something big and heavy, smear butter or other shortening on the floor right in front of the appliance. Then, with someone helping you, you should be able to slide the heavy appliance forward. Be sure to clean the floor when you're done!

   Be aware that butter should NOT be used on marble floors—it can stain.

Cleaning Spills Inside the Refrigerator

If food spills are common in your refrigerator, spread a dishtowel on the bottom shelf to catch any drips. Instead of having to clean the bottom shelf every time there's a mess, you can just toss the towel in the wash.

Keeping the Drawer Liner Clean

◆ For easy cleanup (and to prevent messes), line the fruit/vegetable and meat drawers with old plastic place mats. You may have to cut them to fit, but considering how easy they are to wipe clean, it will be worth the effort.

◆ If you do not want to bother with cleaning place mats, line the drawers with some plastic wrap. Or use a few paper towels in the fruit drawer. They will help absorb moisture, which means the fruit will last longer.

Cleaning a Refrigerator Top

Relieve yourself of the very unpleasant chore of cleaning the top of the refrigerator—just line it with plastic wrap. But—unless you keep things on top of the fridge to hold down the plastic wrap—you may want to tape the sides of the plastic wrap to the refrigerator, to keep the plastic in place.

After a reasonable amount of dust-accumulation time, throw away the dirty plastic and rewrap the top of the fridge with fresh wrap.

Put Jelly on the Racks

If the slide-out racks or trays in your refrigerator are not gliding as smoothly as they should, simply apply a thin layer of petroleum jelly to the edges—they'll whiz in and out.

Optimizing Refrigerator Efficiency

◆ The rubber piping (gasket) inside the door that seals the door should be clean, in good shape and attached properly. If it's dirty or not attached right, it will allow cold air to escape, which wastes electricity and could make your food spoil. Wash it regularly with soapy water, and dry thoroughly.

◆ If a refrigerator is level, it will use less electricity and run more efficiently than if it's a little off-kilter. Test out your refrigerator by placing an almost-full-to-the-rim glass of water on a shelf. Look at it while it's in the fridge—is the water level parallel to the rim, just as when you filled it? If the water is uneven—meaning, it swoops

Easy Refrigerator Deodorizers

Everyone knows about baking soda (we hope!). But do you know that you should keep the open box on the middle shelf in the back of the fridge for it to be most effective?

And when you put a new box in the fridge every other month or so, pour the contents of the old box down the drain while the hot tap water is running. The baking soda will help clean and deodorize the drain pipes.

Here are a few more suggestions for keeping your refrigerator odor-free…

◆ Dab a few drops of vanilla or lemon extract on a cotton ball and put it in a shot glass inside the fridge. Any unpleasant odor will be replaced with an appetizing scent.

◆ Cut a peeled, raw potato in half and place each half—cut side up—on a refrigerator shelf. When the surface of the potato turns black, cut off the top layer and use the clean sections to keep absorbing odors.

◆ Put an open container of natural clay kitty litter in the fridge. (But NEVER put kitty litter down the drain—it will clog.)

◆ A few plain charcoal briquettes will keep the refrigerator smell-free. And they're recyclable —after about 1 month, use a heavy stainless steel pot to heat them. In the heating process, the briquettes release the absorbed odors. When they've cooled off, put them in a container or on a plate and back on the job inside the refrigerator.

◆ When there is a particularly foul odor throughout the refrigerator, stuff a crumpled brown-paper grocery bag on each shelf. The paper will absorb any and all nasty odors. When each bag starts to smell bad, replace it with another until the awful smell is completely gone. (Of course, make sure that whatever caused the nasty smell is gone, too.)

◆ Put fresh coffee grounds in little bowls or in foil-laminated baking cups on each refrigerator shelf. The coffee will deodorize even the worst of smells within 1 or 2 days. Once the bad smell goes, so should the coffee grounds.

to one side of the glass and is not near the rim on the other side—you should adjust your refrigerator. It may only need a small piece of cardboard or a wooden shim to put the fridge on an even footing, but it could make a difference in your next electricity bill.

◆ For a refrigerator to operate at its best, don't overload the shelves—especially the top shelf. It is ideal for air to be able to circulate around each item in the fridge. (Yeah, right! Ideal, but not always very practical.)

◆ Keep leftovers in glass or plastic see-through containers so that you are reminded that they're there. Better yet, set aside a section of a refrigerator shelf for leftovers and eliminate soon-forgotten/long-hidden "UFOs"…*unidentifiable food organisms.*

◆ Putting uncovered food in the refrigerator uses extra energy—the refrigerator has to keep up with the moisture the uncovered food emits. So, when you put food in the fridge, put a lid on it!

Power Outage Guidelines

During a power outage, keep the refrigerator and freezer doors shut. If you can determine when the power outage began (check a clock that runs on electricity), you can figure out how long the food will be good. *As a general rule…*

◆ Food kept cold in an unopened refrigerator will last about 4 hours.

◆ Food in a full, unopened freezer will stay frozen for about 48 hours.

◆ Food in a semi-full, unopened freezer will stay frozen for up to 24 hours.

Cleaning and Defrosting A Freezer

◆ To get the inside of your freezer clean, wipe it with a sponge that has been dampened with rubbing alcohol.

◆ If your freezer needs to be defrosted regularly, try this before turning the freezer back on—wipe the interior surfaces with a light layer of glycerin (available at most drugstores), or give it a light spritz of nonstick vegetable spray. The next time you defrost, the excess ice will slide off easily.

 Very Cool Freezer Hints
◆ If your ice cube trays stick to the surface they're on, let them sit on pieces of waxed paper, and they will glide in and out smoothly.
◆ If there's a really bad food smell coming from your freezer, put ½ cup of freshly ground coffee on a plate, and place the plate in the freezer. In a day or so, the coffee will absorb the smell completely.
   An open box of baking soda may do the same thing and cost less than coffee.

Optimizing Freezer Efficiency

◆ Your freezer will work best if it's at least ⅔ full. But don't run out to the grocery store just to fill your freezer. Instead, put water in plastic bottles, bags or food containers, and use them to occupy the empty space.

   Keep in mind that water expands as it freezes, so leave a little expansion space in the containers.

◆ Put a label with the date and the contents on each food container you freeze. Do not delude yourself into thinking that you'll remember what you've frozen and when. We speak from experience.

◆ When you freeze food in a resealable plastic bag—the less air, the better. The trick to getting the air out is to insert a straw in the bag with the food. Close the bag as much as you can, except for the straw. Using the straw, suck out the air from the bag. Now this is the tricky part—quickly remove the straw and close the bag completely before air gets back in. Be sure to label the bag with the date and contents before you suck the air out of it.

◆ Do not wrap food that's headed for the freezer with reused aluminum foil. Crinkled foil can create little holes. Those holes will let air get at the frozen food and may cause freezer burn or spoilage. Splurge with a new piece of foil each time you wrap food for the freezer.

 NOTE: We take safe storage a step further by first wrapping the food in plastic wrap and then in aluminum foil.

If you're wrapping single-serving items like burgers or hot dogs, wrap them individually for easier future separation.

Cleaning a Dishwasher

Believe it or not, even a dishwasher needs to be cleaned once in awhile. If you notice that your freshly washed dishes and glasses have a film on them, the time has come to clean the machine.

◆ Empty it out and place a dishwasher-safe bowl on the bottom rack. Add 2 cups of distilled white vinegar, and run the wash and rinse cycles only. When completed, open the door and let it air-dry.

◆ Sprinkle a few tablespoons of a lemon- or orange-drink powder (something like Tang will fill the bill) inside the empty dishwasher, then run the wash and rinse cycles.

◆ If there are tough stains inside the dishwasher that will not wash away with other methods, you should be able to rub them off with baking soda on a damp cloth. (How can we talk "cleaning" without bringing baking soda into the conversation?)

◆ Speaking of baking soda…sprinkle some on the bottom of the dishwasher before each use to enhance the cleaning power of your regular detergent.

◆ If your dishwasher has a musty smell—and it probably will if you keep it closed most of the time—empty it, then pour ¼ cup of lemon juice or 2 tablespoons of baking soda in the detergent dispenser. Let it run through the rinse cycle.

Dishwasher Performance Booster

If you've noticed that the ol' dishwasher just ain't what it used to be, the holes in the upper and lower spray arms may need unclogging.

Depending on the size of the holes, use an open safety pin…or an open paper clip…or pipe cleaners…or a knitting needle…or an ice pick to *carefully* clean them out.

If you can remove the spray arms (take out the racks and undo the hubcap that holds the arms in place), you can clean them more thoroughly. But please don't remove anything unless you're sure you can put it back without any problem. (We don't make house calls, and plumbers are expensive.)

 Better Washing with Detergent

◆ If your clean dishes and glassware often come out of the dishwasher with streaks and spots, you may have hard water.

Prevent the streaks by adding 2 tablespoons of baking soda to your regular dish detergent, or adding ¼ cup of distilled white vinegar to the rinse cycle.

◆ If you used too much detergent—or the wrong type of detergent—and the machine is spewing suds, add 1 capful of fabric softener. Let the washer run for a few seconds, then select the drain cycle. The softener will break up the suds and allow them to drain off.

◆ You can also liberally sprinkle table salt over the suds to disperse them. Then toss in a few dozen ice cubes. This will lower the water temperature, getting rid of more suds. If you still have a mess, soak up the rest of the water and suds with dry towels.

Cleaning a Garbage Disposal

Degrease the innards of the disposal unit every other month with 1 cup of baking soda. (Use the old baking soda from the refrigerator when you're ready to replace it.)

Turn on the hot water in the disposal and slowly pour in the baking soda. Let the water continue running for a minute or so after the soda is gone. It's easy and effective. Do it!

Garbage In...Odors Out

◆ Don't throw out lemon peels—use them to deodorize your disposal and sharpen its blades. Put the peel from 2 small lemons or 1 large one, plus 10 ice cubes in the garbage disposal compartment. Turn on the water and run the disposal. The lemon will deodorize while the ice cubes sharpen the blades.

◆ You can just deodorize by pouring in ½ cup of table salt, adding hot water and running the disposal. It's like dermabrasion of the pipes.

◆ You can also mix 1 cup of distilled white vinegar with enough water to fill an average-sized ice cube tray. Once the cubes have frozen, grind them through the disposal and flush it with cold water.

◆ If you're going to be gone from home for a week or more, before you leave, pour ½ cup of baking soda down the disposal. But here's the trick—*do not run the water.* Let the baking soda stay in the disposal so that when you come home, you will have an odor-free sink.

POTS & PANS

 The late author Susan Sontag once observed that "fewer and fewer Americans possess objects that have a patina...old furniture, grandparents' pots and pans—the used things, warm with generations of human touch, essential to a human landscape."

If you're lucky enough to have your grandparents' pots and pans—or if you have your very own collection—here are ways to take care of them as they develop that rich patina Ms. Sontag spoke of...

The following suggestions are reserved for more dramatic scenarios like burned-on gunk, scorches and discoloration, as well as for cast-iron and clay cookware.

✪ Be Dishwasher Safe

It's safe to put anodized aluminum, stainless steel, enameled cast-iron and glass cookware in a dishwasher. But never put aluminum, copper or cast-iron cookware in a dishwasher.

Removing Stuck-on and Almost-Burned Food

◆ For most types of cookware, just fill the gunked-up pot or pan with water and 1 or 2 tablespoons of liquid dish detergent. Put the pot back on the stove, and bring the water to a boil. Then shut off the heat and let it soak until the water cools completely. Rinse out the water, and don't be surprised if the food comes out with it. Whatever is left should sponge off easily.

◆ To clean burned-on food from a cast-iron pan...fill the pan with water and 1 or 2 teaspoons of liquid dish detergent. Let it simmer until you see pieces of food starting to lift off the bottom. Then wait until it's cool enough to touch, and scour off whatever didn't come completely loose. You may want to reseason the pan again. (*See* "Caring for Cast-Iron Cookware" on pages 13–14.)

◆ To loosen food stuck on an enamel pot, mix 2 tablespoons of baking soda with 2 cups of water, bring it to a boil and let it boil for 10 minutes. Once the water cools down, scrape off the food and wash the pot.

Cleaning Burned Pots/Pans

◆ If the burn is moderate—meaning, not easy to clean, yet not burned to a crisp—put about 2" of water in the pot and bring it to a boil. Once it starts boiling, cover the pot and let it boil for another 5 minutes.

As soon as it's cool enough to touch, scour off the burn. If it doesn't come right off, add a few tablespoons of baking soda and/or distilled white vinegar. Give it a few minutes to sink in and scour again.

◆ For moderate burns, boil 1 cup of cola in the pot, wait for it to cool and then you should be able to scrub off the burn.

◆ If the burn is severe…fill the pan halfway with water. For a small pan (up to 7" in diameter), add ¼ cup of baking soda…for a big pan (8" or larger), add ½ cup of baking soda. Bring it to a boil, then watch as it continues boiling. The burned pieces should float to the top.

If it doesn't happen within a reasonable amount of time, chances are it's never going to happen because the pan was scorched beyond salvation. Sorry!

◆ If you really love the pan and are willing to try *anything* to save it, fill it with mud—from your yard or a garden-supply store—and keep it that way overnight. The next day, use the mud to scrub the pan (look out for rocks and small stones!). This remedy may not work, so you should go in knowing that it is very iffy. *Iffy* it works, though, you'll be glad you tried it.

★ **Burn-Stopping Secret**

Before you fill a double-boiler with water, put a few glass marbles in the bottom half. Then set it up as usual. If the water level gets too low, the marbles will start to make noise. Their clatter will be a loud and clear warning for you to add more water, which will prevent the pan from burning.

Caring for Aluminum Pots

◆ To remove stains…fill the pot with enough water to cover all of the stains. Then gently boil the peel of an apple or some rhubarb stalks… or slices of grapefruit, lemon or orange…or slices of tomato. After about 5 minutes, take the pot off the fire, spill out the water, dispose of the food, wash the pot with a little liquid dish detergent, rinse and dry.

◆ To clean up a blackened pot…put 1 teaspoon of cream of tartar (available at the supermarket's spice or baking section) and 2 cups of water in the pot. Boil the mixture for about 3 or 4 minutes. Then wash and dry as usual. That should get rid of the blackened area.

Caring for Stainless Steel Pots

While rainbows are beautiful, you don't necessarily want them on your pots. Rainbows on stainless steel pots will disappear if you rub them with a drop of olive oil.

Caring for Cast-Iron Cookware

◆ Even though cast-iron cookware is an excellent source of dietary iron, you don't want food that tastes like cast iron. And it won't if you season the pot or pan before you cook with it for the first time. Seasoning it will also help prevent food from sticking to the pan.

Season it by rubbing on a thin layer of vegetable or mineral oil with a soft cloth or piece of paper towel. Then put the pan in a 250°F oven for 2 hours, until it's smoky and blackened.

◆ To remove rust from your cast-iron cookware, mix sand (available at hardware stores, nurseries, pet shops…and the beach) with enough vegetable oil to form a thick, gritty paste. Smear the paste on the rusty portions of the cast-iron pan. Then scour it with steel wool. When the rust is gone, wash the pan thoroughly and reseason.

Rust-Free Cast Iron

Moisture causes rust. To absorb moisture when any piece of cast-iron cookware is not being used, let it sit on a coffee filter.

Caring for Clay Cookware

 CAUTION: Clay cracks. Do not wash it in the dishwasher. Do not scrub it with steel wool. When a piece of clay cookware is very hot, do not put it on a cold counter.

Soak the cooker with warm water and 1 to 4 tablespoons of baking soda, depending on the size of the smelly, stained clay piece. Let it stand for a few hours, then rinse thoroughly and dry.

Add Paper to Clay

Line a clay cooker with parchment paper to prevent food from staining its porous surface.

GLASS & CRYSTAL

Glass is mainly made of *silica* (sand). When Englishman George Ravenscroft added lead oxide to the glass composition, he created a highly refractive (more sparkly) and softer glass that's easier to cut. And so, in 1676, lead crystal was born.

It's NEVER a good idea to clean crystal pieces in a dishwasher. They may crack or chip, and they may lose their sparkle. So always be sure to handwash your good glass and crystal pieces. *Here are some other ways you can clean glass and crystal…*

Caring for Glassware

We fill an empty plastic liquid dish-detergent bottle with 1 part dish detergent, 1 part distilled white vinegar and 3 parts water, and shake it a few times.

We use this solution daily—a little on a sponge—to do the dishes and glasses. It's a winning combination that leaves everything clean and sparkling, and lasts a long time.

Best Way to Clean Up Broken Glass

When you break a glass, the first thing to do is put on shoes if you're barefoot. Then put on rubber or latex gloves. Start the cleanup by picking up the bigger pieces and putting them into a trash bag.

To collect all of the tiny scattered slivers of glass, carefully use wet paper towels. Also, check the bottoms of your shoes for little shards of embedded glass. If you have a vacuum cleaner handy, a final suck-up is a good idea.

Glass-Breaking Celebration

Whenever a glass broke at our home, we'd all yell "Mazel tov!" as though it was a good thing. And we thought it was, because of the custom of breaking a glass at the very end of a Jewish wedding ceremony. The custom comes from several different traditions…including a medieval belief that making loud noises will ward off evil spirits. (Ringing church bells comes from the same era and idea.)

So, if and when someone breaks a glass, take it as a sign of good luck and the banishment of evil spirits—you will make the glass-breaker feel less guilty for the little accident.

Unstick Drinking Glasses

Don't you hate it when your stacked glasses stick together? Submerge the bottom glass in hot water, which will expand it…then pour ice-cold water in the top glass, which will contract it. Once you have the hot-and-cold thing happening, you should be able to pull the glasses apart easily.

◆ When you are washing glass dishes in hot water, always put them into the water *sideways*. This will prevent them from cracking due to expansion (from heat) and contraction (from cold).

Caring for "The Good Crystal"

◆ We're talking about the tumblers and stemware and serving pieces you only take out for company…special company…and on special occasions. To clean these irreplaceable treasures, fill a basin or the sink with a 3:1 combination of hot water and distilled white vinegar.

 NOTE: For crystal that is really grimy or filmy, use 3 parts hot water to 2 parts distilled white vinegar.

    Once all the crystal is clean, rinse and dry each piece with a lint-free cloth. Your best bet in terms of *lint-free* is a linen towel, or a cloth made of least 25% linen.

 Protect Your Breakables
When you wash glasses in the sink, line it with a fluffy towel or a rubber mat in case a piece of crystal slips out of your hands.

◆ If your crystal has ornate and deep decorative etching, clean it with an old-fashioned shaving brush. If you do not have a brush lying around, they're available at The Art of Shaving Shops (nationwide, *www.theartof shaving.com*). You can also use a big makeup brush (used for rouge or powder, available wherever cosmetics are sold). These brushes are stiff enough to get into the dirt-collecting crevices, but are also soft enough to not damage the crystal.

◆ To repair hairline scratches on your crystal, put a dab of non-gel white toothpaste on a cloth and rub the scratches. The mild abrasive paste should smooth out the glass without a trace of a scratch. Rinse and wipe dry.

◆ If you don't use your crystal for long periods of time, consider covering each piece with plastic wrap. Then, the next time you take out the good stuff, each piece will be spotless and ready to use.

Cleaning Crystal Vases

◆ If you're reading this, it means that you don't have a bottle brush with which to reach the bottom and sides of your narrow-necked vase. Hopefully, you do have 2 or 3 tablespoons of dry, uncooked rice (either short-grained white or brown rice), and about ¼ cup of distilled white vinegar.

    Put the rice and vinegar in the vase, and then use a circular motion to shake it. The idea is to have the vinegar clean as the rice scours—without scratching the crystal.

◆ If your vase has caked-on crud on the inside, measure the amount of liquid it will hold, then mix 2 parts strong black tea to 1 part distilled white vinegar to fill it. Let the mixture stay in the vase overnight. The next day, spill out the solution and wash the vase with regular dish detergent. Rinse, dry and bring on some fresh flowers!

◆ Fill the vase with just-boiled water, then toss in 2 Alka-Seltzer tablets and let the citric acid and sodium bicarbonate bubbles scour your vase clean. Rinse as usual and dry.

CHINA

As you probably guessed, china dishes originated in the country of China, but it is now produced in many countries throughout the world. *China* generally refers to hard, white, translucent pottery. When it has a soft glaze, it is known as *porcelain*. This glaze can be produced in many different colors and designs, but purists tend to prefer it in white or ivory.

If you have fine china, it's important to wash it by hand. The heat from the dishwasher's drying cycle may do damage.

For more suggestions on how to wash china, *see* the remedies under "Caring for Glassware" on pages 14–15.

★ Keep China Safe

◆ If you are going to stack your fine china dishes, put a coffee filter or a paper plate between each piece. Doing so will prevent damage to the dishes' decorated surfaces.

◆ Every thrift shop has china teapots with chipped spouts. Prevent your teapot's spout from chipping by keeping a toilet paper tube over it, especially when it's in storage or during a household move.

You can also cut off the thumb from a big, thick, old glove and put it over the spout.

Seek and Thou Shalt Find

Are you missing a cup or saucer from your collection of good china? Will 1 dinner plate complete the set you inherited from your grandmother?

You may be able to fill in discontinued patterns of fine china, silver or crystal pieces from Replacements Ltd. Visit them at *www.replacements.com* or call 800-737-5223.

Cleaning Stains

For coffee, tea and most other stains, any of the following tips should work…

◆ Sprinkle baking soda on a damp sponge or cloth, and rub the cup or saucer.

◆ Rub the stain with white non-gel toothpaste, then rinse thoroughly with warm water.

◆ Fill the stained cup with warm water, drop in a denture-cleaning tablet and let it stay overnight. The next morning, wash, rinse and dry as usual.

◆ For a tough tobacco stain, mix a few drops of water with 1 tablespoon of table salt, then stick a cork in it. Use the salted cork to rub away the stain.

★ Cook Away Cracks with Milk

Put a cracked china cup or plate in a pan and pour in enough whole milk to cover it—and then some. Let it simmer on the stovetop for 45 minutes. That allows enough time for the milk protein (casein) to do what it needs to do, which is to fill in the fissures. When the time is up, take the china off the stove and let it cool. Then rinse and marvel at the restored piece.

CORNINGWARE

This kitchenware classic was developed by a company whose history dates back to 1851, and which has made contributions that have affected—and continue to affect—our lives on a daily basis.

For instance, in 1880, Corning provided the glass for inventor Thomas Edison's first lightbulb. By 1915, Corning had developed its Pyrex heat-resistant glass tableware. And in 1957, Corning's innovative glass-ceramic technology made the production of CorningWare possible.

With such a rich history, it pays to keep your CorningWare looking its best.

Cleaning CorningWare

You can remove grease and stains by pouring ¼ cup of distilled white vinegar and 1 teaspoon of liquid dish detergent in the piece of CorningWare. Fill the rest with hot—but not boiling—water. Let it stand for about 5 minutes, then wash and rinse it out.

EVERYTHING *AND* THE KITCHEN SINK

While researching this section, we were so amazed to discover that many of the kitchen accessories and appliances that are considered to be *modern* conveniences have actually been around since the 1800s.

How much do you know about the things that help you prepare food on a daily basis? See if you can select a kitchen item from the following list that was NOT invented in the 19th century—electric mixer, toaster, potato peeler, pressure cooker, waffle iron or coffee grinder.

If you said "pressure cooker," you are right. It was not invented in the 1800s. It was invented by French physicist Denis Papin—in 1679!

Well, enough fun and games. *Here are some hints to help you keep your kitchen tools in good shape and working well...*

Cleaning a Porcelain Sink

To remove yellow stains from a porcelain sink, make 1 of 2 pastes—either add lemon juice to borax powder (available at supermarkets and drugstores)...or add 3% hydrogen peroxide to cream of tartar (available at supermarkets).

For both pastes, use a ratio of 1 teaspoon of the dry ingredient to ¼ teaspoon of the wet ingredient—the paste should be the consistency of soupy oatmeal. Rub the paste into the stained sink with a clean, dry washcloth. Let the paste dry, then wipe it off with a wet cloth or sponge and rinse the sink.

Unclogging a Sink Drain

If your drain is starting to back up, it may be clogged. First, pour 1 cup of baking soda down the drain. Then, in a pan, warm up 1 cup of distilled white vinegar, and pour *that* down the drain. Wait about 10 minutes, then let the hot water run for a minute.

Preventing Clogged Drains

◆ If you have used coffee grounds, pour a little bit down the drain, then let the hot water run for a minute.

◆ Mix ½ cup of salt in 1 quart of hot water, then pour the salt-water solution down the drain. Do this every other week, and it should prevent grease buildup and deodorize as well.

Hang Your Hat—or Rings

If you normally wear rings, a watch, a bracelet or any other jewelry that shouldn't be worn while cooking or cleaning, it's good to have a safe, reliable place in the kitchen where you can stash it.

Put up a hook large enough to hang a watchband on (or whatever jewelry you wear on a regular basis). Position it near enough to be convenient when you start to work in the kitchen, but out of harm's way when the stove, microwave, dishwasher or garbage disposal are in use. Putting up that little hook will be something you wish you had thought to do years ago.

 Weigh In More Accurately
Check the accuracy of your food scale by putting 9 pennies on it. If the indicator points to 1 ounce, the scale is accurate.

Nothing to Sneeze At

Instead of having plastic produce bags taking up lots of space in a drawer waiting to be recycled, or floating around loose in a cabinet, pack them into an empty tissue box.

If you do not want to use the cardboard kind, look for a plastic tissue dispenser that matches your kitchen.

Cute Cookie Cutter Creation

Use some ribbon that matches your kitchen's color scheme to string together your cookie cutters. If you have a lot of them, tie together the ends of the ribbon to make an attractive cookie-cutter wreath—hang it on a hook as a decoration in your kitchen.

Of course, if you just have a few and don't want them on display, you can hang the ribbon on a hook inside a cabinet.

No More Rust Rings

Cans stored for a long time on a kitchen shelf or counter may sometimes leave rust rings. To prevent this, place small lids—such as from plastic containers of yogurt, cottage cheese, butter/margarine, etc.—under the cans as coasters. You'll never have to deal with a rust ring on your shelf or counter again.

Removing Jar Labels And Glue

◆ Remove a label from a jar by first rubbing regular (not reduced-fat) mayonnaise, butter or cooking oil into the label. Then soak the jar in very hot water. After about 10 minutes, peel off the label.

◆ If the label or price tag is off, but a sticky glue spot remains, massage vegetable oil or peanut butter into the spot until all the glue is gone. Clean the jar with soap and water.

Jar Opening Made Easy

◆ To open a stubborn jar, put on a pair of rubber gloves. Then, get a good grasp, and twist the lid counterclockwise.

◆ Put a thick rubber band around the lid of the jar and another rubber band around the middle of the jar. Grasp a band with each hand, and twist the lid counterclockwise.

◆ Turn the jar upside down and let the hot tap water run over it for about a minute. Then turn it right-side up, put on rubber gloves and try to open it.

◆ Vacuum-sealed jars are often hard to budge, but they may be opened with the help of a small screwdriver. Slip the tip of the screwdriver under the edge of the lid and turn it a little to allow air to seep in and unseal the lid. It should open easily.

◆ If you're dealing with a jar of something sticky—such as honey, maple syrup or jam—after it's opened, rub a coat of petroleum jelly lightly over the rim of the jar and the screw part of the lid. The jar will be easy to open from then on.

Make Life Easier for the Chief Bottle Washer

After rinsing out a bottle or jar, turn it upside down and shake it in a circular motion, creating a whirlpool effect.

The air rushes in, the water rushes out and your bottle-rinsing time is cut in half. This saves both time and water.

One to Grow On

Use a terra-cotta flowerpot as a lovely kitchen caddy for spatulas, wooden spoons and other utensils that don't fit in silverware holders.

Flowerpots are inexpensive, come in a variety of sizes and, if you're craftsy, you can have fun decorating them.

Starchy Protection

To prevent light grease stains from messing up your beautiful new pot holder or oven mitt, just spray it with spray starch. You won't need to wash the pot holder very often, but each time you do, spray it after each washing. The starch forms a coating that protects the potholder or mitt—it prevents the oil from seeping through the fabric.

Washing Wood Salad Bowls

It's important to remember that wood is porous and may absorb some dish detergent. If you don't want to wash your mouth out with soap when you eat dinner, then don't wash wood food bowls with detergent!

Instead, rinse out the bowls with plain water, then wipe the inside with a light coating of cooking oil on a paper towel.

Instant Apron!

It's easy to make a homemade apron that's a CUT above the rest! Here's an easy and inexpensive way to coverup in the kitchen (it can also be used as a smock for painting or any other messy job).

Just take a big plastic trash bag and cut out about 12" to 15" along the center of the sealed edge (this is where your head goes through). On the side edges near the head hole, cut a few inches to make holes for your arms to go through. Pull the bag over your head, insert your arms and *voilà*!

Stacking Cookware

Get a few cardboard boxes and use them to cut out circles that fit inside the bottoms of your nonstick cookware.

To prevent one pot's outer bottom from scratching another pot's inner surface, be sure the cardboard circles are in place before you stack one pot on top of another.

You can also use big plastic lids (like those from a set of Tupperware) as pot coasters instead of the cardboard.

Junk Drawer Safety

Keep a pulled cork on the end of a corkscrew, especially if the corkscrew is loose in a drawer with other things you often seek out.

Cleaning a Garbage Can

Clean the garbage can with ½ cup of distilled white vinegar mixed with 1 tablespoon of liquid dish detergent and 2 cups of hot water. Rinse well and wipe dry or air dry. Then sprinkle a thin layer of borax powder (available at supermarkets and drugstores) on the bottom of the can.

Doing this should inhibit the growth of bacteria and mold, and will also prevent the dreaded reeking garbage can. Resprinkle the borax about once a month, and use the vinegar solution every 6 months—or at the first sign of a garbage smell.

Taking Care of Kitchen Knives

♦ To sharpen a knife, find a coffee mug with an unglazed rim on the bottom, or turn a terracotta (clay) flowerpot upside down. Hold the knife at an angle and run the blade (starting at the knife's handle) down the bottom of the mug or flowerpot.

Then turn the knife over and do the same thing to the other side of the blade. Repeat the procedure until the knife is as sharp as you want it to be. Just be careful!

♦ To sharpen a small knife blade, slide it back and forth on a matchbox's strike panel.

◆ If you have a set of knives that are kept in a wood container, that's good. But if you have knives floating around in a kitchen drawer, that's not so good. But you can make easy sleeves for the knives—just flatten a few empty paper towel rolls, fold over 1 end and close it off with tape or a staple. Insert the knife into the open end, with the blade side pointing away from you (toward the closed end of the sleeve). The sleeves will protect the knife blades as well as your fingers.

◆ To remove rust on a good kitchen knife, cut an onion and rub the cut onion on the blade several times. If all the rust doesn't come off, stick the knife into the onion and let it stay that way for about 1 hour. Then rinse and dry the knife and throw away the onion.

Taking Care of Scissors

◆ To sharpen a pair of scissors, fold a piece of aluminum foil in thirds, then cut it with the scissors at least a dozen times. Then cut a piece of paper and see if the scissors' blades are sharper. If they *still* aren't as sharp as you want them to be, take another piece of foil and do it again. If they <u>still</u> aren't sharp enough, then take a sheet of fine sandpaper and cut it up.

If, after you've cut foil and sandpaper several times, the scissors STILL aren't as sharp as you want, consider buying a new pair of scissors.

 CAUTION: Sandpaper sharpening is not recommended for a good pair of sewing shears. Always have them sharpened by a professional sharpener.

◆ Scissors that stick might have some gooey residue from something they cut, such as tape or glue. Clean the scissors' blades with rubbing alcohol on a cotton ball. If doing that doesn't unstick them, rub the blades with an emery board.

◆ If the scissors stick after the blades have been cleaned, they may need to be lubricated. But you don't want to put oil on scissors because the oil will stain everything you cut.

Instead, use the natural oil on your fingers. Gently massage the blades—being careful not to cut yourself—until the blades move more smoothly. (If you have dry skin, you may be busy rubbing your scissors for the next year or so.)

Caring for a Cutting Board Or Butcher's Block

◆ To sanitize your plastic cutting board or your wood butcher's block, coat it with a light spray of distilled white vinegar, followed by a light spray of hydrogen peroxide. Let it sit for 10 minutes, then rinse and dry thoroughly.

 NOTE: Most bacteria cannot survive without moisture. Keep all surfaces in the kitchen dry...especially cutting boards and butcher's blocks.

◆ To remove a stain from your plastic cutting board or wood butcher's block, sprinkle table salt on it, then rub it with a wedge of lemon or lime. Rinse and dry. The salt draws out the grease and acts as an abrasive, while the lemon/lime helps bleach out the stain.

◆ Cuts in a wood cutting board? Well, uh, *yeeeah*. But those cuts can be home to germs. Every now and then, smooth away the cuts with a piece of fine sandpaper.

To remove a strange smell from your wood board or block, rub it with a piece of lemon. Rinse. Dry. Sniff. No smell!

 NOTE: These suggestions also apply to caring for a wood rolling pin.

Caring for All Types of Countertops

◆ If you border on obsessive-compulsive when it comes to having your countertop and other kitchen surfaces clean and disinfected, keep 2 spray bottles handy—fill 1 with 3% hydrogen peroxide and the other with distilled white vinegar.

Lightly spray your counter with the peroxide, and wipe it clean. Follow up with a light spray of the vinegar, and wipe it clean. Then relax, knowing that your countertop and other kitchen surfaces have been treated with antiviral, antifungal as well as antibacterial agents.

◆ Food stains on your nice, clean countertop can be eliminated with a sprinkle of baking soda. Just add some water to make a paste and, after a few minutes, rub off the stain with a damp cloth.

◆ For coffee or tea stains, rub the countertop with a piece of lemon rind.

◆ How many times has the purple ink from a stamped-on price stayed on your countertop? Rub off the ink with rubbing alcohol or the inside of a piece of lemon rind. If the alcohol or the lemon doesn't do it, try nail polish remover. Then wipe with a damp cloth or sponge.

NOTE: If you have any hesitation about using nail polish remover on the surface of your counter, either don't use it…or test a tiny can't-be-seen-area before using it on the whole countertop.

 Make More Space!
When you need more counter space for a party or special occasion, set up an ironing board. Make sure it's secure and won't tip over, then cover it with a nice tablecloth to make it look more festive.

Or, open a kitchen drawer and put a cutting board, cookie pan or serving tray on it.

Cleaning a Grater

◆ How yucky is it to clean a grater, especially after grating cheese? Instead, grate a piece of raw potato and let it do the cleanup for you.

◆ Running cold water on the grater will harden the cheese, making it easier to clean off. Hot water melts the cheese on.

◆ If you're into *zest* (the outermost part of a lemon or orange) and frequently grate rind, set aside an old toothbrush to use as your grater cleaner.

 "Grate" Cleanup Advice
Spray the grater with nonstick cooking spray before you use it. It will take the yuck out of cleanup.

Cleaning a Thermos

◆ Fill the thermos about 2" from the top with warm water, then add 2 tablespoons of baking soda. Put the top on and shake vigorously. Then rinse and dry.

◆ If the thermos is really dirty, add equal parts of baking soda, cream of tartar and lemon juice—enough to fill about ⅓ of the thermos. Put the cover on and shake vigorously, or use a bottle brush to scrub with the mixture. Then rinse and dry.

Sweeten Your Thermos

If you don't use your thermos for long periods of time, store it with 1 white-sugar cube or with 1 teaspoon of white sugar (make sure the thermos is clean and dry and that the top is screwed on *tight*!). The sugar will stop any stale odors before they start.

What's That Smell?

◆ To freshen up a stinky metal or plastic lunchbox, moisten a slice of bread with distilled white vinegar and let it stay in the lunchbox overnight. The next morning, throw away the soggy bread, wash out the lunchbox with warm soapy water, rinse and dry thoroughly —then load it up with your child's sandwich and fruit.

◆ Depending on the size of the plastic container you want to de-skunk, put in anywhere from 1 to 3 tablespoons of baking soda. Add hot water to the brim, cover the container and let it stay that way overnight. The next morning, rinse and dry. Instead of baking soda, you can also use ¼ to ½ teaspoon of mustard powder.

◆ Crinkle up a page of black-and-white newspaper, put it in the smelly plastic container, cover it and let it stay that way overnight. The next morning, take out the paper, wash, rinse and dry.

Keep Smells from Sticking

Line a container with plastic wrap before you put in foods—such as cheese, peanut butter, salami, sour pickles or tuna fish—that might leave lingering smells.

Removing Stains from a Plastic Container

Apply a little lemon juice on the stain, then let the container sit in the sun for a couple of hours. Then wash, rinse and dry.

Contain Your Stains

If you have stain-causing leftovers—such as tomato sauce, curry or chili—lightly mist the container with nonstick cooking spray before putting in the food. The *lecithin* in the spray acts as a repellent to stain-setting pigments.

Cleaning a Highchair Tray

You can wipe off food splatters on your baby's highchair with a bit of baking soda sprinkled on a damp cloth or sponge.

To disinfect the eating surface (tray), just wipe it down with antiseptic mouthwash (such as Listerine).

And while you're at it, you can wipe down teething toys this way, too. ■

■ Products ■

Touchless Trashcan

Whoever thought that we'd get excited about a trashcan? Fair warning—if you see this product in action, you'll want to own it.

Why? It's a sleek, stainless steel can with a brushed-chrome silver finish and a black lid that opens and closes automatically. You do not need to touch anything…you do not have to step on anything. You just hold your hand over the Smart-Chip, and technology does the rest (and it can operate manually, if you choose). The unit uses four "D" batteries (not included), which last for about 3,600 openings…or 6 months at 20 openings a day.

Source: iTouchless Innovation Housewares & Products, Inc., 800-660-7978, *www.touchlesstrashcan.com.*

Talking Timer

If you need to keep to a schedule or remember when to take the baking dish out of the oven, this device can help you. It's both a clock and a timer, and it's smaller than a deck of cards.

A female voice announces the time and counts down (for example, "One minute remaining…"), and counts up, too. The timer has 6 different alarm sounds. It has a waistband clip, a magnet and a stand so you can use it anywhere.

If you can set a digital watch, you can follow these simple instructions.

Source: Dynamic Living, Inc., 888-940-0605, *www. dynamic-living.com.**

*The company has a free monthly e-mail newsletter that offers ideas and tips to make living at home a little easier.

CHAPTER 2

The Best-Ever Food Secrets

Whether you are a gourmet chef or you need a map to find your kitchen, we hope there are lots of helpful ideas here that will make food preparation a delicious, safe and successful experience.

FOOD A TO Z

Anybody who is into food should enjoy reading this A-to-Z listing—and hopefully, you will learn a lot in the process. If you're not a food person, then instead of overwhelming yourself by reading through ALL of this information, we suggest that you just look up the foods you intend to use—everything is arranged alphabetically for your convenience. That way, you'll be able to use the appropriate information when you're in the supermarket or in your kitchen.

Apple Cider

Before drinking fresh apple cider, find out if it has been pasteurized. Unpasteurized cider has been linked to food poisoning from bacteria, such as *salmonella*, *E. coli* and *listeria*. If you aren't sure about the jug of apple cider in your refrigerator, boil it for 1 full minute before drinking it (of course, make sure it has cooled first). Better safe than sorry!

Apples

◆ Apples will keep for weeks in a cool, dark place. Your refrigerator's fruit bin is perfect as well as your basement or garage. And it seems to be true that 1 bad apple spoils the rest. So, if there's room, don't let the apples touch each another, just in case 1 of them is bad.

◆ To keep cut apples from turning brown, try these suggestions…

  ◆ Dunk the cut pieces in a mixture of ¼ teaspoon of salt and 1 pint of water.

  ◆ Spritz citrus juice—either lemon, orange or grapefruit—on the cut apple pieces.

  ◆ Cover cut apple slices with apple juice and refrigerate them for about a half-hour. They won't turn brown, and the juice will make dry, flavorless apples crunchier and tastier.

25

◆ To prevent a mess when baking apples, there are 2 ways to prevent pressure from building in the apple's core...

   ◆ Remove ½" of peel around the middle of the apple and then bake it.

   ◆ Make 8 shallow slits around the apple before baking it. The slits will allow steam to escape, which prevents the rest of the peel from splitting.

◆ If you sprinkle the apple's bare midriff (or the 8 slits) with lemon juice, the citric acid may help stop the breakdown of proteins that can cause a mealy texture.

Asparagus

◆ Once you get these spears home, cut about ½" off the bottom. In a tall drinking glass or small vase, stand the bunch upright in about 1" of water. Cover them gently with a plastic bag, and refrigerate until they're ready to be used.

◆ Our instinct tells us to open the *top* of a can. But when it comes to canned asparagus, open the *bottom* of the can. That way, the spears will slide out, leaving the delicate asparagus tips intact. Hey, you'll have tip-top tips.

Avocados

◆ Avocados ripen best when kept at room temperature. The cold air in the refrigerator can turn them black.

◆ If you want an avocado to ripen quickly, place it in a brown paper bag along with an apple slice, a banana peel or a tomato. Keep the bag closed, but check often so that the avocado doesn't get overripe and turn into mush.

◆ If you only use ½ an avocado, keep the pit in the remaining half, then lightly brush lemon juice on the open side. Cover it with plastic wrap and refrigerate. (The same goes for guacamole—add some lemon juice, cover and refrigerate to keep it fresh.)

Avocado Bravado

The avocado is a great source of heart-healthy monounsaturated fat, which helps increase the body's absorption of antioxidants known as *carotenoids* (nutrients that help reduce the risk of cancer and cardiovascular disease).

And, as if that wasn't enough, avocados are also loaded with dietary fiber and other healthy stuff like folate and vitamin K. And they taste great!

Bacon

◆ When you bring home the bacon (literally), roll the package lengthwise, and put a rubber band around it to keep it that way.

Then refrigerate it. When you're ready to use it, the bacon slices will be easier to separate.

■ Recipe ■

Bacon Sticks

To create a will-be-gobbled-up-in-seconds treat, you'll need 1 package of prebaked, store-bought bread sticks and 1 pound of low-sodium bacon (also works with soy bacon or turkey bacon). Adding 1 cup of parmesan cheese is optional.

Wrap ½ slice of bacon around each bread stick, barbershop-pole style. Line up the sticks on a broiler pan and put them in the oven at 325°F for about 30 minutes, or until the bacon is crisp.

When you take them out of the oven, roll them on paper towels to blot them. Here comes the optional part—you can then roll them in the parmesan cheese. With or without the cheese, they're scrumptious.

◆ Rinse the slices in cold water before frying, and they won't curl in the pan.

◆ If you throw a few celery leaves into the pan along with the bacon, the grease will stay in the pan instead of splattering.

◆ To minimize the shrinkage of the bacon, do not preheat the skillet. Just plop in the bacon and let it cook over a medium flame.

Bananas

◆ To ripen bananas, poke holes in a brown paper bag, then put the bananas and 1 ripe apple in the bag. It should speed up the ripening process of the banana before you peel it. Check often so that you use the banana and the apple before *ripen* turns to *rotten*.

◆ If you brush an unpeeled banana with lemon, orange or pineapple juice, it won't turn brown …for a while.

◆ Forget the myth about not putting bananas in the refrigerator. If you put a ripe banana (with the peel) in a sealed jar or a plastic bag, getting out as much air as possible, and then put it in the fridge, you'll slow down the ripening process.

 NOTE: If you use this method, the peel will turn yucky brown, but the banana itself will be banana-color and delicious.

◆ Here's how to make a yummy frozen snack— peel a ripe banana, cut it into 1" to 2" pieces, wrap it in aluminum foil and put it in the freezer. When you want to eat the banana, just take off the foil and eat it like any frozen dessert.

◆ If you have a powerful blender or juicer, put several pieces of frozen banana into it, and whip up a surprisingly good banana custard.

Bay Leaves

Make it a snap to remove the bay leaves from your sauce, soup or stew by putting them in a tea ball (available at kitchen specialty stores). The holes let the flavor out, but keep the herb contained inside.

Beans

We love beans, but we hate the intestinal gas they create! These suggestions range in effectiveness from partial flatulence prevention to totally gas-free. The only way to know which works best for you is to put them to the test… when you're dining alone.

◆ Soak dry beans overnight in a pot of water along with ⅛ to ¼ cup of apple cider vinegar. The next morning, thoroughly rinse the beans, put fresh water and 1 or 2 tablespoons of apple cider vinegar into the pot, and cook the beans as usual.

◆ Soak dry beans overnight in water with 1 teaspoon of fennel seeds (tied up in a piece of cheesecloth). The next morning, take out the seeds, spill out the water and cook the beans as usual in fresh water. During the cooking process, toss in a few pieces of raw peeled potato. When the beans are done, remove the potato pieces.

◆ If you want to add salt when you're cooking beans, add it when they are almost finished cooking. If you add salt too early, it will impede the beans' softening process. Ah, so that's why it takes forever for the beans to get done!

◆ While beans are cooking, pour in ½ can of cola to the water. Wouldn't you think that carbonated soda would *add* gas? It's good to know it actually *prevents* gas. Kitchen magic—that's what we're talking about.

◆ Avoid boil-over mess by adding 1 tablespoon of olive oil to the beans' cooking water.

◆ Keep weevils away from your supply of dry beans—put a dried hot pepper in the container in which the beans are stored.

Beef

◆ When you're grocery shopping, make the meat counter your last stop—that way, whatever you buy will stay cold as long as possible. Also, put the meat into a plastic bag so that if there's any dripping or leaking of the raw meat's juices, the other food in your cart and grocery bag will be protected.

◆ Marinate meat in a self-sealing plastic bag. This disposable container distributes the marinade evenly and there's no cleanup needed. After the marinating is done, simply throw away the bag.

◆ Let steak or ribs marinate in cola for 3 to 4 hours before cooking. The results are a more tender and tasty meat treat.

◆ A marinade made from distilled white vinegar will destroy bacteria as it tenderizes meat. Use ½ cup vinegar on a 4- to 6-pound roast. If you use herbs in your usual marinade, add them to the vinegar. Let it marinate overnight, and then prepare the meat without draining or rinsing it.

◆ The tannic acid in tea makes meat tender and juicy. Add 2 teabags (without the strings or tabs) of Pekoe black tea to the pot roast pot and cook as usual. Remove the teabags when the roast is done.

◆ It's tough to reheat a roast without drying it out. The idea here is to moisturize the roast as it reheats. Start by wrapping washed lettuce leaves around the roast, and wrap aluminum foil around the whole thing—pinch it closed.

Heat the oven to 425° to 475°F and put the roast in for 2 to 10 minutes (depending on the size of the roast). By flash-heating it, you get the meat warm without overcooking it.

◆ Put raw beef in the freezer for about 15 minutes, and it will be much easier to cut the slim slices needed for a stir-fry.

◆ If you don't have a sharp knife—or you're not comfortable using one to cut thin strips of beef—use kitchen scissors to get the job done safely.

Also see "Thermometers/Cooking Temperatures" on pages 64–65 for guidelines on cooking beef properly.

Beef (Ground)

◆ Use a strainer (with a close weave) to rinse cooked, crumbled ground beef under hot water. By doing this, you will actually be able to wash away up to 50% of the fat.

◆ If you do not want to rinse your cooked ground beef, you can also use paper towels to blot off a lot of the excess grease and fat.

◆ Make a package of ground beef easy to stack in your freezer. Take the meat out of the package and put it in a plastic freezer bag, then flatten it with a rolling pin. When you want to use it, the flattened-out beef will thaw quickly.

 NOTE: Cut the label off the original meat wrapping and attach it to the new freezer bag so that you know what it is and when you got it.

◆ Put patties in the freezer for about 3 minutes right before you put them on the grill. It will help them keep their shape from grill to bun to mouth.

◆ Before piling on the raw patties to be grilled, cover your platter with plastic wrap. Then put the patties on top of it. Once you've transferred the patties to the grill, remove and discard the plastic wrap. You can now use the clean platter for the finished product...the grilled patties. This way, you have to wash the platter only once, and you save a trip inside to get another platter.

◆ Before broiling or grilling, poke holes in the center of the burgers, which will let in the heat—they will cook surprisingly fast. How do you think White Castle is able to fill orders as quickly as they do? It's all about poking holes in the patties.

◆ Cut slices of white and yellow American cheese into 3" x ¾" strips. (If you're into soy cheese, you can use white Swiss or American and yellow cheddar.) Weave these strips (3 white and 3 yellow) into a checkerboard pattern and plop it on top of the burger for the last minute of grilling time. It's a creative way to serve cheeseburgers.

✳ **Healthier Beef Alternatives**

For those of you who want to cut down on your intake of high-cholesterol foods and/or reduce your intake of fat, replace traditional ground-beef products with *textured vegetable protein* (TVP), soy crumbles or cooked bulgur. All are available at supermarkets and health-food stores.

While you're there, check out the wide variety of beef substitutes in the form of burgers, nuggets and steaks. Be adventurous. You may actually enjoy eating these meat alternatives. (For starters, we recommend Sunshine Burgers, found in the refrigerated section.)

Meatballs with a Twist

Put a new ingredient in an old standard—meatball hors d'oeuvres. When making the meatballs, start with a little chunk of something—sautéed mushroom, pitted olive, cheese, dried apricot, grape tomato or come up with something even more creative—and pack the meat around it, forming the meatball.

Then cook, grill, broil or fry the meatballs as usual. *Ahh*, but there will be nothing "usual" about them! Guests will love tasting and comparing the fillers in these meatball hors d'oeuvres.

If you want to stick with the standard meatball, but want them perfectly moist, place a small ice cube in the middle of each before cooking.

◆ For easier meatloaf mixing, put the ingredients in a sturdy, resealable plastic bag and zip it closed. Then knead the outside of the bag, thoroughly blending the ingredients together. Then unseal the bag, plop the meat out into the meatloaf pan and discard the bag. Everything—especially your hands—will stay clean. And no concerns about raw-meat contamination.

◆ When making meatloaf, place 1 or 2 slices of uncooked bacon on the bottom of the pan. This will prevent the meatloaf from sticking, and it will add a little more flavor.

Also see "Thermometers/Cooking Temperatures" on pages 64–65 for guidelines on cooking burgers properly.

 Make Extra-Tender Fruity Beef

Many people are sensitive to *monosodium glutamate* (MSG), a substance that is commonly used in cooking as a meat tenderizer. Fortunately, MSG is not the only tenderizer available. *Papain* is an enzyme found in papaya that can help tenderize meat. Let the meat sit in papaya juice (available at grocery stores) in the refrigerator for 3 or 4 hours. Then blot the meat dry and prepare as usual.

Berries

OK, so you got a ton of berries for a bargain price. Instead of eating all of these little beauties so quickly that you can't look at them anymore—freeze them.

If space allows, the best way to do this is to spread them on an ungreased cookie sheet. Cover the sheet with plastic wrap, and freeze the berries for about 20 minutes, until they're frozen solid. Then put them in a plastic freezer bag, and seal it closed with as little air in it as possible. This freezing system will prevent the berries from squishing and sticking together.

Bread and Biscuits

◆ Aluminum reflects heat, so line your breadbasket with foil, then cover the foil with a napkin. The bread will stay warmer longer.

◆ When mixing the dough for whole-wheat bread, add 1 tablespoon of lemon juice. The bread will rise higher and be lighter, and you won't taste the lemon.

◆ About 5 minutes before your bread finishes baking, brush the top with distilled white vinegar—this will make the loaf shine.

◆ To enhance the rising time of your bread's yeast, run the dishwasher on its hot cycle, and dry it with a towel. Then place the bowl of bread dough in the dishwasher. Within no time, it should rise.

◆ To make stale bread fresh again, spray it with a bit of water or milk and wrap it in aluminum foil. Put it in a 350°F oven for about 8 minutes, and the bread should taste as though it just came out of the oven…for the first time.

◆ If you want to freshen a stale loaf of Italian or French bread, follow the steps above, then carefully open the foil and leave the bread in the oven for another 3 to 5 minutes.

◆ When a recipe calls for stale bread, but your bread is fresh, put the slices in the toaster on the lowest setting—this will dry out the bread. Let it cool for a few minutes, then it will be stale enough for the recipe.

◆ If you like your biscuits to be crusty, space them out on the baking sheet. If you like soft-sided biscuits, line them up next to each other with the sides touching. For browner biscuits, lightly spray the tops with butter-flavored cooking oil.

Bread Crumbs

◆ When you want to prepare your own bread crumbs and don't have any stale bread, lightly toast slices of fresh bread. Cut them in pieces and toss them into the blender or food processor.

◆ If your loaf of bread is frozen, you can grate it into crumbs.

◆ Consider seasoning the bread with your favorite dried herbs and/or powdered spices. But be sure to do a taste test before mixing anything into the entire batch of bread crumbs.

◆ For every cup of bread crumbs called for in a recipe, use ¾ cup of cracker crumbs.

 Great Use for Cereal

Instead of bread crumbs, consider using oatmeal or instant mashed potatoes (ground in the blender) as a filler for meatloaf and veggie burgers.

You can also use any whole-grain flaked cereals (unsweetened, of course) or soda crackers (also ground in the blender) as a substitute for bread crumbs in stuffing or as a casserole topping.

Brown Sugar

See "Sugar" on page 63.

Butter

◆ It takes only seconds for butter on the stove to go from *good* to *gone*—as in burnt and no longer usable. The secret to sautéing butter and not scorching it is to add a little olive oil.

 NOTE: Olive oil contains healthy monoun-saturated fats, so consider using just the olive oil and forget the butter altogether.

◆ When your cookie recipe calls for butter, do not melt it...especially in a microwave. The melted butter will make the cookies flat and greasy. Soften butter at room temperature. If it's cut into small pieces, it's easy to blend.

◆ Use a cheese grater to shred your too-hard butter, making it easier to work with and more blendable.

◆ For your next dinner party, serve a bowl of butter balls instead of putting out sticks or individual pats of butter. Simply place a melon ball cutter in very hot water for about 5 minutes.

   While it warms up, prepare a bowl of cold water with lots of ice cubes in it. Then, when the melon ball cutter is hot, scoop out the butter balls from a large container of butter, and drop each of them in the bowl of ice-cold water. Keep the balls cold in the refrigerator until you're ready to put them on the table for your guests.

Buttermilk

◆ An alternative for buttermilk in a recipe is to use the same amount of plain yogurt.

◆ Or you can mix 1 tablespoon of lemon juice into 1 cup of regular milk, and let it stand for 10 minutes before using—this is the equivalent of 1 cup of buttermilk.

 NOTE: Instead of putting lemon juice in the milk, you can use 1 tablespoon of distilled white vinegar. Let it stand for 10 minutes before using it in your recipe.

Cabbage

◆ To wash away any small insects that may be nestled between the cabbage leaves, fill a basin or sink with cold water, add 2 or 3 tablespoons of distilled white vinegar, and soak the cabbage for 10 minutes. Then rinse the cabbage with plain water and use those lovely, bug-free leaves.

◆ To remove leaves easily, freeze the head of cabbage. Once it's completely frozen, take it out of the freezer, and let it thaw completely. The leaves will be soft and easy to pull apart.

◆ Any of these suggestions may eliminate—or at least reduce—the smell of cabbage's volatile sulfur compounds...
   ◆ Add a stalk of celery to the cooking pot.
   ◆ The minute you begin cooking cabbage, toss a walnut—with the shell still on— into the pot.
   ◆ Add a pinch of baking soda to the cooking water.
   ◆ While the cabbage is cooking, place a heel of bread on top of it.
   ◆ Add ½ lemon to the cooking water once it starts boiling.

Cake

◆ Believe it or not, there is a fat substitute for some (not all) cakes. It works best with recipes that include *wet* ingredients, such as milk or fruit. Just substitute an equal quantity of applesauce or other fruit purée for the oil, butter or margarine called for in the recipe.

Smart Sauce Idea
Buy small snack-packs of applesauce, and use them as you need them. It's more efficient than having a big, open jar of applesauce taking up space in your refrigerator.

◆ An easy and efficient way to mix dry ingredients is to put them together in a plastic bag and *shake-shake-shake*.

◆ When mixing nuts and/or dried fruit, put them in a plastic bag, add a little flour and shake the bag so that the ingredients get fully coated with flour. When added to the cake batter, these coated pieces will be distributed evenly instead of sinking to the bottom.

◆ Is it done yet? If you don't have a toothpick —or if a toothpick isn't long enough to test whether or not the cake is ready to take out of the oven—use a strand of uncooked spaghetti to get the job done.

◆ To prevent your cake from sticking to the serving plate, sprinkle the cake plate with powdered sugar before setting down the cake. Now you're ready to cut and serve!

Cake Frosting

◆ You want to cover a cake with plastic wrap, but don't want it to stick to the cake's icing. Just spray the inside of the plastic wrap with a nonstick spray before covering the cake.

◆ If you're a big fan of the chocolate–peanut butter combination, just mix 1 tablespoon of creamy peanut butter into chocolate frosting. Because of all the good-for-you fats that peanut butter contains, it's a healthy addition… not to mention how delicious it tastes.

◆ If you don't want to frost a cake, you can decorate it with the help of a paper doily. Here's what to do…after the cake has cooled, center a doily on top of the cake and sprinkle powdered sugar on it. Be sure all the openings in the doily's pattern are covered with sugar.

Then gently lift off the doily to reveal a lovely, lacy design on the cake.

 NOTE: If you are so inclined, use a piece of paper to cut your own lacy pattern and decorate the cake with it.

◆ The secret to slicing a frosted cake easily and neatly is to dip the knife in hot water before you make the first cut.

Candy

◆ If you make your own candy, do it on dry days to get the best results. Candy made on rainy or damp days won't set properly—this is because sugar blots up humidity.

◆ When preparing to boil homemade candy, butter about 1" around the inside of the top of the pot. This will help prevent liquid from boiling over.

Cans

Before opening a can of soda or soup or beans, rinse the top with water and then dry it off. This quick, easy step can help prevent undesirable bacteria from getting into the can when you open it.

Carrots

Put the crunch back into raw limp carrots by letting them soak in some ice water for about 30 minutes.

Cauliflower

◆ Soak a head of cauliflower in salted ice water with the florets facing down for at least 30 minutes. Any little bugs that have taken up residence will float out.

◆ To maintain cauliflower's bright white color, cook it with 1 tablespoon of distilled white vinegar...or a little lemon juice...or some milk added to the water.

Caviar

With this section, we're straying from the practical and introducing the extravagant. It's meant for those who want to try caviar for the first time, as well as for those of you who have had a long-running *roe-mance* with this delicacy. *Here are a few suggestions to help you select, store, serve and eat these salted sturgeon eggs...*

◆ There are several high-profile types of Russian caviar, with *beluga* being considered the best (it's the most expensive). There is also the fine-flavored *osetra*...as well as *sevruga*, whose eggs tend to clump together...and the almost-extinct *sterlet sturgeon*. The choice is up to you, your budget and the availability of these precious little glistening eggs.

When you're ready to splurge, keep in mind that caviar connoisseurs generally agree that *pasteurized* caviar—which is not refrigerated and is sold in vacuum-packed jars—cannot begin to compare to the taste of fresh caviar.

> **NOTE:** Caviar on crackers is sinful...in a bad way. According to some food mavens, crackers are too crisp for the tender fish eggs. Then again, there are some beluga buffs who wouldn't eat it any other way.

◆ Caviar should be served simply with *crème fraîche* (a cultured cream with the texture of a rich cream cheese, but with a taste that is more tart, like a fine yogurt) and fresh handmade *blini* (yeast-risen buckwheat pancakes)—both tend to be available at specialty gourmet shops that also sell caviar.

◆ The top 3 most traditional potables paired with caviar are champagne (chilled), vodka (chilled) and dry white wine (cool).

◆ Caviar is delicate and perishable. Read all of the labels on the packaging before serving.

◆ Take caviar out of the refrigerator 10 to 15 minutes before serving. If it's going to be on a buffet table and may not be eaten for a while, keep it in its original jar or tin, and wedge that container into a bowl of crushed ice.

◆ Once the caviar container has been opened, finish it within 2 to 3 days.

◆ *Never* use a metallic spoon for scooping out, serving or eating caviar. The metal will taint the taste, giving it a horrid, unsavory flavor. The utensils of choice should be made from mother-of-pearl, bone or tortoise shell. The spoons are usually available wherever caviar is sold. (Of course, if you've spent too much money on the caviar, *crème fraîche* and *blini*, it's perfectly fine to use plastic spoons.)

Celery

◆ Peel the stalks with a vegetable peeler to get rid of the strings and minor boo-boos. The peeled-off strips of string are wonderful for decorating dishes of prepared food. Peel a celery stalk, and you'll see what we mean.

◆ If you want to dice up celery, use a pair of kitchen scissors and you won't have to peel it or deal with the string thing.

◆ To revive wilted celery, place the rubbery stalks in a bowl or pickle dish with ice water and a few slices of raw potato. In about 1 hour, the stalks should be nice and crisp and ready to serve.

◆ You can also cut about ⅛" from the bottom of the stalks, stand them up in a tall drinking glass or small vase that is filled with cold water, and let them stay in the refrigerator for a couple of hours.

◆ When you buy celery that still has its leaves, put the entire bunch in a plastic bag and keep it in the refrigerator...leave the leaves on until you're ready to use the stalks. If you buy celery that's been trimmed, put the stalks in aluminum foil. They should keep fresh in the refrigerator for weeks.

Cheese

◆ To prevent a chunk of cheese from getting moldy, place it in a resealable plastic bag along with 1 or 2 cubes of sugar (try to squeeze any excess air out of the bag). The cheese should stay fresh longer, and the sugar deters mold.

◆ You can also dampen a piece of cloth with apple cider vinegar, wrap it around the block of cheese, and seal it in a plastic bag. The acid in the vinegar will help prevent the growth of mold.

◆ Keep shredded cheese in an airtight, resealable bag in the freezer—where no mold can grow.

◆ If the cheese has mold, cut off a 1" square around the moldy area, and you can safely eat the rest.

◆ To prevent cheese from hardening, coat the exposed edges of the cheese with a thin layer of butter—the moisture from the butter will prevent the cheese from getting hard and inedible. Wrap and store the buttered cheese in the refrigerator. When you're ready to eat the cheese, just wipe off the butter...or not.

◆ Bring out the full flavor of your favorite hard cheese by putting it in the microwave. Nuke it for about 10 seconds on a high setting or 15 seconds on a medium setting.

◆ To prevent grated cheese from sticking to the bowl you're grating it into, lightly coat the bowl with flour.

◆ Before you cut or grate a block of cheese, put the wedge in the freezer for about 20 minutes. This will prevent it from clinging to the knife or the grater.

◆ If you're grating just a little bit of cheese, spray the grater with a nonstick vegetable spray. The spray helps prevent the cheese from sticking to the grater, but not for long (you may have to reapply).

◆ Once you open a container of cottage and/or ricotta cheese, you can do 1 of 2 things to prolong its staying power—either transfer the unused portion to a glass jar with a screw-on lid and refrigerate...or, after you've opened the container, close the lid securely and store it upside down in the refrigerator.

◆ It's not a good idea to zap cream cheese in the microwave—it can melt. Instead, put the cream cheese in a resealable plastic bag and zip it closed. Then dunk it in warm water for about 4 minutes...until it's soft and workable.

◆ If you're counting fat grams and want an alternative to cream cheese, line a strainer with a coffee filter and place it over a bowl. Fill the center of the filter with plain, low-fat yogurt. Cover it with plastic wrap and refrigerate it.

(i) **FYI: Yummy Creamy Yogurt**
Yogurt cream is delicious mixed with any number of things, including fruit, honey, vanilla extract, almond extract, carob powder, cocoa powder, flaxseed and wheat germ. Or, you can add herb seasonings and use it as a healthy dip for vegetables.

About 8 hours later, most of the moisture will have drained out, and the yogurt should have a spreadable consistency like cream cheese.

Cheesecake

◆ If the surface of your cheesecake is cracked— or just not presentable enough to serve to guests—spread an attractive and delicious topping of fresh fruit...or pie filling...or 1 cup of sour cream mixed with 1 tablespoon of sugar...or shaved shards of chocolate.

 NOTE: To make chocolate shavings, use a vegetable peeler on a chocolate bar. And try to make your shavings from dark chocolate—it's healthier than milk chocolate.

◆ Unflavored dental floss will cut a cheesecake better than most knives. Take a piece of floss that's a few inches longer than the diameter of the cake. Hold an end in each hand, and hold your hands as far apart as possible, making the floss taut. Then cut the cheesecake in half. Slide the floss out from the bottom of the cake. Now that there are 2 halves, you can cut slices—1 at a time—using the same method.

Chicken

◆ The "use by" or expiration date on a package of chicken is there for your safety. Abide by it unless you freeze the chicken. And even then, be sure to note the date you put the chicken in the freezer. If the freezer is set at 0°F, chicken can be frozen for 9 months to 1 year. If you've already cooked the chicken, either eat it or freeze it within 1 or 2 days.

◆ Always thaw a chicken in the refrigerator ...in its original package...on a plate on the lowest shelf. This will help the chicken retain its moisture and reduce the possibility that it will grow harmful bacteria, while the plate will catch any juices that may trickle out of the packaging.

◆ Do not put raw chicken alongside any food that is usually eaten raw, such as salad greens or fresh fruit.

◆ Wash everything that touches raw chicken —such as your hands, the cutting board, knives, counter, plates—with hot, soapy water before handling any other food.

◆ Raw chicken skin is usually slippery. To remove the skin easily, grab hold of it with a paper towel and give it a firm pull. *But...*

◆ If possible, leave the skin on the chicken— there's a membrane between the skin and meat of a chicken that keeps moisture in and fat out while it's cooking. So, for juicier, more flavorful chicken, remove the skin *after* it has been cooked.

◆ For crispier and more delicate fried-chicken coating, add about 1 teaspoon of baking soda to the batter.

◆ For extra-crispy fried chicken, add 1 rounded tablespoon of cornstarch for each cup of flour used.

Also see "Thermometers/Cooking Temperatures" on pages 64–65 for guidelines on cooking chicken properly.

Chili

Have a chili party and impress your guests by hollowing out crusty loaves of whole-grain bread and using them as the chili bowls. Put the chunks of bread that are taken out of the hollowed loaves in a breadbasket on the table —your guests can use them to dip in the chili. They can also eat the chili-soaked bowl once the chili is gobbled up.

Chocolate

◆ If a recipe calls for unsweetened squares of chocolate and you don't have any, you can substitute 3 tablespoons of powdered cocoa and 1 tablespoon of shortening for every square needed.

◆ When baking chocolate-based cakes, cookies or bread, use cocoa powder instead of plain flour to dust whatever needs dusting—the work surface, the rolling pin, the pan, etc.

◆ When you have cookies or cake or any dessert that would be more complete with some chocolate design on top, use chocolate chips. Put the chips in a heavy-duty resealable plastic bag and zip it shut. Dip the bag in a pot of very hot water (about 140°F) and keep it there for a few minutes…until the chocolate feels soft.

Carefully dry the outside of the bag, and cut a tiny hole in a bottom corner of the bag. Now you're ready to squeeze out the chocolate and do your creative dessert decorating.

 NOTE: You will probably want to practice on something *other* than the cake until you get the feel for it, and can coordinate your concept with your execution.

Chopsticks

If you sometimes have problems using chopsticks efficiently, bind them together with a rubber band set just above the halfway point. And then bring on the vegetable lo mein!

Coconut

◆ Select a coconut that sounds like it's full of liquid. When you're ready to open it, take out a hammer and a big nail or screwdriver. Place the nail or screwdriver on 1 of the 3 small, hairless black eyes or indentations on the coconut. Then tap the top of it with the hammer, piercing the eye. Ouch! Repeat the process on the other 2 eyes, and pour the liquid into a bowl.

◆ A coconut has a natural fault line. If you have a feel for these things, you may be able to crack the coconut open by using a hammer to tap around the widest part until there's a crack in the shell. Then continue turning and tapping the coconut on that fault line to make a clean break.

◆ Instead of depending on your *Survivor* abilities, you may want to put the coconut in a 375°F oven for 20 minutes. Take it out and let it cool for about 5 minutes. Then put a towel on top, and tap on it with a hammer until the coconut breaks.

◆ Instead of putting the coconut in the oven, try this—after you've pierced the eyes and purged the liquid, put it in the freezer for 1 hour, then cover it with a towel and tap on it with a hammer to break it open.

◆ Whichever method you use, you still have to pull the meat away from the shell with your hands and a screwdriver. It's dirty work, but it's worth it. The coconut meat will keep fresh in the refrigerator for about 5 days.

Coffee

◆ If you have ground coffee or coffee beans, but don't use them often, keep them in a tightly sealed container in a cool, dark place (like your kitchen pantry). By keeping air out, the coffee will retain its strong flavor. (As a last resort, you can also store coffee in the freezer.)

◆ If you gotta have that "cuppa joe" and you're out of filters, you can use 2 paper towels or 1 thick paper napkin instead of a filter.

◆ Before brewing ground coffee, try spicing it up with a pinch of cinnamon or a couple of drops of almond or vanilla extract.

◆ Freeze leftover coffee in an ice cube tray. Then you can use it to cool *hot-hot-hot* coffee...or to make iced coffee...or to add great flavor to eggnog.

Condiments

For a fun and colorful way to serve condiments (especially at a backyard barbecue), try this—hollow out a red bell pepper and fill it with ketchup...hollow out a yellow bell pepper and fill it with mustard...hollow out a green pepper and fill it with relish. Serve with a spoon.

Cookies

◆ Refrigerate your cookie dough. After about 30 minutes, the dough should be easier to work with. If it's still too sticky to manage, slowly knead in 1 or 2 tablespoons of flour.

◆ Before scooping up cookie dough with a spoon, dip the spoon in milk or olive oil to coat it. That way, the dough will glide off the spoon onto the cookie sheet.

◆ If you use your hands to shape the cookies, keep wetting them with cold water to prevent the dough from clinging. Better yet, spray your hands with cooking spray.

◆ When you're preparing peanut butter cookies, use a plastic fork to flatten them. The batter will not stick to plastic.

◆ If your kitchen is like most counter-scarce kitchens, and you need more space to cool your cookies, set up the ironing board. Put the cookies on paper plates and put the paper plates along the ironing board.

◆ Cookies will stay moist if you put a slice of apple in the container with them.

◆ Cookies will stay soft if you put a slice of bread in the container with them.

◆ Cookies will stay crisp if you crumple up a piece of tissue paper and place it on the bottom of the cookie container. Keep the cookies on top of the tissue and be sure the container stays closed—except when you're taking out a crisp cookie.

◆ To get neat, smooth squares when making cookie bars, use a pizza cutter to do the job.

Cookie Sheet

◆ Consider using parchment paper instead of greasing a cookie sheet. Not only will you save yourself the job of cleaning the cookie sheet, but the cookies will bake more evenly on the parchment paper. Plus, it's easy to transfer the finished product to the cooling rack.

◆ Also consider taping some parchment paper to the work surface on which you roll out the cookie dough.

Cooking Spray

Hold the pan (or whatever you're going to spray) over the kitchen sink, then spray. This will prevent you from spraying a slippery spot on the kitchen floor, and the over-spray in the sink will get washed away.

You can also spray over the open door of your dishwasher to achieve the same effect.

Corn

◆ Don't consider buying a cob of fresh corn unless it has husks—nature's freshness seal. The husks should be moist (rather than dried out) and bright green, with a little brown tassel on top. The kernels should feel full and plump.

 NOTE: Do not remove the husks until you are ready to prepare the corn for eating.

◆ As soon as you've taken off the husks, remove the silk threads by wiping them off, in a downward motion, with a damp paper towel.

◆ Do not add salt to the water when boiling corn—it will toughen the kernels. If you want to enhance the corn's natural sweetness, add 1 tablespoon of sugar or 1 or 2 packets of sugar substitute to the cooking water.

Cornstarch

If you've run out of cornstarch and need it for a recipe, use double the amount of flour instead.

Crackers

If your crackers are soggy, spread them out on an ungreased baking sheet, and put them in a 250°F oven for 15 minutes. Let them cool before serving the crispy treats.

Cranberries

Many recipes call for cranberry halves, which prevents whole cranberries from bursting while they're cooking. To halve them quickly, use a cutting board that has a gutter, line up the berries and cut them in half with a long knife.

 NOTE: Since the fresh-cranberry season is short—just November and December—buy them in season and freeze them. That way, you'll have the luxury of eating them all year-round.

Crumbs

Put whatever you want to turn into crumbs (such as cookies, crackers, nuts) in a resealable plastic bag. Make sure it's closed securely. Then roll over it with a rolling pin until the contents are as crummy as you want them to be. Use as much as you need, and then refrigerate the remaining crumbs in the plastic bag.

Cucumbers

If you keep cucumbers in the vegetable bin on the bottom shelf of your refrigerator, you're doing the right thing. It's the warmest place in the fridge. When cukes get too cold, they get mushy.

Cupcakes

◆ Do you love chocolate cupcakes with cream inside? Here's how to do it yourself—use a drinking straw to poke a hole in the middle of the top of each cupcake (when cool).

Then fill a clean plastic bag with vanilla frosting and cut a tiny hole in 1 corner of the bag. And now for the fun part—carefully pipe in the frosting from the bag into the hole in the cupcake.

 NOTE: If you want the cream to come as a surprise to the eater, place a chocolate chip...or a raisin...or a piece of walnut on top of the cupcake to hide the cream hole.

◆ About 3 or 4 minutes before the cupcakes are ready to be taken out of the oven, put a marshmallow on top of each. Then watch as the cupcakes finish baking with their instant frosting. Remove them from the oven when the melted marshmallows are just slightly brown.

◆ Once the cupcakes are out of the oven and cool, place a small chocolate-covered mint on top of each, and zap it in the microwave for a few seconds. Take out the cupcake and spread the melted chocolate mint around, just as you would spread frosting.

Deodorizers for the Kitchen

Whether you want to cover up cooking smells or create a fresh, appetizing scent in the kitchen, here are some suggestions…

◆ Keep a small bowl of leftover coffee grounds on the counter. They will help absorb cooking smells.

◆ In a pot, combine ½ cup of lemon juice, 1 cup of water and 3 or 4 whole cloves and/or a few cinnamon sticks. Let it simmer on your range for about 20 minutes…enough time to freshen the air in your kitchen.

◆ If it's cool outside, and you don't mind heating up your kitchen a little—and your smoke detector won't go crazy—preheat your oven to 300°F. With the oven door open a little, bake 1 whole (unpeeled) lemon for 15 minutes (poke a few holes in it first).

◆ If you like the lemon scent, but don't want to do the open-oven-door thing, slice up 1 whole lemon, put it in a pot of water and let it simmer on the stove for about 15 minutes.

◆ Put 1 teabag (make sure there's no metal staple), 2 teaspoons of cinnamon or another favorite spice and 1 cup of water in a microwave-safe bowl. Nuke it on *high* for 2 minutes. Then open the microwave door and wait a few minutes before removing the scented bowl and setting it on the counter.

◆ If you prefer a room spray, you can prepare your own. It will be healthier than commercial chemical sprays and also more economical. Combine 2 cups of distilled water (available at supermarkets), 2 cups of rubbing alcohol and 3 drops of natural lemon oil (available at health-food stores) in a large spray bottle. Shake it until the mixture is completely blended, and then it's ready to freshen the air.

Eggplant

◆ Choose an eggplant that's heavy for its size…or 1 that seems heavier than others that are the same size. To tell if an eggplant is ripe, gently press its flesh. If the dent bounces back and disappears, the fruit is ripe. If the dent stays a dent, the eggplant is too ripe.

On purple eggplants, look for smooth, taut skin that's glossy. If you're looking for white eggplant, discard any that seem to have a tinge of yellow.

◆ When you buy an eggplant in summer, during the fruit's peak season, it will be less bitter and have a thinner skin than when you buy it off-season.

◆ To take the bitterness out of a mature, out-of-season eggplant, chop or slice it and put it in a colander in the sink…or in a strainer over a bowl…or on a cooling rack on a baking pan. Sprinkle all of the eggplant pieces with table salt and let it stay that way for 1 hour. Then rinse well and pat dry before sautéing, grilling or baking.

 NOTE: The salt causes the release of the fruit's bitter juices, and it also helps keep it from absorbing excess oil.

Eggs

◆ As soon as you select a carton of eggs, open it and turn each egg. Make sure the egg moves within its little cubbyhole. If an egg doesn't move, it may be cracked and the leaked egg has glued to the carton. Or it may mean that it's stuck to the carton because of the dripping of another egg. In any case, you want a carton in which all of the eggs move freely when you turn them.

If a recipe (for example, Caesar salad) calls for a raw egg, be sure to use an egg that has been pasteurized (heated)—or do not use an egg at all.

> ⚡ **CAUTION 1:** NEVER eat a raw egg! The main risk is *salmonella*, a bacterium that can contaminate eggs through microscopic imperfections in their shells. The only way to kill the bacteria is through adequate heating.

> ⚡ **CAUTION 2:** NEVER use an egg that's cracked. Even if it's not oozing, just the fact that it has a crack means it could be contaminated with bacteria.

◆ Every hour that a carton of eggs is left out at room temperature is said to be equivalent to a week stored in the refrigerator. With this in mind, when you come home from the market, put those eggs in the fridge ASAP!

◆ Do not wash eggs before refrigerating them…not that we think you would. But keep them in their original carton, not in the refrigerator door's egg section. It's too warm there, and there's too much shaking going on each time the door opens and closes.

◆ Stored properly in the egg shelf of the refrigerator, fresh eggs will keep for up to 5 weeks.

◆ If your eggs have been in the fridge for a while, you may want to test their freshness. To do this, place each raw egg in a pot of water. If the egg floats, it's rotten. If it stands on its pointy end, it's 10 to 14 days old. If the egg tilts, it's about 3 or 4 days old.

You want an egg to sink and lie on its side. That means it's fresh—any fresher, and a live chicken will be walking out of your kitchen.

◆ When a recipe calls for 1 or more eggs but doesn't specify the size, use *large*—this is the recipe standard.

◆ You need not have egg-separation anxiety if you have a little funnel. Place the funnel in a glass, then crack the egg over it. The egg white will glide into the glass and the yolk will (hopefully) stay in the funnel.

◆ If you want to separate eggs, do it as soon as you take them out of the fridge. They're harder to separate when they're warm.

◆ To get best results when you are whipping egg whites, whip them in a glass or metal bowl at room temperature.

> ✎ **NOTE:** If you think the whites are whipped enough, turn the bowl over slowly…if the eggs start to slide out, turn it back and whip some more. If the eggs stay in the bowl when inverted, they're whipped enough.

◆ When a raw egg falls on the floor, discard the eggshell first, then pour table salt over the egg and wait about 5 minutes, until the salt soaks up the egg.

We tried it, and the salt does make for easier cleanup. There's no drippy, gooey slime to contend with. You might have to use a lot of salt, though, and you also have to be careful not to step in the spill during the 5-minute wait.

◆ We discovered an easy way to retrieve a piece of eggshell that falls into the bowl of eggs—just use a larger piece of eggshell to get the little piece of shell out of the bowl. The larger shell attracts the little shell, almost like a magnet.

> ⚡ **CAUTION:** Wash your hands thoroughly after touching raw eggs or eggshells to reduce the risk of spreading harmful bacteria.

◆ When making deviled eggs, put all of the ingredients—egg yolks, onions, mayo, etc.—in a resealable plastic bag. Close the bag and knead it—this blends the ingredients from the outside.

Then cut a small tip off 1 bottom corner of the bag. Line up the empty hard-boiled egg whites, and fill them by squeezing the yolk mixture out of the bag through that little hole. Just throw away the empty plastic bag to clean up.

◆ If you want float-off-your-plate omelets or scrambled eggs, stir in a pinch of cornstarch before cooking.

◆ Eggs should not be frozen in their shells.

◆ Uncooked whole eggs (out of the shell) can be frozen for up to 1 year if you beat them lightly, pour them into a freezer-safe container and seal it tightly. Don't forget to label the container with the number of eggs it contains, and the date they were frozen. To thaw the eggs, let cool water run over the container, or leave it in the refrigerator overnight.

> **CAUTION:** Use frozen whole eggs as soon as they're thawed, and only in dishes that are thoroughly cooked.
>
> Then again, all eggs should be thoroughly cooked before eating.

◆ Raw egg whites can be frozen the same way as whole eggs, except you should not beat them first. Just pour them directly from the shell into a container.

◆ You can also freeze egg whites in an ice cube tray—but be sure to put the tray into a resealable plastic freezer bag to prevent spills. And don't forget to label the bag with the number of egg whites it contains and the date they were frozen.

◆ Thaw egg whites the same way you thaw whole eggs (at left). If you are going to beat the thawed egg whites, keep them at room temperature for about 30 minutes after thawing, and they will have better volume.

◆ To store raw egg yolks, put the yolks in a container, fill it with cold water, put a tight lid on the container, and refrigerate it. The yolks should stay fresh that way for several days.

◆ Wondering whether an egg is raw or hard-boiled? This question comes up more often than you would think...especially when preparing eggs for holidays like Easter or Passover. The secret is to spin the egg. A raw egg will wobble, and a hard-boiled egg will spin.

Blood Spots on Eggs

Blood spots, also called *meat spots*, are found on less than 1% of all eggs produced. Contrary to popular belief, these tiny spots do not mean that the egg was fertilized. The spots are caused by the rupture of a blood vessel on the surface of the yolk. And, according to the American Egg Board (*www.aeb.org*), from both a chemical and nutritional standpoint, these eggs are fit to eat.

As an egg ages, the blood spot gets diluted as the yolk absorbs water from the *albumen* (the gooey egg white). While that's probably more information than you need to know, the ironic significance is this—a blood spot in an egg is an indication that the egg is fresh.

Eggs (Hardboiled)

◆ To prevent an egg from cracking during the hard-boiling process, first carefully puncture either end of the egg with a clean pin or thumbtack. Then gently place the egg in the water to boil.

◆ You can also add 1 tablespoon of distilled white vinegar to the water to prevent cracks. If the egg does crack, the vinegar should keep it from creeping out of the shell.

◆ Another crack-prevention idea is to cover the eggs with water in a yet-to-be-covered pot that has a tight lid. As soon as the water comes to a rolling boil, turn off the heat, cover the pot with the tight lid, and let it sit for 12 minutes. The eggs will come out hard-boiled and uncracked.

◆ Hard-boiled eggs that are overcooked tend to take on a greenish hue. To avoid this, place the egg in a pot, cover it with water, bring it to a boil, then set the timer for 12 minutes. When the buzzer rings, take the egg off the stove, then drain and rinse under cold water until the egg is cool.

◆ To peel a hard-boiled egg, gently roll it between your palm and your kitchen counter, making hairline cracks in the shell. Then hold the egg under cold running water and, starting at the large end, carefully pull off the shell.

◆ Do not freeze hard-boiled whole eggs or egg whites. When you defrost them, they're tough and watery.

🕲 Substitute Egg Poacher

Remove both ends of a tuna can, and wash it thoroughly. Put some water into a skillet... when the water starts to simmer, place the can in the skillet and then crack an egg into the can. Within no time, you'll have a perfectly poached egg.

Eggs (Substitutes)

◆ If you buy into the "no yolks because of the cholesterol" theory, substitute 2 egg whites for each whole egg called for in a recipe.

◆ If you're baking a cake and you're short 1 egg, mix 1 teaspoon of distilled white vinegar with 1 teaspoon of baking soda. Add this to the cake recipe to make up for the missing egg.

◆ For a recipe other than a cake, try this when you're minus 1 egg—use 1 teaspoon of cornstarch in its place.

Extracts

When your recipe calls for a small amount of vanilla, almond or any other extract, don't risk pouring straight from the extract bottle. Use a separate dropper (available at kitchen-supply stores) so that you can control the exact extract amount needed.

Prevent Foodborne Illness

Every year, an estimated 76 million Americans get sick because of foodborne illness, and more than 5,000 people die from it. But those numbers could be lowered if people heeded the "2-hour food rule."

Basically, food that is exposed to the open air for longer than 2 hours will grow bacteria to harmful levels. So at a party or a picnic—or wherever you serve food—keep track of the amount of time the food has been out of the refrigerator or oven. And after 2 hours, wrap the food properly and put it in the refrigerator or freezer.

Also, when a platter is empty (or almost empty) and you want to refill it, DO NOT just dump new food on top of the old food—in fact, don't even put new food in the empty-but-used platter. Each time you want to set out new food, wash the platter before you refill it, or serve the new food on another clean platter.

Fish

◆ To determine the proper cooking time for your fish, lay out the whole fish, fish fillet or fish steak. Pinpoint the thickest part of the fish, and then measure it with a ruler. For each inch of thickness, figure on 10 minutes of cooking time.

◆ Thaw frozen fish in milk or in 1 cup of nonfat dry milk mixed with 3 cups of water—this will remove the freezer taste, and the fish will cook up as though it was just reeled in.

◆ Neutralize the fishy smell of fresh fish by restoring its pH balance. You can do this by soaking fish fillets in a mixture made from 4 cups of water and 2 tablespoons of baking soda. Let the fish soak for at least 10 minutes. Then rinse under running water, and bake, broil or sauté.

◆ If there's a frying-fish smell when you're frying fish, add 1 teaspoon of peanut butter to the pan to eliminate the smell. The peanut butter will also add an interesting taste.

⚠️ **CAUTION:** If you're preparing peanut-butter fish for guests, be sure none of them has a peanut allergy.

◆ Fish-cooking smells can be absorbed—just place a small bowl of distilled white vinegar or fresh coffee grounds near the stove or wherever the fish is being prepared.

◆ If your fish fillet gets a little too blackened, it's minced parsley to the rescue! It's the go-with-everything herb that will cover up the whoopsies…and it tastes good, too. When cooking for company, always keep a stash of parsley on hand.

◆ After your fish is prepared, get rid of the fishy smell by washing the pan with distilled white vinegar.

◆ When you open a can of sardines, salmon or tuna and it has a strong fish-oil smell, drizzle distilled white vinegar on it. Let it stay that way for about 5 minutes, then spill it out. Chances are, the too-fishy taste will be gone too.

Flour

◆ If you keep your flour in bins without labels and you keep forgetting which is plain and which is self-rising—taste them. Plain flour is tasteless…and self-rising is a little salty because of the baking powder in it.

◆ Once you open a bag of flour, it's on its way to tasting stale. OK, it probably won't happen for a few months, but if you transfer the flour from the bag to an airtight container and keep it in a cool place, it will stay fresh for YEARS. The *coolest* place, the freezer, will keep it super-fresh as well as bug-free.

◆ To keep flour handy, fill a large salt shaker or an empty, clean spice container with flour and keep it in the freezer. When you need just a little bit for dusting or coating, it's easier to reach for the freezer-shaker instead of opening a sack of flour or the airtight container it's stored in.

◆ If you keep flour in a canister, also keep a clean, new powder puff in with it. Whenever you need to dust a surface—or lightly coat something—the powder puff will do the job.

Flour (Substitutes)

◆ *All-purpose flour*—You can use 1 cup plus 2 tablespoons of cake flour for each cup of all-purpose flour.

◆ *Cake flour*—Use 1 cup less 2 tablespoons of all-purpose flour for each cup of cake flour.

◆ *Self-rising flour*—Combine 1½ teaspoons of baking powder with ½ teaspoon of table salt, and fill up the rest of the cup with an all-purpose flour. Make sure it's level.

Fruit

◆ The use of pesticides to kill bugs on produce has become a big concern for many people. However, until organic fruits and vegetables are more affordable and readily available, you may have to remove the pesticides yourself at home.

Jay "The Juiceman" Kordich recommends this method—clean your sink and fill it with cold water, then add 4 tablespoons of salt and the fresh juice from ½ of a whole lemon. This will make a diluted form of hydrochloric acid.

Soak most fruits and vegetables for 5 to 10 minutes…leafy greens, 2 to 3 minutes…strawberries, blueberries and all other berries, 1 to 2 minutes. After soaking, rinse the produce thoroughly in plain cold water and dry each piece. Now, it's pesticide-free and ready to eat!

◆ Another way to remove pesticides is to soak your fruit in a clean sink or basin with ¼ cup of distilled white vinegar. Then, with a fruit/vegetable brush, scrub the fruit under cold water. Give it a final rinse, dry it and it's ready to be eaten.

◆ You can also mix 1 teaspoon of baking soda with 1 cup of plain water, and wash the produce with the solution. Then rinse and dry.

◆ And a final pesticide-removal suggestion— in a sink or basin of cold water, add ¼ cup of 3% hydrogen peroxide. Wash the fruits and vegetables in it, then rinse with water and wipe dry.

◆ According to the United States Department of Agriculture (USDA), fruit should be ripened at room temperature. *When it is ripe*

and refrigerated, you can plan on it staying edible for the following amounts of time…

◆ Apples—1 month
◆ Apricots, bananas, grapes, nectarines, peaches, pears, plums—3 to 5 days
◆ Berries and cherries—2 to 3 days
◆ Citrus fruit—2 weeks
◆ Cranberries and melons (except watermelon)—1 week
◆ Watermelon—3 to 5 days

◆ Many fruits—including apples, pears, peaches, avocados and tomatoes—will ripen faster in a brown paper bag. The paper bag helps the natural fruit-ripening gases do their job.

 NOTE: If you're very eager for your fruit to ripen, put a banana in the bag with it. The banana's gases will speed up the ripening process.

◆ When you refrigerate fresh fruit, the ripening process stops.

Fruit (Dried)

If you need to cut up dried fruit, make this sticky chore easier by freezing the dried fruit for 45 minutes. Then spray a kitchen scissors with nonstick vegetable spray or dip the scissors in flour before cutting the dried fruit.

 NOTE: If you insist on using a knife to cut dried fruit, spray it with cooking spray or dip it in flour to help prevent sticking.

 Quick Funnel
If you need a funnel and don't have anything handy, cut a 20" piece of heavy-duty aluminum foil, fold it in half and then roll the double thickness into a cone shape. Cut off the pointed end, and it's ready to be used as a funnel that's perfect for filling bottles.

Garlic

◆ There are several ways to peel individual cloves of garlic. *Choose the method that works best for you...*

   ◆ Put the clove on its side, and smack it with the bottom of a large can. Or put the flat side of a wide knife's blade on top of the clove. Make a fist and quickly pound the blade, or press down on the blade with the heel of your hand.

   ◆ Immerse the clove in a bowl of cold water for 20 minutes.

   ◆ Put the clove in hot water for 5 seconds.

   ◆ Microwave the clove for 20 seconds.

◆ To remove the odor of garlic from your hands, use a piece of silverware (stainless steel works fine) like a bar of soap, and wash with it under cold water. Or wash your hands and rub the stainless-steel faucet at the same time.

◆ To remove the smell of garlic from your breath, mix a touch of sugar in a little lemon juice and swill it around your mouth, then swallow it.

◆ When a recipe calls for both fresh garlic and fresh ginger, work with the garlic first, then ginger. The ginger will remove the garlic smell from your hands, utensils and cutting board.

Gelatin

◆ When preparing gelatin, add 1 teaspoon of distilled white vinegar for every 4 cups of liquid—this way, the gelatin will stay firm longer than usual.

◆ Do not add kiwi or fresh pineapple to gelatin...not unless you want it to be runny. The enzymes in both fruits keep gelatin from setting properly.

Roast Your Own Garlic

Roasted garlic is a versatile treat. You can use it as a healthy spread (and butter substitute) on bread...or as a paste in sauces, soups, grain dishes, dips and dressings. It's easy to prepare.

Start with a large head of garlic. Flake off the outer layers of skin, but leave the peels on the cloves intact. Cut off about ¼" of the pointed tops so that the individual cloves of garlic are exposed, while the head of garlic is still intact.

Place the head of garlic in a small baking dish, with the cut side up. Drizzle about 1 tablespoon of olive oil on the cloves. Cover the dish and let it bake in a 400°F oven for about 30 minutes, until the cloves feel soft when pressed.

Let the head get cool enough to handle. Then use the tip of a small knife (or a fork) to remove the softened garlic from each clove. Or, you can simply squish out the garlic and discard the skins.

Roasted garlic will keep for 1 week or longer if you refrigerate it in an airtight container.

> ✎ **NOTE:** You can also roast garlic in the microwave. Prep the head of garlic the same way as for oven-baking.
>
> Then place the head in a small, deep, microwave-safe dish, along with 2 tablespoons of water. Cover the dish with microwave-safe plastic wrap, and cook it on *medium* for 7 to 7½ minutes.
>
> Then remove the garlic from the microwave and let it stand for 10 minutes before taking off the plastic wrap. Use the garlic the same way you would use it if it were oven-roasted. *Bon appetit!*

Garbage Bowl

When you're preparing food, keep a large bowl on the counter and use it for food scraps and waste. It will help keep things neat during the food-preparation process, and it will save you from making countless trips to the garbage can.

Ginger

◆ Fresh gingerroot can last indefinitely if it's stored in sherry and sealed in a covered jar in the refrigerator. The ginger will not take on the taste of sherry, but the sherry will taste like ginger. Use both the ginger and the sherry to cook with—and to drink.

◆ You can also store a piece of fresh gingerroot in the freezer. When you want to use it, just lop off a piece and grate it. It's so much easier to grate frozen ginger than ginger that's at room temperature (or even refrigerated).

Glass

If you break a drinking glass—or anything made of glass—put on rubber gloves, then pick up the shattered pieces with a few slices of bread. It's thicker than paper towels and it's also safer to use.

Once you think you've cleaned up all of the glass, throw out the bread and carefully go over the area using the hose attachment of your vacuum cleaner.

Grapes

◆ Wash and dry bunches of grapes, then freeze them for a yummy cold snack.

◆ For your next party, add frozen grapes to the punch bowl in place of ice cubes. You will have a lovely garnish, and they will not dilute the punch.

◆ On a hot day, take frozen grapes out of the freezer, lightly sprinkle them with confectioner's sugar and serve them as an unusual, refreshing and sensual snack.

Grater

◆ Before grating lemon, lime or orange zest, wrap 2 layers of plastic wrap around the grater. Then when you grate the fruit, the zest will stick to the plastic wrap, not the grater. When you're done, gently remove the plastic wrap from the grater and shake the zest onto a plate.

Zest Conversion
One medium lemon should provide about 1 tablespoon of zest.

◆ When a recipe calls for grated zest, only grate the thin outer layer…the colored portion of the fruit. The white pith will give the dish a bitter taste.

Protect Your Digits
Nobody wants grated finger in his/her food. Go to a sewing-supplies store and get thimbles that fit the fingers that are in jeopardy each time you use the grater.

With the thimbles in place, you will be able to grate faster and more completely. And no more leftover stubs of potato, carrot or cheese!

Gravy

◆ To remove fat that's floating on top of gravy, blot it up with a piece of dry bread.

◆ You can also remove fat by putting the gravy in a container in the freezer for about 30 minutes. After that time, the fat will have formed a solid layer on top, and you can easily spoon off the fatty layer.

◆ When adding wine to gravy, cook it for about 10 minutes longer than usual—doing this will boil off the alcohol, but not the flavor of the wine in your gravy.

Greens

Here's a great way to keep collard greens, kale, mustard greens, lettuce and other salad greens fresher longer—keep them in a covered container in the refrigerator, along with a piece of stainless-steel silverware. (If you don't think this will work, try it for yourself and see.)

Hair Dryer

Yes, keeping a hair dryer in the kitchen is a good idea. It can help you dry just-washed salad greens…soften too-frozen ice cream…set icing on a cake…dry a big water splotch you got on your blouse right before your guests are due to arrive…and probably a dozen more useful things that you'll think of when the dryer is within reach in the kitchen.

Ham

Due to their high salt content, leftover ham and other cured meats do not freeze well. Wrap sliced ham tightly in plastic wrap, then cover it with aluminum foil and freeze it for no more than 1 to 2 months. Leftover ham can generally be kept in the refrigerator for 3 to 5 days.

Herbs (Fresh and Dried)

◆ Before using any herb, crumble it by rolling it around in the palms of your hand. Doing this will release the herb's flavor—not just in your hand, but for the dish it's going into.

◆ Freeze fresh herbs by washing and cutting them into pieces that are small enough to fit in an ice-cube tray compartment. Once the entire tray is filled with pieces of herb, carefully add a little water to each compartment.

Then it's ready for the freezer. Once the herbs are completely frozen, transfer these cubes from the tray to resealable plastic freezer bags. Label the bag with the name of the herb. Then, when a recipe calls for that herb, figure on 1 ice cube yielding 1 teaspoon of it. To defrost the cube, just put it in a small strainer and run hot water over it.

◆ Add dried herbs to what you're cooking about 30 minutes before the dish is done. To help the fresh herb keep its color and flavor, add the herb 10 minutes before you turn off the heat.

Herbal Plate Decoration
Spread the rim of each dinner plate with a light, even coating of margarine. Select an herb that goes with the entrée, chop it finely and sprinkle it on the margarine, creating an herbal border around the plate. Put your entrée in the middle of the plate, add your side dishes and serve.

DID YOU KNOW?

You can keep lettuce fresh in a re-sealable plastic bag with a piece of almost-burnt toast. When the toast gets soggy, replace it with another piece.

Lettuce should stay crisp in the fridge for a couple of weeks this way.

◆ If your recipe is not specifically written for microwave cooking, keep in mind that *fresh* herbs tend to be milder when microwaved, so you may want to *increase* the amount you use. And the flavor of *dried* herbs is heightened in the microwave, so you may want to *decrease* the amount you use.

◆ To make fresh herbs into dried herbs, place them on a paper towel and cook them in the microwave on high for about 1 minute. When dry, store them in labeled resealable plastic bags. They should retain their flavor for up to 1 year.

◆ Here's a helpful guideline—when a recipe calls for a fresh herb, but you want to use a dried herb instead, use ⅓ the amount. So, if the recipe says to use 1 tablespoon of fresh basil, use 1 teaspoon of dried basil.

Of course, the reverse is also true. If the recipe calls for 1 teaspoon of dried basil, use 3 times as much (1 tablespoon) fresh basil.

Honey

◆ If your jar of honey has crystallized, reliquefy it by putting the jar in a bowl filled with very hot water. Let it stand for about 5 minutes, then stir until it's the consistency of honey.

◆ You can also remove the lid and put the uncovered, metal-free jar or container in the microwave and heat it on *medium* for 10-second increments. Stop the microwave as soon as the honey is liquefied.

◆ Always store honey in a dark place at room temperature.

Jelly/Jam

Transfer jelly or jam to a clean squeeze bottle to make it more manageable for young children.

Juice Boxes

In hot weather, when you plan on packing a juice box in with lunch, freeze the juice box overnight. Pack the frozen juice box in with lunch in the morning, and by the time lunch rolls around, the juice should be thawed to a slushy consistency.

 NOTE: As a bonus, the frozen juice box will keep the rest of the lunch contents cold.

Ketchup

◆ *Shake, O shake the ketchup bottle...none will come, and then a lot'll.* Insert a straw into the bottle of ketchup—all the way to the bottom—and then remove it. Doing this lets in air, which breaks the vacuum and helps the ketchup come out quickly.

◆ To get the last few splurts out of the almost-empty ketchup bottle, try this—first make sure the cover is tight on the bottle. Then get a good, strong grip of the neck of the bottle and swing it in a circular motion. Every last drop will come to the top.

Kiwi

◆ To ripen a kiwi quickly, put it in a brown paper bag with a banana or an apple. Close the bag and let it stay that way overnight. The banana or apple's ethylene gas will help ripen the kiwi quickly.

◆ If you want to peel a kiwi quickly, first slice off the top and bottom of the kiwi. Then insert a teaspoon or tablespoon (depending on the size of the fruit) between the flesh and the peel. Gently turn the spoon around the inside of the kiwi, which will separate the flesh from the peel.

 Smart Way to Peel Kiwi
It helps to use an egg slicer to peel kiwi quickly and evenly.

Lasagna

◆ If you don't want to cook the lasagna noodles before you start layering the pan, add more liquid in the form of tomato sauce, and a little more cheese. How much more sauce and cheese? We wish we could tell you, but there are so many variables, that the only way to know is by using your own judgment.

So, if you're a courageous cook, layer the pan with the uncooked lasagna noodles, add extra sauce and cheese and hope for the best. (You may not want to have dinner guests the first time you try this method.)

◆ If your lasagna tends to stick to the aluminum foil with which you cover it, try this—spray the foil with nonstick cooking spray *before* you cover and bake the lasagna. Or, check the supermarket for nonstick aluminum foil.

Leftovers

Never put hot leftovers right into the refrigerator—doing so requires the refrigerator to use extra energy to cool the food, which makes it less efficient. Instead, place leftovers in shallow containers (with the lids securely fastened) and set them out on your counter until they reach room temperature.

 NOTE: The leftovers will cool faster in the shallow containers, which means there's less of a chance that harmful bacteria will grow, and the food will stay safely edible for a longer period of time.

Lemons and Limes

◆ When all you need is a squirt of juice, don't dry out the entire lemon or lime by cutting it open. Just puncture the peel with a toothpick and squeeze out the little bit you need. Then put a piece of masking tape over the hole…or cover the fruit with plastic wrap…or put it in a resealable plastic bag.

◆ You can also take the lemon/lime out of the refrigerator, and when it's reached room temperature, use your palm to roll it back and forth on a hard surface. This will break the fruit's inner membranes, and you'll get close to twice as much juice that way.

◆ If you can't wait until the lemon is at room temperature, let hot water run over it for 1 minute, then do the palm-rolling thing.

◆ To get the most juice out of a lemon (or lime), jab it with a fork, then microwave it for about 15 seconds on medium power. Juice as usual.

◆ For fresh-squeezed juice, it's best to use an old-fashioned and low-tech juice reamer (the kind with the conical-ridged center). But if you don't have a reamer, try this—cut the lemon/lime in half and then stick a fork in its center, where the conical-ridged center of the reamer would go.

◆ Turn the fork around and around in the center of the lemon that you're holding in your palm. Then turn the fork in the opposite direction, until no more juice comes out. Repeat the entire procedure with the other half of the lemon.

◆ When a recipe calls for the juice of 1 lemon, figure that you'll need to use 2 to 3 tablespoons of lemon juice.

Lemon (Substitutes)

When a recipe calls for lemon juice and you don't have any, you can substitute equal amounts of lime juice or white wine.

Lentils

One of the oldest cultivated crops in the world, lentils may be dusty and have tiny pebbles mixed in. There are no shortcuts when it comes to sorting and cleaning them…start by spreading them out in a single layer on a cookie sheet. Pick out and discard the pebbles as well as any shriveled or discolored lentils.

Transfer the remaining lentils to a bowl of water. Clean the beans by swishing them around with your hand. Throw out all the ones that float to the top. Transfer the rest to a strainer and rinse them under running water. Then 1 more transfer…to a pan for cooking as usual.

Lettuce

◆ To make lettuce last longer, take it out of its plastic bag and store it in a brown paper bag—this will allow moisture to escape, and the lettuce will last longer. But do NOT store lettuce with apples, pears or bananas. Their ripening gases will cause the lettuce to turn brown and yucky.

◆ Soak limp lettuce leaves in ice-cold water with a splash of lemon juice. After about 15 minutes, they will be crisp again.

Marshmallows

◆ It's best to store marshmallows in your freezer—put them in a plastic container with a tight-fitting lid. They will stay fresh and not mush together.

◆ When you open a bag of marshmallows and don't seal them closed again, they will get hard and stale.

   If that happens, put the hardened marshmallows in a resealable plastic bag along with 2 slices of very fresh bread. Seal the bag closed and let it stay like this for a few days…until the marshmallows are soft again.

 Phenomenal Pumpkin Pie Topping

Put a layer of marshmallows on the bottom of a pie crust, and pour the pumpkin pie filling on top of it. Bake the pie as usual, and keep checking it—you'll want to witness the moment when the marshmallows make their way to the surface of the pie, where they will form a tufted topping.

Measuring Spoons/Cups

◆ Spray measuring spoons with cooking spray before you measure a sticky ingredient. Then go ahead and scoop up the molasses or peanut butter or chocolate syrup. Each will glide right off the sprayed spoon.

◆ You can spray a measuring cup with cooking spray before you pour in a gooey ingredient, or you can line the cup with a piece of plastic wrap and spray the wrap with cooking spray. That way, after you've poured in the honey or whatever, you can simply discard the sticky plastic wrap and rinse out the cup.

◆ Is it hard to read the faded markings on your measuring cup? Carefully repaint the lines and numbers with bright-red nail polish.

◆ To be super-organized, measure all of the recipe's dry ingredients first, then measure all of the wet ingredients. Put everything in its own little dish or bowl…in the order you'll need it for the recipe. That way, you will be able to use the same measuring utensils several times over, without having to wash and dry them for each measured ingredient.

 Makeshift Measuring Cup

Clean, empty yogurt containers make good measuring cups. Filled almost to the top, a 4-ounce container = ½ cup…a 6-ounce container = ¾ cup…and an 8-ounce container = 1 cup.

Milk

◆ Buy milk in a cardboard carton or in a jug that's opaque. See-through (translucent) containers let light seep in. That can cause milk to spoil…especially if it stands out on the sidewalk in hot weather, waiting to be brought into the supermarket.

◆ Keep containers or jugs of milk on a shelf inside the refrigerator, not in the door. The door keeps opening and closing, exposing

Common Kitchen Measurements

A dash of liquid = A few drops
3 teaspoons = 1 tablespoon
½ tablespoon = 1½ teaspoons
1 tablespoon = 3 teaspoons
2 tablespoons = 1 fluid ounce
4 tablespoons = ¼ cup
5⅓ tablespoons = ⅓ cup
8 tablespoons = ½ cup
8 tablespoons = 4 fluid ounces
10⅔ tablespoons = ⅔ cup
12 tablespoons = ¾ cup
16 tablespoons = 1 cup
16 tablespoons = 8 fluid ounces

⅛ cup = 2 tablespoons
¼ cup = 4 tablespoons
¼ cup = 2 fluid ounces
⅓ cup = 5 tablespoons plus 1 teaspoon
½ cup = 8 tablespoons
1 cup = 16 tablespoons
1 cup = 8 fluid ounces
1 cup = ½ pint
2 cups = 1 pint (16 ounces)
2 pints = 1 quart
4 quarts (liquid) = 1 gallon
8 quarts (dry) = 1 peck
4 pecks (dry) = 1 bushel
1 kilogram = approximately 2 pounds
1 liter = approximately 4 cups or 1 quart

the items in the door to warm air from the kitchen. The cool air inside the refrigerator remains more constant.

◆ When boiling milk, rinse the pot with cold water right before you pour in the milk. That little step will prevent milk from scorching and sticking to the pot.

◆ Put a clean marble or stone in the pot to prevent milk from boiling over. Just be sure to remove the marble or stone before pouring the milk!

◆ Also, don't ever let milk come to a rolling boil. Turn off the heat as soon as little bubbles form around the edge.

Milk (Substitutes)

For baking or cooking…

◆ Substitute 1 cup of whole milk with 1 cup of skim milk plus 2 tablespoons of (melted) unsalted butter or margarine.

◆ Substitute 1 cup of whole milk with ½ cup of evaporated whole milk plus ½ cup of water.

◆ Use ¼ cup of dry whole milk plus ⅞ cup of water in place of 1 cup of whole milk.

Muffins

◆ To avoid over-baking your muffins, take them out of the oven when they have a few minutes left to bake. They'll finish baking on their own, outside of the oven.

◆ Instead of using the milk that's called for in a muffin recipe, use the same amount of plain yogurt or buttermilk. Also add ½ teaspoon of baking soda for each cup of milk you're replacing. These muffins are so light, they will practically float out of the pan!

◆ If, after you've poured the muffin batter into the baking tin, there are empty compartments, fill them halfway with water. This will prevent the tin from smoking or warping while baking.

◆ Muffin mavens advise against cooling muffins in their pans. They say that the bottoms will get soggy. Instead, take the muffins out of the oven and put the pan on a wire rack…let the muffins sit there for 10 minutes. Then take the muffins out of the pan, and put them on the rack until they have finished cooling. When muffins have been allowed to cool this way, they are less likely to fall apart.

◆ Use a clean shoehorn to help you take warm muffins out of the tin easily.

◆ If the muffins are stuck to the pan, spread a wet towel out on your work surface. Then put the hot muffin pan on the wet towel. After 1 to 2 minutes, you should be able to pop out the muffins without any problem. But next time, consider baking the muffins in paper baking cups.

Mushrooms

◆ To keep fresh mushrooms fresh, keep them in a basket or in an open brown paper bag in the refrigerator. Dried mushrooms should be stored in an airtight container.

◆ Do not wash or soak fresh mushrooms in water. The mushrooms are sponge-like and they will absorb the water. This will make them watery and tasteless.

    Instead, clean them with a damp cloth, or gently scrape them with a paring knife. OK, if stubborn dirt is clinging to a mushroom, you can rinse them with water. Just be sure to dry them thoroughly. Also, cook

them immediately or the water will cause them to decay.

Nuts

◆ Keep Brazil nuts and other hard-shelled nuts in the freezer. Frozen nuts are generally much easier to crack.

◆ Soak shelled walnuts in salted water overnight, and they'll be a cinch to crack.

◆ Hot water makes pecan shells more porous and creates air pockets, making them easy to crack. Here's how to do it—place pecans in a microwave-safe container, cover them with water and zap them on high for about 3 minutes. Then take the pecans out of the water and, once they're cool, their shells should be easy to crack.

 NOTE: You can also soak pecans in a covered pot of just-boiled water for about 15 minutes before cracking them.

◆ When a recipe calls for *unsalted* nuts, but the ones you have are salted, cook the *salted* nuts in boiling water for 2 minutes. Then drain them and spread them out on an ungreased baking sheet. Bake them in a 200°F oven until they're dry…no more than 5 minutes. Then continue on with your recipe and your unsalted nuts.

◆ To skin almonds, first boil a pot of water. Then put the shelled almonds in a strainer and plunge the strainer into the water. After a couple of minutes, take the almonds out of

Toasting Nuts

Toasting brings out the full flavor of nuts. And it's easy to do. Start with nuts that are shelled and about the same size. *Then decide whether you want to toast them in the oven or in a skillet...*

♦ *Oven*—Spread the nuts in a single layer on a baking pan and cook them at 400°F for 7 to 10 minutes, or until the nuts start to turn golden. Halfway through the toasting, carefully rotate the nuts by shaking the pan.

♦ *Skillet*—Place nuts in a single layer and put the skillet over medium-high heat. Stir or shake the nuts while they're toasting for 5 to 7 minutes, or until they start to turn golden. Always aim for *golden*. Toasted nuts taste best if they're not darker than light brown.

the water. When they're cool enough to handle, pinch the lower portion of each almond and watch it slip right out of its skin.

♦ Macadamia nuts are a real treat. Because they're pricey, people tend to buy a jar and dole out the nuts over a period of time. But that's *not* a good idea. These nuts turn rancid rather quickly. Make sure the lid is on the jar tightly, keep it in a cool place, and eat them sooner than later!

Oil

♦ If the new bottle of cooking oil you open has a foil seal, cut a small slit in it—instead of removing it completely. The slit will give you more control over the amount of oil you pour...and should eliminate any extra drips or the occasional spill.

♦ To make a bottle of cooking oil easier to use, transfer it to a clean, empty mustard bottle— you know, the kind you squeeze.

♦ Lids from plastic containers—such as yogurt, cottage cheese or margarine—can be used as coasters for bottles of oil. Using them will save you from having to clean oil drips off your countertops and cupboard shelves.

♦ Before heating oil, add 1 tablespoon of distilled white vinegar to the frying pan. It will help cut down on the amount of fat absorbed by the frying food, and the food will taste less greasy.

 Quick Oil Absorber

If you spill oil on the floor, pour some flour on the spill. Wait 1 or 2 minutes for the flour to absorb the grease, then clean it all up with a few paper towels.

Oil (Substitute)

Cut the number of calories and fat grams in your baked goods by using the equivalent amount of applesauce instead of oil (in other words, 1 cup of oil equals 1 cup of applesauce).

 Smart Sauce Idea

Buy snack-packs of applesauce, and use them as you need them. It's more efficient (and less wasteful) than keeping a big, open jar of applesauce in your refrigerator.

Onions

♦ When you cut a raw onion, a compound called *propanethial-s-oxide* is released in a vapor. When the vapor comes into contact with a person's eyes, it is converted into a form of sulfuric acid. No wonder it causes stinging and tearing!

To slow down the enzymes that cause this unpleasant chemical reaction, put onions in the freezer for 15 minutes—or in the refrigerator for 1 hour—before you have to cut them. *But if you don't plan ahead, here are some other suggestions...*

◆ Work with the onion under cold running water, or fill a basin with cold water and submerge the onion while you cut it.

◆ Wear a pair of safety goggles while working with onions.

◆ Try to breathe through your mouth instead of your nose.

◆ Burn a candle in the area where you are cutting. The tear-causing vapor from the onion is drawn to the heat source from the flame, and it will burn off some of the noxious fumes.

◆ Bite on a slice of bread and have the rest sticking out of your mouth to absorb the tear-making fumes.

◆ Here's a great way to peel onions quickly—and it's particularly useful if you have a lot of small onions to peel. Soak them in just-boiled water for a few seconds. Then soak them for another few seconds in cold water. The skins should slip right off.

◆ Let's suppose you want to use a milder and sweeter-tasting onion in your salad, but all you have is a regular, strong yellow onion. Slice the yellow onion and soak it in cold water for 30 minutes, along with 1 teaspoon of distilled white vinegar. The pungent acid will dissipate in the water, and the onion will have a milder, sweeter flavor.

◆ You can also make an onion sweeter this way—cut it into thin slices and put them in a bowl, then pour just-boiled water over them. Let the slices stand for 2 to 3 minutes, then drain and refrigerate until the onion is cold...and sweet.

◆ If your onions are sprouting *and* it's springtime *and* you have a garden—plant them! Or plant them in a flowerpot and place them in a sunny window. Use the green stalks in recipes the same way you would use scallions.

◆ If you bought onions in a mesh bag, keep them in that bag so that the air can circulate around them. If you bought the onions loose, keep them in the leg from an old, clean pair of pantyhose, knotted on the open end.

◆ You can get the onion smell off your hands by rubbing them with table salt, then rinsing and drying your hands.

◆ Another way to remove the onion smell is to squeeze a dollop of regular non-gel toothpaste in your palm, then distribute it over your hands. Then wash off the toothpaste under running water and dry your hands. There shouldn't be a hint of the onion smell left.

Onion (Substitute)

When a recipe calls for 1 small onion, it's equivalent to ¼ cup of chopped, fresh onion. You can substitute it for 1 to 2 tablespoons of instant minced onion...or 1 tablespoon of onion powder...or 1⅓ teaspoons of onion salt.

Pancakes

◆ Here's a simple way to make your pancakes super-light and fluffy—instead of using the milk or any other liquid called for in the recipe, use the same amount of seltzer or club soda (at room temperature). The carbonation bubbles will cause the pancakes to rise higher and stay airier.

Be sure to use all the batter you make as soon as you prepare it. Batter made with seltzer or club soda doesn't have staying power.

◆ If mornings are hectic and you welcome all the time-savers available, then prepare pancake batter the night before (but not with seltzer or club soda!). Put the prepared batter in a squeeze bottle (clean out and re-use an empty ketchup or mustard bottle), and keep it in the refrigerator. It will be good to go in the morning.

Prepare Perfect Pancakes!

Put batter in a clean plastic squeeze bottle or a turkey baster, and you will have an easy time forming perfect pancakes.

While you're at it, have some fun with it ...make odd-shaped pancakes, or pancakes in the shape of big letters for the names of the people who will be eating them.

◆ For very decadent pancakes, use eggnog instead of the milk (or any other liquid that's called for in the recipe). It's a real once-in-a-blue-moon treat.

Parsley

◆ When your parsley has wilted, cut off ½" from the stems and let them stand in the refrigerator in a glass of ice-cold water for 1 to 2 hours.

◆ When you are serving food or spices that stay on the breath—such as garlic, onions or curry—garnish the food with parsley. It looks nice and, if your guests eat it, it will help freshen their breath.

Paper Towel Alternative

When you need to wipe up a spill and there are no paper towels handy, reach for a couple of coffee filters.

You may be thinking, "Chances are, I'd sooner have paper towels within reach than coffee filters!" This is probably true most times, but on the off-chance that you've run out of paper towels and you spilled something *right near* where you keep coffee filters, you'll know what to do.

Pasta

◆ Pasta won't stick together if you add 1 tablespoon of olive oil (or any vegetable oil) to the water while it's cooking.

◆ Always add the pasta *after* the water starts boiling. If you add the pasta before the water boils, it will slow down the boiling process... which causes the pasta to clump together.

◆ To avoid having the pasta water boil over, coat 1" of the inside top of the pot with olive or vegetable oil.

◆ When steam from the just-served, hot pasta condenses, there will be a puddle pooling on the plate. To prevent the puddle, wait a few minutes until the pasta stops steaming before putting it on the plate.

Better Pasta Storage

If pasta is a real passion for you, invest in a spaghetti canister for proper storage. They are available at some supermarkets as well as kitchen and cookware stores.

◆ Why don't spaghetti boxes close on their own without having to be taped shut? When you have uncooked spaghetti, transfer it from the original box to a clean potato-chip can.

This kind of can is tall enough to hold spaghetti, and when it's closed, it's airtight. Store in a cool, dry place.

 CAUTION: Do not put uncooked pasta in see-through (plastic or glass) containers. Exposure to light contributes to the breakdown of the vitamin content that's in fortified pasta. Stored in airtight, non-see-through canisters in a cool, dry place, fortified pasta will retain its benefits for up to 18 months.

Peanut Butter

Natural peanut butter (available at supermarkets and health-food stores)—which is made only from peanuts (no sugar or other additives…and no preservatives—nothing to interfere with the wonderful peanut butter taste)—has a layer of oil on top. *The oil should not be spilled off!* It's necessary to make the solid portion spreadable and even more delicious. The oil should be mixed in before the jar is refrigerated.

The best way to do that is to leave the jar on its side for a few days before you want to open it. Then the mixing process will be fairly easy. Just mix it until the oil is fully integrated into the solid portion, and refrigerate it.

 Keep PB Fresh Longer

Once you open a jar of natural peanut butter, store it upside down in the refrigerator. It will stay fresher longer.

Peppers

When preparing stuffed bell peppers—especially if you're going to serve them to guests—have them look their best even after they soften during the cooking process. Just place them in muffin tins and they will keep their shape.

 Smart Pepper-Baking Hint

If there are empty compartments in the muffin tin, fill them halfway with water to prevent the tin from smoking or warping in the oven.

Pepper Shaker

To keep the holes in a pepper shaker from getting clogged, toss in a few whole black or white peppercorns. Doing this seems to make the pepper taste fresher, too.

Pies

◆ Custard-type pies, including pumpkin pie, should *always* be refrigerated…even if that means rearranging everything on the shelves

to make room. Left out at room temperature, pies can grow dangerous bacteria.

◆ To prevent the juice from oozing out of a pie and making a mess in the oven, stand a 4" piece of uncooked macaroni in the middle of the pie while it's baking.

Piecrust

◆ When a pie recipe calls for 1 tablespoon of ice water, instead use 1 tablespoon of distilled white vinegar—this will make a crispier crust.

◆ For a flakier piecrust, substitute the same amount of sour cream or plain yogurt for the liquid called for in a pie recipe.

◆ Before you put the pie in the oven, dip a pastry brush in cold water and lightly paint the crust with it. The crust will become nice and flaky.

Pineapple

When you're cutting a whole pineapple, wear oven mitts to hold on to it more securely.

Pita

Here's an easy way to cut open a pita—heat it in the microwave for about 20 seconds, long enough for it to puff up. Watch it every second, though, and as soon as it looks like a blowfish, stop the cooking.

When you open the microwave door, the pita will unpuff almost entirely. Even so, it

Make Your Own Pita Chips

Preheat the oven to 350°F. Cut each large pita into 16 triangles—first, by cutting the pita in half, then by cutting each half in half, then cutting each quarter in half. That leaves you with 8 double triangles. Now, turn them into 16 single triangles.

Put them on a tray and bake them at 350°F until they're crisp…about 5 minutes. Let them cool, then you can use them for dips…or spray them lightly with vegetable spray and sprinkle on your favorite seasoning(s). They're great with a little garlic powder.

should be easy to cut the pita neatly along the edge without tearing into the middle of it.

Hands-Free Phone

When you're involved in food preparation, it's usually inconvenient to answer the telephone. You can solve that problem the same way that professional chefs do—keep a small plastic bag next to the phone. Just put the plastic bag over your hand, and you'll never miss another call. Plus, your phone receiver will stay clean.

Popcorn

◆ If you air-pop popcorn and want to add salt, garlic powder or any other seasoning, lightly spray the popcorn with vegetable spray first to help the seasoning adhere to the popcorn.

◆ If you use a hot-air popcorn maker, preheat it to get the very best results.

◆ An hour before popping corn, sprinkle a little warm water on the kernels. Or keep your popcorn kernels in the freezer. Either way—warm water or freezer—your popcorn will be fluffier and have fewer duds.

 CAUTION: Never leave the kitchen when popping popcorn. It can scorch and burn unexpectedly.

◆ If you don't have an air popper, but you do have a microwave, you can still prepare fresh popcorn. Put ¼ cup of popcorn kernels in a lunch-sized brown paper bag. Fold the top over twice and secure it closed with tape. Microwave the bag on high power until you hear the kernels finish popping…they usually take anywhere from 1½ to 4 minutes.

◆ When the popcorn is done popping, carefully open the bag…facing away from you. Then put the popcorn in a bowl, and add salt or curry or any seasoning of your choice. You can also drizzle melted butter on it. Stir and enjoy!

Prevent Popcorn Pain

Don't you hate biting down on an unpopped popcorn kernel? *Ouch!* Here's a way to prevent that from happening ever again. After you've popped the corn and it has cooled, transfer it to a resealable plastic bag. Cut a small hole in 1 bottom corner of the bag, and shake it over the sink—the duds (unpopped kernels) should all fall out of the hole.

Potatoes

◆ To store potatoes, keep them in a cool, dark place with a piece of fresh gingerroot. Both will stay fresh longer.

◆ If you peel potatoes and you don't want to use all of them, put the leftovers in a bowl. Then add 1 teaspoon of distilled white vinegar and enough cold water to cover them completely. Put plastic wrap across the top of the bowl and refrigerate. The peeled spuds will stay good this way for 2 to 3 days.

◆ Keep the skins on the potatoes while you boil them. The skins help hold in the flavor and the nutrients. Also, potatoes are easier to peel once they've boiled.

◆ If you do peel the potatoes before you boil them—and you want them to remain firm and whole and white—add 1 tablespoon of distilled white vinegar or white wine to the water. The vinegar or wine will help form a light skin on the potatoes, which will prevent them from falling apart when you work with them.

Potatoes (Baked or Mashed)

◆ After scrubbing and puncturing the potato skins, stand the spuds in a muffin tin and they will bake quickly.

 Smart Potato-Baking Hint
Be sure to fill any empty muffin compartments halfway with water to prevent the tin from smoking or warping while baking.

◆ Get an aluminum nail—they are specifically made for baking potatoes, and are available in some supermarkets, cookware stores and hardware stores. Then, starting at the top of the potato, stick the nail in through the center, lengthwise.

Bake the potato in a 400°F oven for about 35 minutes (the nail shaves off about 20 minutes of baking time), directly on the oven rack. When it's crisp on the outside and tender on the inside, it's done. Oh yes, don't forget to take out the nail before serving.

 CAUTION: NEVER put a potato in the microwave if you've used the nail or the muffin-tin cooking method.

◆ Brown-skinned russet and Idaho potatoes are the same, and they are said to make the fluffiest, creamiest mashed potatoes. To make them extra-fluffy, add a pinch of baking powder as you mash them. The powder mixes with the heat and forms tiny air pockets.

Rice

◆ Have your white rice stay white by adding 1 teaspoon of lemon juice for each quart of water used to cook the rice.

◆ To prevent a messy boil-over when making rice, add 1 teaspoon of butter or oil to the cooking water.

◆ Prevent rice from getting mushy and clumping together—add 1 teaspoon of lemon juice for each quart of water used to cook the rice.

◆ Instead of preparing rice with water, substitute a delicious rice "go-with"—try onion soup...or vegetable or beef broth...or miso soup...or low-fat chicken soup...or tomato juice. Experiment. You may discover a wonderful new dish.

◆ OK, you've cooked the rice, but you're not ready to serve it...you want to keep it warm, but you don't want it to get sticky. So, here's what to do—take a few sheets of paper towel, stretch them across the top of the pot and then put the lid on it.

The towels will absorb the condensation that accumulates on the lid. This will prevent it from dripping back into the rice, which is what would make the rice too sticky...and the rice will stay warm.

◆ When reheating rice, put it in a microwave-safe bowl and place an ice cube on top of the rice. Cover the bowl with plastic wrap, and puncture a few holes in it to allow the release of steam. Heat the bowl on high power for about 90 seconds per cup of rice. The rice should taste as though you just cooked it for the first time.

Rolls

◆ Here's a great way to freshen stale rolls—put them in a small, brown paper bag, moisten the bag with water and put it in the oven (pre-heated to 300°F). When the bag is dry—in just a few minutes, so don't leave the kitchen—take out the bag and remove the rolls. They should taste like they did when they were baked the first time.

◆ Another way to freshen stale rolls is to lightly spray them with water and wrap them loosely in aluminum foil. Then put them in the oven (preheated to 350°F) for 10 to 15 minutes. Keep watch because it could take less than 10 minutes to reheat the rolls.

> **NOTE:** If you're warming croissant-type crusty rolls, put them in the oven uncovered and on a piece of foil.

◆ If you want to warm rolls in the microwave, first wrap each in a dry paper towel. The towel will absorb moisture and the rolls will not come out soggy.

◆ If you are serving warm rolls, place a piece of aluminum foil under the napkin in the serving basket. The foil will help the rolls retain their heat longer.

Efficient Recipe Holder

If you are always collecting recipes, there is a unique, organized and efficient way to keep them protected—get a large Rolodex (available at office-supply and stationery stores) and put the recipes on cards in plastic sleeves.

This is more user-friendly than a cookbook because the page won't turn while you're preparing a recipe. The Rolodex recipe card stays in place.

If your recipes are pulled from magazines or printed on sheets of paper, put the pages in plastic holders in a 3-ring notebook.

Salads

◆ The drier the salad ingredients, the better the dressing will coat them. To dry your rinsed salad greens efficiently, use a salad spinner (available at kitchen-supply stores). Put a few paper towels in the spinner along with the wet greens, and they'll dry even faster.

◆ If you want to prepare a salad in advance, place a saucer or plate face-down on the bottom of the salad bowl, covering as much of the bowl's bottom as possible. Then prepare the salad in the bowl. Water from the rinsed salad greens will drain off and slide down the sides of the plate to the bottom of the bowl. The plate will keep the salad stuff from sitting in water and getting soggy.

◆ Tossing a big salad can be messy, but not if you toss all of the salad ingredients into a big plastic bag. Hold the top closed and shake the bag until everything's perfectly integrated.

◆ Control portion size and neatness by giving your guests individual salad bowls with the salad already in them. Put the remaining salad in a bowl on the table so that guests can help themselves to more.

Salsa

If your salsa is too intense, mix in a few drops of vanilla extract. It tames the heat, making it seem less spicy.

Salt

◆ Highly salted foods—also highly spiced foods and foods with vinegar, as well as highly acidic foods, such as tomatoes—have an adverse reaction with aluminum foil. They cause the food to be damaged and the foil to rust.

◆ If a dish is over-salted, gradually add ½ teaspoon of distilled white vinegar and ½ teaspoon of sugar to the food. Do a taste test, and if it's still too salty, add another round of vinegar and sugar. Keep tasting and adding until the saltiness has been neutralized.

◆ An easy way to reduce saltiness in over-salted stews, soups or sauces is to add a potato. Just peel a raw potato, cut it into about 6 pieces and put them in the pot with the over-salted food for the last 10 minutes it needs to cook. As the potato gets soft, it will absorb some of the salt. When the dish has finished cooking, discard the potato. If it's still very salty, discard the dish.

◆ Most everyone knows that putting grains of raw rice (about 10 of them) in a salt shaker will soak up moisture and prevent the salt from clumping up. But you may not know that the grains of rice should be replaced once a year.

◆ If you don't want to bother with the grains of rice, mix 1 tablespoon of cornstarch into a 1-pound box of salt. The cornstarch will keep the salt clump-free.

◆ Kosher or coarse salt has large grains and requires a shaker that has larger holes. A cheese shaker (available at kitchen-supply stores) works well.

◆ To keep kosher salt from caking, add a few dry beans to the shaker. The beans will absorb moisture, and they won't fit through the shaker's holes as grains of rice would.

Sandwiches

Two things usually make a sandwich soggy—the dressing (such as ketchup, mayonnaise and/or mustard)...and the wet add-ons (such as lettuce, tomato, pickles and/or cucumber). Instead of smearing the dressing on the bread, which is what gets the soggiest, smear it on the main ingredient (the meat, cheese, fish, veggie patty).

 Smart Sandwich Prep

If your sandwich needs to be prepared hours before it will be eaten, wrap the wet things separately. Then, when it's time to eat, assemble the sandwich.

Sausage

When a recipe calls for loose or bulk sausages and you only have link sausages, just remove the casings. Do this by using a knife or kitchen scissors to slit the casing lengthwise from top to bottom, and then peel it off.

Seafood

◆ Refrigerate any seafood you buy as soon as possible. If you have not eaten the seafood within 48 hours, freeze it. Depending on what type of fish it is, it should keep frozen for no more than 6 months. Don't forget to label it with the date of purchase. (Fresh crab and lobster should NOT be frozen.)

◆ For fresh-tasting shrimp, consider buying them frozen, since most shrimp are frozen at sea. Right before you want to cook them, thaw the shrimp by running cold water over them for a few minutes. They will taste fresh, as though you just got off the shrimp boat with them.

◆ To get the fullest flavor from shrimp, prepare them with their shells on. If the shells are already off, then simmer the shrimp in beer for a real taste treat!

Shortening

Measuring out shortening can be a messy job, and don't you hate washing the greasy measuring cup? A standard-sized ice cream scoop holds ¼ cup of shortening—use it to plop out the amount of shortening called for in a recipe. With the scoop, cleanup seems easier.

Shortening (Substitute)

In a never-ending effort to cut calories and fat grams, we found a good way—instead of using butter or lard—to substitute ⅓ less vegetable oil. If a recipe calls for 3 tablespoons of butter, use 2 tablespoons of vegetable, canola, olive or coconut oil instead.

✳ Removing Kitchen Smells

- **Burned food**—Wet a large towel with plain water, and imitate a cowboy swirling a lasso for a couple of minutes...until the smell is gone. If there's smoke in the air from the burned food, wet the bath towel with distilled white vinegar instead of water and start lassoing. Be careful not to knock any knick-knacks, mugs or dishes off nearby shelves.

- **Plastic container**—Crumple a sheet of newspaper and stuff it into the plastic container. Then put the lid on and let it stay that way for a few days. When the time is up, remove the newspaper and wash the container with soap and water. Rinse and dry.

    You can also make a paste from baking soda and water, and rub the inside of the container with it. Let it stay that way overnight. The next morning, rinse and dry the odor-free container.

Soup

There are several ways to help remove some of the fat from soup. *Use whichever method is most appropriate...*

- Wash and dry 1 or 2 lettuce leaves. Once the pot of soup is done cooking, place the lettuce leaves on the surface of the soup. Within a couple of minutes, the leaves will be coated with fat. Remove and discard them.

- Add 1 raw egg white on the top of soup that's in a pot. As the soup cooks, all the fat will be collected by the egg white. Then, just scoop out the egg. Bye-bye egg...and bye-bye fat.

- If you have fatty broth, strain it through a paper coffee filter.

- If time permits, refrigerate the soup. A layer of fat will form on top, and you can simply scrape it off with a spoon.

- If you can't wait for the soup to cool in the refrigerator, put 6 ice cubes into the soup pot. They act like fat magnets. In seconds, grease solidifies around the cubes. Use a slotted spoon to remove the fatty ice.

    Chances are, you will need to warm up the soup again before serving it.

- When you need to thicken soup, the standard thickeners—flour, cornstarch, or arrowroot—can add lumps to the soup. Experiment by using a more creative thickener, such as crustless bread crumbs...or quick-cooking oatmeal...or leftover cooked oatmeal. Mashed potatoes (or instant potato flakes) also make a good thickener.

 NOTE: If you insist on using flour, cornstarch or arrowroot as a thickener, mix it with a liquid (such as water, broth or wine) before adding it to the soup. This will prevent it from getting lumpy.

Sour Cream (Substitute)

- As a substitute for 1 cup of sour cream, combine 1 cup of cottage cheese, 1 teaspoon of distilled white vinegar plus ¼ cup of skim milk in a blender.

- You can also use plain yogurt as a substitute for sour cream—the amounts are equivalent. If you use the yogurt in cooking, add 1 tablespoon of cornstarch to each cup to prevent it from separating.

Spices

◆ Red spices—such as chili powder, cayenne pepper and paprika—lose their color and potency faster than other colored spices. It's best to keep them refrigerated to help prevent loss of color and flavor.

 NOTE: Most spices will keep their flavor even longer if they're kept in the freezer.

◆ If storing spices in the fridge or freezer is not convenient or practical, then keep them in airtight containers in a cool, dark place—far away from the stove.

◆ The conventional wisdom says that spices should be replaced 1 year after they've been opened. Unless you regularly use a large quantity of a specific spice, it's a good idea to buy the smallest available size. Date the jar the first time you open it, so that you will know when to replace it.

◆ When you cook using spices that are not meant to be eaten (such as bay leaves or whole cloves), put them in a metal tea ball or in a piece of cheesecloth tied with string. Then drop them into whatever you're cooking. When the soup or stew is done, fish out the tea ball or cheesecloth, and then discard the contents.

◆ Whether you pour your spices into a shaker or a measuring spoon, do it over a small piece of waxed paper. When the inevitable spill happens, just fold the piece of waxed paper and pour the spice back into its container.

Spinach

◆ This may not come up too often, but we thought it was interesting enough to mention—a *carbon-steel* blade will cause discoloration to spinach leaves, but a *stainless-steel* blade will not. So, now you know which knife to use next time you cut fresh spinach.

◆ When cooking spinach, use a stainless-steel pot. An aluminum pot will give the leaves a metallic taste, and they will also turn a dark, dismal color.

Spray Bottles

It's a good idea to keep several small spray bottles in the kitchen. If you know that they're there, we're sure that you will find many uses for them. The next time you want to moisten, mist, coat, sprinkle or spritz something, you'll be glad you have a spray bottle handy.

Squash

It's generally hard to cut into a butternut or acorn squash—but it's easy if you use a serrated knife. Try it yourself and see.

Also, when you slice squash (or any other round, awkwardly shaped food), do it on a non-skid cutting board or plastic mat to reduce the chance that you'll inadvertently cut yourself.

Strawberries

◆ Want to cut washed strawberries quickly? Use an egg slicer to do it.

◆ Frozen strawberries will stay good up to three months. First, spread the unwashed strawberries on a baking sheet and put them in the freezer. Once they are frozen solid, transfer them to a resealable plastic freezer bag and put them back in the freezer. (Don't forget the label with the date they were frozen.)

Stuffing

◆ It's best not to cook stuffing inside a turkey. When stuffing is in the bird, heat penetration is reduced. And if the inside temperature doesn't reach at least 180°F, bacteria can survive in the innermost part of the turkey and the stuffing. To make sure the meal is as safe and healthy as possible, cook the turkey and stuffing separately.

◆ Here's a unique way to cook prepared stuffing—fill clean coffee cans with the stuffing, cover the cans with aluminum foil and bake for about 2 hours at 350°F.

 NOTE: You can store leftover stuffing in the coffee can—just cover it with the can's plastic lid and put in the fridge.

Sugar

◆ When you check labels for the food's sugar content, you may not see the word "sugar" listed. But that doesn't mean the food is sugar-free. There are other words to look for—*dextrose, fructose, lactose, maltose* and *sucrose* are all forms of sugar. Other sugary sweeteners include corn syrup, honey, maple syrup and molasses.

◆ Keep sugar on your table in a large shaker. This will make it handy for sprinkling on food.

◆ Clean and dry a plastic 1-gallon milk jug, and use it to store granulated white sugar. The closed container will not attract bugs, the sugar will not clump up and the jug's handle makes it easy to pour.

◆ If you store sugar in a canister, keep a chopstick inside it. It will come in handy each time you want to level off a measuring cup.

◆ Put a couple of saltine crackers in the sugar container to help prevent the sugar from lumping up.

Sugar (Brown)

◆ If you can wait a day or so for brown sugar to unclump, then place a few slices of apple in the bag, box or jar of sugar. Close it tightly and wait.

 NOTE: A slice of fresh bread or a few marshmallows will also help to keep brown sugar unclumped.

◆ If you're in a hurry, put the brown sugar on a rimmed baking sheet and bake it at 225°F for 5 to 10 minutes—until it's soft enough to mash down and be normal consistency.

◆ If you're in a really big hurry, put the brown sugar in a microwave-safe bowl, cover it with plastic wrap and poke a few holes in the plastic. Zap it on high power for 30 seconds. Then test it to see if it is unclumped. If not, let it go for another 30 seconds.

◆ To prevent brown sugar from hardening in the first place, try this—after opening a package of brown sugar, put in a strip of orange zest (about 1" wide and 3" long) or a few prunes. Close up the package securely, then store it inside a resealable plastic bag in your cupboard or pantry.

◆ You can also prevent brown sugar from hardening by keeping the package in a resealable plastic freezer bag in the freezer.

63

Sugar (Brown, Substitute)

Use 1 cup of white sugar plus 2 tablespoons of molasses in place of 1 cup of brown sugar.

 NOTE: If you substitute brown sugar for white sugar when baking, the baked goods may be a little moister and have a slight butterscotch taste. What could be bad?

Sugar (Confectioners', Substitute)

In a blender, combine 1 tablespoon of cornstarch plus 1 cup of granulated sugar. Blend at high speed until it's a fine powder consistency. It's not an exact copy of the real thing, but it comes close.

Sweet Cream

If you have sweet cream that's just starting to turn sour, but you're intent on using it anyway, you can bring back the sweetness by adding a pinch of baking soda.

Tacos

Tacos can be messy to eat, but not if you use a coffee filter as a holder. Once you try it, we're sure you'll agree…it's neat.

Tea

◆ When preparing water for tea, turn off the heat as soon as you see little bubbles forming—*before* the water comes to a rolling boil. This prevents oxygen from being boiled out of the water, which would result in flat-tasting tea.

◆ For a slightly spicy taste, stir a cup of hot tea with a cinnamon stick.

◆ If you made a pot of tea and have some left over, freeze it in an ice cube tray. Then use the tea cubes when you make iced tea—they won't dilute the flavor.

Thermometers/Cooking Temperatures

There are several types of meat thermometers available. Before using a thermometer, make sure it's accurate. To test it, boil water and pour a few inches into a glass. Then submerge the thermometer in the water. The temperature should read 212°F. If it does, then you know that the thermometer is accurate. *Here are some general guidelines for cooking meat…*

◆ **Beef roast**—The thermometer should be inserted into the side of the roast, with the stem reaching the center. For a medium-rare beef roast, cook until the thermometer reads 145°F.

◆ **Chicken**—The thermometer should be inserted into the thickest part of the thigh, away from the bone. The chicken is properly cooked when the thermometer reads 180°F.

◆ **Hamburgers**—The thermometer should be inserted into the side of the burger, so the stem reaches the center. Cook until the thermometer reads 160°F.

◆ **Pork roast**—The thermometer should be inserted into the side of the roast, with the stem reaching the center. Remove the roast from the oven when the thermometer reads 155°F, and then let it stand, tented, until the thermometer goes to 160°F for medium.

◆ **Steaks**—The thermometer should be inserted horizontally, into the side of the steak so that the stem reaches the thickest part, not near fat or bone. For medium-rare, the thermometer should read 145°F…for well done, the reading should be 170°F.

◆ **Turkey**—The general rule when cooking a whole defrosted turkey is 25 minutes for each pound at 325°F. When a turkey reaches an internal temperature of 180°F, it is considered done.

 NOTE: If the turkey doesn't have a little button that pops up—and you don't have a meat thermometer—make a discreet incision between the bird's back and thigh. If the juice that seeps out is clear, it's time to *gobble-gobble* the cooked turkey.

Tomatoes

◆ To ripen tomatoes quickly, place them in a brown paper bag with a banana or a couple of apples. The ethylene gas emitted by the banana or apples will help the tomatoes ripen.

◆ Tomatoes have ovary walls and when you cut into them, the pulp and juice tend to slosh out. But if you slice a tomato vertically—from the top of the stem down to the bottom of the fruit—the slices will stay firmer, which will keep your sandwich drier. Also, vertically cut tomatoes will not dilute salad dressing from the excess juice.

◆ If you want to peel fresh tomatoes, here's a simple way to get the job done—dunk the tomatoes in just-boiled water for about 30 seconds, then in cold water for another 30 seconds. The skins will practically fall off!

Tomato Sauce/Paste

◆ Most cooks know to add 1 teaspoon of sugar to sweeten acidic-tasting tomato sauce. But a more nutritious way to get the same result is to add 1 whole carrot to the sauce during the last 30 minutes of cooking. The natural sugar from the carrot will offset the tomatoes' acidity. Before serving the sauce, remove the carrot...or not.

◆ Does anyone use an entire can of tomato paste at once? Use what you need, then put the rest in a small resealable plastic bag. When you're spooning it into the bag, make note of the total number of tablespoons that are going into the bag. Flatten out the paste to about ¼" thickness and freeze it. Then, whenever a recipe calls for 1 or 2 tablespoons of paste, just break off an appropriate-sized piece.

 NOTE: Remember to label the bag of paste with the number of tablespoons it contains as well as the date you put it in the freezer.

Tuna Salad

Oops! Too much mayonnaise in the tuna salad? Soak up the excess mayo by mixing in some breadcrumbs.

Turkey

◆ There are basters (available at some supermarkets or at cookware and hardware stores) that separate the fat from the juice. Be sure to baste with the juice and discard the fat.

◆ You can also baste turkey by soaking a large piece of cheesecloth in melted butter or olive oil, and then covering the turkey with it. This way, the bird will baste itself.

Remove the cheesecloth during the last 30 minutes of baking so that the skin can brown.

◆ For nonstick roasting, let clean celery stalks be your roasting rack, preventing the turkey from sticking to the bottom of the pan.

Line the bottom of the roasting pan with the stalks, and place the turkey on top of them. The gravy will drain to the bottom of the pan and, once the turkey is cooked, it will lift out easily.

◆ When you want to transfer the turkey from the roasting pan to the serving platter, insert a long-handled wooden spoon in each end of the turkey (top and tail), and it will lift out easily.

Also see "Thermometers/Cooking Temperatures" on pages 64–65 for guidelines on cooking turkey properly.

The Place to Talk Turkey

The turkey specialists at the United States Department of Agriculture (USDA) are available to answer cooking questions from 10 am to 4 pm (Eastern time), Monday through Friday, excluding holidays—except Thanksgiving. They also have recorded information that is available 24 hours a day.

The toll-free Meat & Poultry Hotline is 888-674-6854. Or you can visit the USDA's Food Safety and Inspection Service Web site at *www.fsis.usda.gov.*

Turnips/Turnip Greens

- While cooking turnips, add 1 teaspoon of sugar to the water to help prevent that unappetizing turnip-cooking smell.
- When cooking turnip greens, always use a stainless-steel pot. An aluminum pot will give the greens a metallic taste, and it will also turn the greens a dark, dismal color.

Vegetables

- Always store fresh vegetables in your refrigerator (preferably, in the lower fruit/vegetable bin) to keep them crisp and fresh. *The United States Department of Agriculture (USDA) recommends these optimum storage times for fresh vegetables…*
  - Asparagus, beans (snap or wax), cauliflower, celery, cucumber, eggplant, green peppers, salad greens and tomatoes—1 week
  - Beets, carrots, parsnips, radishes, rutabagas and turnips—2 weeks

- Broccoli, brussels sprouts, greens (spinach, kale, collards, etc.), okra, green onions, peas and summer squash—3 to 5 days
- Cabbage—1 to 2 weeks
- Corn—Eat as soon as possible
- As soon as you bring home root vegetables—such as carrots, beets, ginger, potatoes, parsnip, radish, turnip, yam, jicama, horseradish, rutabaga—cut off their leafy tops. If you leave the leaves on, they will rob the roots (the edible part) of their nutrients. And then what's the point of eating your veggies?
- To revive wilting greens, gather them in a bowl filled with ice-water plus 2 or 3 tablespoons of lemon juice. Cover the bowl with plastic wrap and put it in the refrigerator. Wait about 1 hour for your greens to perk up again.

Vinegar

Food that contains vinegar (such as vinaigrette dressing, cucumber salad or coleslaw) should not be served on painted plates. The vinegar may leach out the lead from the plates, and that can be dangerously toxic, especially to children. If you have any question about the plates you use, buy a lead-testing kit (available at home-improvement stores) and check them out.

Water

If your water filter is out of kilter, get out the vitamin C! A pinch of vitamin C powder—or a tiny piece of a vitamin C tablet added to a glass of water right before you drink it—will eliminate any chlorine taste and smell.

Watermelon

Here's a yummy, healthy treat for the summer! Remove the seeds from a chunk of watermelon, and purée the melon meat in the blender. Transfer the puréed pulp into popsicle makers and put them in the freezer. These watermelon pops make a thirst-quenching treat on a hot day.

Whipped Cream

◆ One cup of heavy or whipping cream will provide 2 cups of whipped cream.

◆ To speed up the process of turning heavy cream into whipped cream, chill the bowl, beater and cream before you start whipping—and/or add a pinch of salt or ¼ teaspoon of lemon juice to the cream.

Yogurt

While this is not a cookbook, we wanted to share a quick and easy, satisfying and nutritious dessert recipe. *We'll give you the basics in the hope that you will take it from there and turn it into a treat to suit your specific taste...*

Start with 6 to 8 ounces of plain low-fat yogurt, 1 level teaspoon of carob powder (or 1 teaspoon of unsweetened cocoa powder) and 1 to 2 teaspoons of sugar (or 1 packet of artificial sweetener).

 NOTE: Instead of carob or cocoa powder, you could add your favorite flavor of gelatin. For example, lemon tastes great with yogurt. Have fun experimenting. Add little bits at a time and taste as you go. It's easier to *add* more sweetener than to...well, you know.

DID YOU KNOW?

The Legend of the Zucchini Fairy

Have you ever opened your front door and seen a basket of fresh-grown zucchini waiting there? You probably wondered where it came from—perhaps your neighbor with the lovely garden and the green thumb gave you some overflow from his/her bumper crop. Well, we have a secret to share with you—you've been visited by the Zucchini Fairy!

So pull out the recipe book and make some stuffed zucchini, zucchini quiche or *ratatouille*...and maybe invite your neighbor over for dinner, anyway.

Mix all the ingredients until they reach a marvelous *mousse* consistency. For a little extra pizzazz, add a few drops of almond extract.

Zucchini

Size *does* count. In zucchini's case, the smaller the vegetable, the more flavorful. Look for zucchini that's 2" to 8" in length. They can be stored in a plastic bag in the refrigerator for up to 4 days, but it's best to use them the same day you buy them. ■

CHAPTER 3

Magical Recipes

Our mother and both of our grandmothers were truly kitchen magicians. We always appreciated their to-die-for foods and baked goods, and now we marvel at the strength it took these 3 short, chubby dynamos to conjure up great eats.

They grated and ground and kneaded and rolled and mixed and shook and strained and drained and mashed and sliced and diced and minced and beat and pummeled and stirred and whipped. These were the days before food processors, blenders, electric mixers, graters and peelers. In short, they had no shortcuts.

Inspired by our mother and our grandmothers, but making full use of today's conveniences, we've created this eclectic collection of dessert recipes, ranging from easy (get out the cake mix!) to complex (using more than a half dozen ingredients). We feel that each recipe has a magic of its own.

And by *magic* we mean...

◆ A unique preparation method (let the cookies stay in a turned-off oven overnight)

◆ Something strangely wonderful (a singing cake...cancer-fighting muffins)

◆ An ingredient you may never have used before or even heard of (miso...coconut flour)

◆ Something outrageously decadent (Creamy Coffee Cheesecake)

◆ A surprising ingredient (a cake made with baked beans and tomato sauce, another with eggplant and a believe-it-or-not scrumptious cake made with cherry cola, cocoa powder, mayonnaise and sauerkraut)

With most of these recipes, you may want to play "Guess What's in It?" with your guests... but *after* they've enjoyed eating it.

A few of the recipes that were contributed by family and friends come with their own glaze or frosting. Other recipes refer you to the "Toppings" section so that you may select another that's more to your liking.

Remember, these recipes are for dessert and party treats! They are not recommended for daily consumption...not if you want to eat healthily—and especially not if you want to lose weight. These are for special occasions... for gift-giving...or for that occasional break-the-rules binge. If a child is having a sleepover party, preparing 1 of these recipes would be a fun togetherness project. What kid wouldn't enjoy making Popcorn Cake?

But before you begin, you may want to breeze through these...

BASIC BAKING TIPS

Here are some general baking recommendations to keep in mind when preparing these recipes. We hope these hints make your culinary experiences easier and more enjoyable.

◆ Preheat the oven for at least 15 minutes before baking.

◆ When a recipe calls for eggs, unless otherwise specified, use *large eggs*. The general rule (again, unless otherwise specified) is to use them when they're at room temperature for greater cake volume.

◆ When a recipe calls for the juice of 1 lemon, figure on 2 to 3 tablespoons of juice. When a recipe calls for lemon zest, figure on getting 1 tablespoon from an average-sized lemon.

◆ When a recipe calls for melted chocolate, you want to melt it *slowly* to avoid scorching it. Break the chocolate into small pieces, and either put it in a glass cup or ramekin and let it sit in a pan of hot water, or place the chocolate pieces in a double boiler over hot (not boiling) water and stir.

You can also melt chocolate in a microwave. Be cautious and follow the recommended *time* instructions that come with your microwave.

◆ When a cake recipe calls for nuts or dried or candied fruits, and you want to prevent them from sinking to the bottom of the pan while baking, be sure to *dredge* them. That means toss them with flour, sugar or other dry ingredients so that they are coated before putting them in the cake batter.

◆ For beating cake batter—use an electric mixer and keep it going for at least 2 minutes.

◆ Any cake batter that contains butter or other fat should be baked in a greased pan. If it's an extra-rich batter, grease and flour the bottom of the pan, even if it's a nonstick pan and even if you use parchment paper.

Unless otherwise specified, there's no need to grease the sides of a pan. If a cake can cling to ungreased pan sides, it will rise more evenly all around.

◆ Batter should always be put in a cool pan. The batter should not fill the pan to the top. It is ideal for the pan to go in the oven ½ to ⅔ full.

◆ When making a layer cake, use a soup ladle or ice-cream scoop to divide the batter between the 2 cake pans to ensure that the layers end up being the same size.

◆ For best results, bake on the oven's middle rack—not the top or bottom racks.

◆ To test if a cake is done, insert a toothpick (or a piece of uncooked spaghetti) into the center. If it comes out clean, it's done. If you touch the cake and it springs back, that also means it's done.

◆ When baking cookies, keep in mind that a cookie sheet that is not filled to capacity will take less time to bake than a sheet that is full.

◆ When a cookie recipe calls for butter or margarine, the stick form is best. When a label says *spread*, *whipped*, *light* or *diet*, chances are the butter or margarine contains water or air and less fat by volume. Using it will cause cookies to spread excessively during baking, and they will be less tender.

We hope you have as much fun making these recipes as we did, and that you derive as much pleasure from pleasing the people around you by feeding them these extremely yummy treats.

CAKES

Ok, get ready to bake some fun (and slightly unusual) cake recipes! You should definitely tell your guests what's in these wonderful confections—however, you may want to wait until *after* they've told you how delicious they are.

Avocado Cake

> 1 cup sugar
> ½ cup butter
> 2 eggs
> 1 cup mashed avocado
> ½ cup buttermilk
> 1 teaspoon baking soda
> 1½ cups all-purpose flour
> ½ teaspoon nutmeg
> ½ teaspoon cinnamon
> ½ allspice
> ½ cup raisins
> ½ cup chopped walnuts

1. Preheat oven to 350°F.

2. Cream sugar and butter, add the 2 eggs and avocado and mix well.

3. Add the baking soda to the buttermilk and add to the batter.

4. Add spices to flour and add to the batter all at once and mix well.

5. Dust the raisins and walnuts lightly with flour and add to the batter.

6. Pour into well-greased Pyrex pan (8" x 10") and bake for 35 to 40 minutes. (This can be stored or frozen. It is also delicious served warm with or without a tart lemon sauce.)

> **NOTE:** To ice this cake, see the recipe for Avocado & Banana Ice Cream on page 77, or use any of the icings in the "Toppings" section on page 78.

Baked Beans in Tomato Sauce Cake

> 1 cup white sugar
> ½ cup vegetable oil
> 1 large egg and 1 egg white
> 1 8-ounce can vegetarian baked beans in tomato sauce
> 1 cup all-purpose flour
> ½ teaspoon vanilla extract
> ½ teaspoon ground cinnamon
> ¼ teaspoon baking soda
> ¼ teaspoon baking powder
> ½ cup chopped walnuts (optional)
> ½ cup chopped raisins (optional)

1. Preheat the oven to 325°F. Lightly grease and flour an 8.5" x 4.5" loaf pan, or spray it with nonstick cooking spray.

2. Empty the can of baked beans (with sauce) in a large bowl, and mash the beans. Then stir in the sugar, oil, eggs and vanilla extract. Mix until smooth.

3. In a separate bowl, combine flour, cinnamon, baking soda and baking powder and mix thoroughly. Then add the mixture to the bean batter, and mix thoroughly until smooth. If you're adding walnuts and/or raisins, do so and mix the batter again.

4. Pour the batter into the prepared loaf pan. Bake for 55 to 60 minutes, until a toothpick inserted in the center of the cake comes out clean.

5. Place the pan on wire rack until the cake cools. When it has cooled, frost it with the Cream Cheese Frosting (recipe below).

Cream Cheese Frosting

> 1 3-ounce package cream cheese
> 1 tablespoon milk
> 2½ cups sifted confectioners' sugar
> ½ teaspoon vanilla extract

Blend cream cheese and milk. Add sugar and blend well, then stir in the vanilla extract. Spread the frosting on cooled cake.

Cherry Cola–Chocolate–Mayonnaise–Sauerkraut Bundt Cake

From the "Foodly Yours" column, *Star-Gazette* (Elmira, NY) by Pat Ernst Dugan, food journalist and recipe creator.

2 cups all-purpose flour

⅓ cup unsweetened Dutch-process cocoa powder

1¼ teaspoons baking soda

¼ teaspoon baking powder

3 eggs

1½ cups sugar

1 teaspoon vanilla extract

1 cup light mayonnaise

1 cup cherry cola

1 cup sauerkraut, washed, drained and chopped

1. Preheat oven to 350°F. Spray a Bundt pan heavily with vegetable cooking spray.

2. Sift flour, cocoa, baking soda and baking powder together on a sheet of waxed paper.

3. In a large bowl with mixer on high speed, beat eggs, sugar and vanilla extract. Reduce speed to low and beat in mayonnaise. Add flour-cocoa mixture alternately with cola. Stir in drained sauerkraut.

4. Bake in prepared Bundt pan for approximately 45 minutes. Cool 10 minutes. Remove from pan onto serving plate.

Chiffon Cake

By Bruce Fife, ND, from *Cooking with Coconut Flour: A Delicious Low-Carb, Gluten-Free Alternative to Wheat*. Piccadilly Books.

This recipe makes either a chiffon or Bundt cake, depending on the type of tube pan used.

12 eggs, separated

½ teaspoon cream of tartar

½ cup butter, melted

½ cup coconut milk

1 cup sugar

1 teaspoon salt

1 teaspoon vanilla extract

1 cup sifted coconut flour

½ teaspoon baking powder

Glaze Frosting (recipe below)

1. Preheat oven to 325°F.

2. Combine egg whites and cream of tartar in a large bowl. Using an electric beater, beat until stiff peaks form. Set aside.

3. In a separate bowl, mix together the butter, coconut milk, egg yolks, sugar, salt and vanilla extract.

4. Combine coconut flour with baking powder and quickly whisk into batter until moistened. Batter will thicken if stirred for too long or allowed to sit for more than a minute or so—before it thickens, pour it gradually over beaten egg whites, folding with rubber spatula until just blended. Do not overmix.

5. Pour batter into a greased tube pan. Bake for 1¼ hours or until knife inserted into cake comes out clean.

6. Turn pan upside down on its center funnel to cool. Let cool for at least 30 minutes, remove cake from pan and cover with the Glaze Frosting.

Glaze Frosting

⅓ cup butter, melted

2 cups powdered sugar

1½ teaspoons vanilla extract

2 to 4 tablespoons hot water

Combine melted butter, sugar and vanilla extract. Stir in hot water, 1 tablespoon at a time until glaze is desired consistency.

Chocolate Potato-Flake Cake

From our uncle, Larry Koster.

2 cups all-purpose flour
2 cups sugar
1 cup instant potato flakes
4 teaspoons baking powder
½ teaspoon salt
1 package instant chocolate pudding
1 cup butter
¾ cup milk
¾ cup water
4 eggs

1. Preheat oven to 350°F. Grease and flour a 10" or 12" Bundt pan.

2. Mix all of the ingredients together, then beat at medium speed for 4 minutes.

3. Pour the batter into the Bundt pan and bake for 55 to 65 minutes, until toothpick comes out clean. Let it stand in the pan, on a cooling rack for 30 minutes. Then spread on the glaze.

Glaze

1½ cups powdered sugar
2 tablespoons cream cheese or butter
½ teaspoon vanilla extract
2 or 3 tablespoons milk or cream
3 to 5 tablespoons chopped nuts

1. Mix all of the ingredients together.

2. Beat on low speed until smooth. Then spoon it on top of the cake. Top it off by sprinkling chopped nuts on it.

Creamy Coffee Cheesecake

By Marie Nadine Antol from *Confessions of a Coffee Bean*. Square One Publishers. *www.squareonepublishers.com*.

Yield: 9" cheesecake

Crust

1½ cups graham cracker crumbs

¼ cup powdered sugar
6 tablespoons butter, melted

Coffee Filling

32 ounces cream cheese, softened
¾ cup sugar
2 teaspoons instant coffee granules
1 teaspoon hot water
2 eggs
1 cup sour cream
3 tablespoons Kahlúa or Tia Maria liqueur (optional)

Topping

1½ cups sour cream
2 tablespoons sugar
½ teaspoon vanilla extract
⅛ teaspoon salt

1. To prepare the crust, place all of the crust ingredients in a medium-sized bowl, and toss with a fork or mix with your hands until well-blended.

2. Place the crust mixture in a 9" springform pan or a deep-dish pie pan. Using the back of a spoon or your hands, press the crumbs firmly around the bottom and sides of the pan. Refrigerate the crust for at least 1 hour, or until very cold.

3. To make the filling, place the cream cheese in a large mixing bowl, and beat with an electric mixer until very soft. Add the sugar and beat into the cream cheese.

4. Dissolve the instant coffee in the hot water, and beat into the cream cheese mixture. Then beat in the eggs, 1 at a time, until well-blended.

5. Add the sour cream and the liqueur, if desired, to the filling, and beat slowly until thoroughly combined.

6. Pour the filling into the chilled crust and bake in a preheated 350°F oven for 40 minutes, or until the filling is set and a knife inserted in the center comes out clean.

7. Place the pan on a wire rack, and cool for 40 to 60 minutes, or until the cake reaches room temperature.

8. To make the topping, place the sour cream in a medium-sized mixing bowl and gently stir in the remaining ingredients. When well-blended, spread the topping over the cooled cheesecake.

9. Bake the "topped" cheesecake in a preheated 425°F oven for 5 minutes, or just long enough to set the sour cream. Allow to cool on a wire rack. Refrigerate for at least 4 hours before cutting into wedges and serving.

 NOTE: This coffee cake actually has coffee in it and takes some doing, but it will be worth it.

Eggplant Pudding Cake

1 package (2-layer size—18.25 ounce) yellow cake mix (DO NOT use mix that has pudding added for extra moisture)

1 package (4-serving size) vanilla flavor instant pudding and pie filling

2 cups peeled and grated eggplant (about 1 pound)

1 cup sour cream

4 eggs

½ cup vegetable oil

½ teaspoon nutmeg

¼ teaspoon cinnamon

⅛ teaspoon salt

1. Preheat oven to 350°F. Grease and lightly flour a Bundt pan.

2. In a large mixing bowl, combine all of the ingredients. Blend, then beat at medium speed with an electric mixer for 4 minutes. Pour into the prepared Bundt pan.

3. Bake for 1 hour and 10 minutes, or until the cake tests done. *Do not underbake.*

4. Remove from oven and cool in pan for 15 minutes. Remove from pan and let it finish cooling on a rack. Dust with powdered sugar.

This cake freezes great…if there's any left.

 NOTE: You don't have to like eggplant to enjoy this cake—you really can't tell there's eggplant in it. It just tastes good.

Popcorn Cake

8 cups dry-popped popcorn

4 ounces chocolate chips

½ cup peanuts, broken in half

¼ cup margarine or butter

¼ cup peanut butter, smooth with no additives (we use Maranatha)

5 ounces miniature marshmallows

1. Line an angel food–cake pan with aluminum foil.

2. In a large bowl, combine popcorn, chocolate chips and peanuts. Set aside.

3. In a saucepan, melt margarine or butter over low heat. Stir in peanut butter and marshmallows. Keep stirring continually until every little marshmallow has melted.

4. Pour marshmallow mixture over popcorn mixture as you gently stir the popcorn, so that it all gets coated.

5. Pack mixture into prepared pan, pressing down firmly. Let it cool completely. Then remove from pan and cut into slices to serve.

Singing Cake

A friend sent us this recipe and said to time it so that you put it in the oven right before your guests are due to arrive. Then, once the cake is baking and your guests are there, invite them into the kitchen to listen to the cake sing.

We were intrigued and—even though we were in the midst of working on this book and weren't about to have company—we wanted to test this recipe and hear the cake sing. We went so far as to set up a tape recorder, thinking we would send the tape to our editor, along with the recipe.

So, we measured out all of the ingredients, then carefully followed the directions and put the cake in the oven. We waited and listened. No singing. No humming. We even would have settled for whining. But nothing. Not a sound.

We left the cake in the oven for close to an hour, hoping at least to hear the refrain from *New York, New York*. But ours was the Marcel Marceau of cakes—absolutely silent. Once it was out of the oven and had finished cooling, we tasted it —and, it was so good, it made *us* sing!

While we can't speak from experience in terms of the cake singing, we've heard that it does work. If you have the time, patience and ingredients, try it and let us know what happens.

> 1 cup butter
>
> 2 cups firmly packed brown sugar
>
> 3 eggs, separated
>
> 2 squares bitter chocolate, melted
>
> 1 cup raisins
>
> 2 teaspoons cinnamon
>
> 1 teaspoon ground cloves
>
> 4 cups flour, sifted
>
> 1 cup strawberry jam
>
> 1 cup chopped walnuts
>
> 2 teaspoons baking powder
>
> 1 cup buttermilk

1. Preheat oven to 350°F.

2. In a large bowl, cream the butter and sugar.

3. Add the egg yolks and stir. Add melted chocolate and stir. Add raisins and stir. Add cinnamon, ground cloves and flour, and stir. Stir in the jam and walnuts. Now, rest your hand from all of that stirring.

4. Beat the egg whites until stiff.

5. Add baking powder to the buttermilk and quickly stir it into the cake mixture.

6. Fold in the stiff egg whites.

7. Quickly pour the mixture into the greased and floured angel food–cake pan. Bake until the cake stops singing—about 45 minutes.

 NOTE: We think that this cake is delicious without any topping. But if you want the "icing on the cake," please select 1 from the "Toppings" section on page 78.

COOKIES

Crispy Potato Chip Cookies

From B. L. Ochman.

Yield: About 4 dozen

> 1 cup vegetable shortening or unsalted butter
>
> 1 cup granulated white sugar
>
> 1 cup light brown sugar
>
> 2 eggs, well beaten
>
> 1 teaspoon baking soda
>
> 2 cups all-purpose flour
>
> ½ teaspoon water
>
> 1½ teaspoons vanilla extract
>
> 1½ to 2 cups potato chips (salted or unsalted), coarsely crushed
>
> 1 (6-ounce) package butterscotch or peanut butter chips

1. Preheat oven to 350°F.

2. In a large bowl, cream the shortening with the sugars until smooth, then add the beaten eggs.

3. In a separate bowl, combine the baking soda with the flour. Mix them together thoroughly. Then slowly pour this dry mixture into the large bowl with the wet mixture. Combine thoroughly.

4. Add the water, vanilla extract, crushed potato chips and butterscotch or peanut butter chips to the large bowl and mix thoroughly.

5. Lightly grease a cookie sheet, or line it with parchment paper. Drop rounded teaspoonfuls onto the cookie sheet 2" apart.

6. Bake for 9 to 12 minutes. Cool cookies on a wire rack.

Bet you can't eat just 1 of these treats!

Overnight-Delight Cookies

Yield: 5 to 6 dozen cookies

2 egg whites
pinch salt
1 teaspoon vanilla extract
⅔ cup sugar
1 cup chopped walnuts
1 6-ounce package semisweet chocolate chips

1. Preheat the oven to 350°F for at least 20 minutes.

2. Beat egg whites, salt and vanilla extract until soft (not stiff) peaks form

3. Add sugar—1 tablespoon at a time—and continue beating until very stiff peaks have formed.

4. Add walnuts and chocolate chips.

5. Drop teaspoonfuls of mixture on a large, ungreased cookie sheet. Turn off the oven. Place the cookie sheet in the oven and leave overnight. Do not open the oven until the next morning.

OTHER GOODIES

Almond Crisped Rice Treats

By John and Jan Belleme from *The Miso Book*. Square One Publishers. *www.squareonepublishers.com.*

Yield: 16 treats (2" squares)

½ cup unsalted almond butter*

Scant ½ cup rice syrup (available at health-food stores and many supermarkets)

2 teaspoons sweet white miso** (available at health-food stores) mixed with 2 teaspoons water

½ teaspoon vanilla extract

⅛ teaspoon almond extract

2½ cups crispy brown rice cereal

1. Preheat the oven to 350°F.

2. Combine the almond butter, rice syrup, miso and vanilla and almond extracts in a medium-sized bowl and mix well.

3. Add the cereal and gently toss until evenly coated.

4. Press the mixture into an unoiled 8" square baking pan. Bake for 12 to 15 minutes or until the edges are lightly browned. Allow to cool on a wire rack.

5. Cut into 2" squares and serve.

*Maranatha Almond Butter—100% organic, raw almonds, no salt added and available at health-food stores—is our favorite.

**Miso is a fermented soy food usually made from cooked soybeans and cultured grains, such as rice and barley. Scientific studies have confirmed miso's reputation as a very healing food. *The Miso Book* goes into detail about the many health benefits derived from incorporating miso into your daily diet, along with tasty recipes.

Avocado & Banana Ice Cream

Yield: 2 servings

1 frozen banana, cut in small pieces
1 ripe, average-sized Haas avocado
3 tablespoons lemon juice
½ cup soy milk
sugar or sugar substitute (before you add sweetener of any kind, taste it after it has been blended)

1. Blend all the ingredients in a blender until creamy.

2. Eat it this way, or put it in an ice-cream maker or in the freezer until it has the consistency of ice cream.

Or you can also use it to make an avocado/banana smoothie. Just add more soy milk and ice and blend.

Or you can use it as a topping on the Avocado Cake (*see* page 71).

Orange Bran Flax Muffin Magic (also known as Breast Cancer–Prevention Flax Muffins)

Yield: 18 muffins (a profound number that symbolizes *chai,* meaning life, according to Jewish numerology).

1 cup oat bran
1 cup all-purpose flour
1 cup flaxseed, ground (we use Barlean's Forti-Flax, available at health-food stores)
1 cup natural bran
1 tablespoon baking powder
½ teaspoon salt

2 oranges, whole, washed, quartered and seeded
1 cup brown sugar
1 cup buttermilk
½ cup canola oil
2 eggs
1 teaspoon baking soda
1½ cups raisins

1. Preheat oven to 375°F.

2. In a large bowl, combine the oat bran, flour, flaxseed, bran, baking powder and salt. Set aside.

3. In a blender or food processor, combine oranges, brown sugar, buttermilk, oil, eggs and baking soda. Blend well.

4. Pour orange mixture into dry ingredients and mix until well-blended.

5. Stir in raisins. (White chocolate chips can be substituted for the raisins.)

6. Fill paper-lined muffin tins almost to the top and bake for 18 to 20 minutes or until wooden toothpick inserted in the center of the muffin comes out clean.

7. Let the muffins cool for 5 minutes, then transfer them to a cooling rack.

 NOTE: According to Christiane Northrup, MD, a leading expert on women's health, flaxseed is the best source of anticancer and phytoestrogenic compounds (lignans), a concentration more than 100 times greater than other lignan-containing foods, including grains, fruits and vegetables.

When you buy flaxseed for these muffins, be sure the label says that the flax is from cold-milled select flaxseed and that it is 100% organic (which means pesticide- and herbicide-free). That milling process gently frees vitamins, minerals, amino acids, lignans and phytonutrients without damaging the delicate omega-3 fatty acids.

TOPPINGS

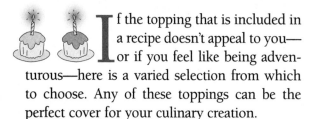 If the topping that is included in a recipe doesn't appeal to you— or if you feel like being adventurous—here is a varied selection from which to choose. Any of these toppings can be the perfect cover for your culinary creation.

NOTE: The level of sweetness in these recipes is controllable by the amount of sugar used. Even though we are in the minority, we think the average topping is too sweet, and so we caution you to gradually add the sugar and keep tasting it, so that you stop before you mix in too much.

Chocolate Fudge Frosting

2 cups sugar
¼ cup light corn syrup
½ butter or margarine
½ cup milk
2 1-ounce unsweetened chocolate squares, coarsely grated
1 teaspoon vanilla extract

1. In a heavy saucepan, over low heat, stir all of the ingredients except vanilla extract. When the chocolate melts, bring it to a rolling boil while constantly stirring. Then boil it for 1 minute.

2. Take it off the heat and beat it until it's lukewarm. Then stir in the vanilla extract and continue stirring, and when it reaches a desirable spreading consistency, it's good to go…enough to frost on 2 8" or 9" cake layers.

Lemon Sauce

1 cup water
⅓ cup sugar
1 tablespoon cornstarch
2 tablespoons butter
1 tablespoon lemon juice
½ teaspoon vanilla extract

Boil until clear and serve warm over cake.

Peanut Butter Frosting (Broiled)

2 tablespoons butter, softened
1 cup packed dark brown sugar
⅔ cup peanut butter
¼ cup milk
⅔ cup chopped peanuts

1. Combine and cream butter, sugar and peanut butter.

2. Add milk and stir well. Keep stirring as you mix in nuts.

3. Spread over warm cake.

4. Place frosted cake under broiler, about 4" to 5" from the heat source. Leave it there until topping bubbles and browns lightly. It will happen quickly, so stay with it every second to prevent it from scorching.

5. Let the cake cool at least 30 minutes before serving it.

Quick-and-Easy Tropical Frosting

1 9-ounce container of Cool Whip
1 small can crushed pineapple
1 package vanilla instant pudding

1. Combine and beat ingredients thoroughly.

2. Frost and refrigerate. ■

CHAPTER 4

Easy Holiday &
Party Plans

roviding you with a start-to-finish guide to entertaining presumes that whatever you're doing now needs improvement. And that's not right (and that's also a whole other book).

We're taking it for granted that you are already a great and gracious host or hostess who's always looking to add to your repertoire of ways to please your guests.

So, although we're sure that you could teach us a few things, we hope that you will discover some helpful tips to enhance your next dinner party, romantic rendezvous, luncheon, backyard picnic, family get-together, holiday celebration or any other special event that's made extra-special because you're in charge.

INVITATIONS

Receiving a creative invitation in the mail is the beginning of the fun for the people who are invited to a party or special event. Be sure that each invitation you send to your guests has all of the pertinent information they need to know—the reason for the event, date, time, location (with directions, if necessary) and RSVP contact information and "respond by" date.

Invitations are the first thing that people see, and they can set the overall tone for your party or gathering. *Here are a few ideas to get you thinking of attention-getting invitations…*

- Print the invitation on T-shirts.
- Make jigsaw puzzles out of the invitations.
- Use a permanent marker to write every invitation on a blown-up balloon (you may want to enlist a helper to hold each balloon while you write on it). Let the air out of the balloon, then put it in an envelope and mail 1 to each person you're inviting.

    Be sure to include in the envelope a separate piece of paper with your phone number and directions to your home.

 NOTE: If you need help with the directions you provide, check out *www.mapquest.com*. (If you're not on-line at home, take advantage of the free Internet connection at any public library.)

If your potential guests have e-mail and Internet access, send them electronic invitations. You can either design an attractive e-mail and write something clever yourself, or use a free e-vite service, such as *www.evite.com*.

PLACE CARDS

Place cards are used to determine the seating arrangement of the guests, and where you place the place cards can signal the failure or success of a dinner party. Since you, the host or hostess, control who sits where, you can arrange people however you think best—for example, the big (and loud?) talkers should sit next to the good listeners, and 2 feuding relatives should be seated at opposite ends of the table—or at different tables.

In addition to arranging people in the best possible way, place cards serve another important purpose…they help remind people of their tablemates' names. (Doesn't everyone seem to be having a hard time remembering names these days?)

When we recently attended a private business dinner at the famed Four Seasons restaurant in New York City, we noticed that each place setting had a tent-shaped place card with the name of the guest printed on BOTH sides of the card. *Very clever.* That way, you can see the names of the people sitting across the table from you, as well as the names of people seated on either side of you—and they can all see your name as well.

Here are some fun place card ideas…

◆ For moderate-sized parties, blow up balloons and write your guests' names with a permanent marker or nail polish (you may want to enlist a helper to hold each balloon while you write on it). Then attach the named balloon to the chair as a unique place card.

◆ Put a fresh (or artificial) rose across each place setting with the guest's name written with metallic ink on a leaf. (If the flower doesn't have leaves, use an adhesive address label—just wrap it around the stem.)

◆ Bicycle nameplates serve as novelty place cards that can be taken home as souvenirs.

If you need to invite 2 people with the same name, use a permanent marker to write in a last name or initial.

◆ Buy miniature picture frames and put each guest's name in a frame—they make great keepsakes. It would be even more fun if you had a photo of each guest to put in the frame.

✳ Fun Photo Place Cards

This is a great idea if you have a digital camera, a printer and a helper (cohost, relative, spouse or close friend)—as each guest arrives, you or your recruited assistant will take a photo of him/her. Then print out the photo, cut out the face, frame it and place it at the appropriate place setting.

◆ For a pasta party, use a permanent marker to write each guest's name on a piece of uncooked lasagna. Place the pasta on each dinner plate setting.

On a buffet table, identify the food in each dish by writing the information on pieces of uncooked lasagna that you then place in front of the appropriate dish.

◆ Buy a rubber stamp (available at crafts stores) that's appropriate for the occasion or that tells guests they are in your home (for example, your initial in an elegant font). Also buy an ink pad in a stand-out color.

Fold an unlined 3" x 5" index card in half (tent style) and stamp it, then write the guest's name on it to make your own creative, personal placecards.

NAPKINS & NAPKIN RINGS

Creative and interesting napkins and napkin rings are a good way of adding personality to your table setting. *Here are some unique suggestions...*

◆ If you're not using cloth napkins, give paper napkins some personality by stamping them with the same rubber stamp you used on the place cards.

◆ If you're baking bread, make an extra portion of dough and use it to make napkin rings. Roll out the dough in 8"-long strips. Use 2 strips entwined to form a circle for each ring. Bake them at 350°F until golden-brown, and when they're cool, set the table with these edible treats.

Barbara, our neighbor and generous friend, shared this idea with us—she uses 3 strips of dough, braids them, makes them napkin-ring shaped and bakes them (also at 350°F until golden-brown). Her napkin rings match the top of the challah (braided bread) she uses on the Sabbath table.

◆ Remember those candy dots on long strips of paper? Many candy stores still carry them, and they make adorable napkin holders, especially for a dessert table or a grown-up's birthday celebration dinner. Each holder requires about 8" of dots-paper, wrapped around the napkin. Close the ends of each strip with double-sided tape.

You can also tie the napkins with long strings of black or red rope licorice.

◆ Make napkin rings from empty tubes of toilet tissue or paper towel (depending on the thickness of the napkins you plan to use). Cover the tubes by pasting on paper that matches your table or room décor. You can use construction paper, wrapping paper, left-over wallpaper, last season's sample wallpaper books (available at your local paint store) or even newspaper—try the comics.

Once the tube is covered, cut it crosswise into equally sized pieces—about 1½" wide. If you use solid paper to cover the tubes, you can also decorate them with stickers, sequins and ribbon—or stamp them to match your rubber-stamped napkins and even your place cards.

We recently set a dinner table with a solid red tablecloth, napkin rings covered in black-and-white magazine excerpts with thin red ribbon tied around them, white linen napkins and white dinnerware. *Dahling, it looked mahvelous!* Conversations started immediately as dinner guests read their napkin rings and shared the articles.

TABLE DECORATIONS

Decorating your table is like putting on sparkling pieces of jewelry after you are dressed—it completes the whole picture. *Here are some decorative ideas that are gems...*

Fruit-Flavored Fun

This simple idea is attractive and smells good, too. Cut a citrus fruit (lemon, lime, orange, etc.) in half. Remove the pulp* and put a votive candle in the middle of the shell. Surround the candle with cranberries to hold it in place.

You can use several oranges, grapefruits, lemons or limes as a centerpiece, or you can space them out around the table.

*Choose the fruit according to its color and scent as well as which fruit pulp you can use in the meal.

To help you decide on which fruit to use, you should know about the results of a recent study conducted by Alan R. Hirsch, MD, neurological director of The Smell & Taste Treatment and Research Foundation in Chicago. According to Dr. Hirsch, "In the presence of the smell of pink grapefruit, women appear [to men] to be 6 years younger than their real age."

A Festive Touch

Scatter some confetti on the table. You can make your own with a hole puncher or paper shredder, or you can buy packages of confetti in a variety of colors and shapes (available at crafts and stationery stores). Use a disposable tablecloth, and cleanup will be a breeze.

Centerpiece Enhanced

Whatever your centerpiece—flowers, leaves, fruit, candles—place it on a mirror to create the illusion that you have twice as many flowers, leaves, fruit or candles. Candles will be especially dazzling because of their reflection in the mirror.

 FYI: Enhance Sparkling Conversation

Think low and wide for your centerpiece. If a floral arrangement is on the tall side—beautiful as it may be—conversation across the table will be blocked, along with your guests' view.

Tablecloth Substitute

For something a little different, use a colorful bedsheet with a great design as a tablecloth. (No, not a fitted sheet.)

Anticipation Preparation

Before her company begins to arrive, Caroline (our neighbor and a gracious hostess) fills an average-sized vase with water, and leaves it in an out-of-the-way place in the kitchen.

Then, if 1 of the guests brings flowers, Caroline is able to quickly put the bouquet into the vase, place it in the living room and continue hostessing.

Glass Dinnerware Extraordinaire

If you have clear glass dinner plates—or a set of clear glass plates and a set of solid colored plates—and you want something unique (and don't mind washing twice as many dishes), then this idea is for you.

Use 2 plates per setting—the clear plate laid on top of the colored plate. In between the 2 plates, press fresh flowers and leaves…or fresh herbs…or make a collage of photos, special announcements/news clippings, or birthday, anniversary or holiday cards…or use a printed or solid napkin to match the tablecloth…or whatever else will fit between the plates. It's your dinner party and your plates, so use your imagination for a memorable idea that will have everyone talking.

 Traditional (and Practical) Food Service

It's traditional for food to be served from the left side of each guest. Because most people are right-handed, they generally tend to gesture more with their right hand.

Therefore, it's safer for food to be served from the left side, so that a plate or serving dish will not be knocked out of the server's hand by any of those right-sided hand gestures.

CANDLES

Candlelight makes skin tones glow and eyes sparkle. It also helps create a festive atmosphere. And doesn't food just taste better when eaten by candlelight? These suggestions will help you handle each candle safely, efficiently and imaginatively.

Lighten Up with Carbs

When you want to light several candles at a time, first light the end of a strand of dry spaghetti. Use it to go from wick to wick to wick.

Relighting a Candle

Before relighting a candle, trim the candle's wick to ¼" in length. The candle will burn longer and without smoking.

Drip Prevention

◆ Beeswax candles do not drip. If your candles are not beeswax, and you don't want them to drip when lit, prepare some saltwater—use 2 tablespoons of table salt to 2 cups of water—and let the candles soak in the solution for about 4 hours. Then dry the candles thoroughly. When lit, thanks to the saltwater soaking, the candles should be dripless.

◆ Keep candles in the freezer for several hours before lighting them. The candles will burn longer and hardly drip, if at all.

Candle Holders

◆ If your candle is a little too big for the holder, dip the last inch of the candle in hot water and keep it there until the wax is soft enough for you to squeeze it and make it thinner so that it will fit into the holder.

◆ Before inserting a candle, lightly spray a holder with cooking spray to help prevent melted wax from sticking to it.

Candle Holder Alternatives

◆ Use apples that are flat on the bottom and won't topple over. Core each apple carefully and insert a candle.

◆ Mini-pumpkins and gourds make colorful candle holders, especially at Halloween and Thanksgiving dinners. Cut out the top, scoop out the inside, then insert a candle.

◆ Using teacups and saucers to hold votive candles, floating candles or tea lights can add a feminine touch to a table setting.

✎ **NOTE:** Tea lights are the candles that are shorter than votives and used in fondue sets, chafing dishes and butter warmers.

◆ Candle holders made from uncooked artichokes will add soft light and panache to your buffet or dinner table. Cut a thin slice off the bottom of the artichoke, so that it stands up straight. Trim the sharp points off the leaves and scoop out the middle and place a votive candle there. If you want some glitz, spray paint the artichokes gold.

◆ If you don't have holders for candles on a birthday cake, use a few gumdrops as colorful holders. You can also use them to spell an appropriate word or name on the cake.

◆ Insert birthday candles in mini-marshmallows and put the marshmallows into the cake. You may wind up with waxy marshmallows, but you'll also have a cake that's free of wax…and that's the whole idea.

✳ Bright Birthday Ideas!

◆ Consider using fuzzy pipe cleaners instead of candles. They're colorful, stiff enough to stand up straight, burn brightly thanks to their metal core, and your cake will stay free of candle wax.

◆ Let everyone get a chance to blow out a candle. Give each guest an individual cupcake or miniature cake with a candle on it. This is especially nice at kids' birthday parties.

Votive Candles

◆ Pour 1 ounce of water on the bottom of each votive holder to prevent the candle's heat from cracking the glass.

◆ Before putting a votive candle in the holder, rub the bottom of the candle with petroleum jelly. When you want to remove the candle, just turn the holder upside down and out it will slide.

◆ Put 6 drops of liquid soap in the votive holder and fill it halfway with hot water. Let it soak for 20 minutes, and you should be able to pop out the wax along with the metal wick holder.

Candle Cleaner

Wipe the surface of a decorative candle with a clean piece of pantyhose to remove dust and fingerprints and to restore its shine.

Candle Storage

Keep your long candles out of harm's way by storing them in cleaned-out, tall potato chip cans (such as Pringles), or paper towel tubes with aluminum foil on both ends and held in place with rubber bands. If you're on a low-carb diet and no longer have use for your spaghetti canister, it's perfect to hold a few long tapers.

ALCOHOL & OTHER BEVERAGES

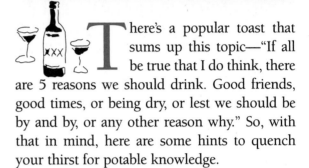

There's a popular toast that sums up this topic—"If all be true that I do think, there are 5 reasons we should drink. Good friends, good times, or being dry, or lest we should be by and by, or any other reason why." So, with that in mind, here are some hints to quench your thirst for potable knowledge.

Wine

Writer and world traveler Ernest Hemingway thought wine to be the most civilized thing in the world. *Here are some civilized ways to treat it…*

Corks Away!

When tiny pieces of cork break off into the bottle, pour the wine through a fine strainer or sieve, or through a coffee filter. Pour the wine into a lovely decanter or other decorative serving bottle, preferably crystal.

Quick Chill for White Wine

Salt keeps ice colder longer. Put ice in a bucket or pail, and mix salt in with the cubes. Then put in the bottle of wine to chill.

White wine kept in a bucket of ice and water will chill faster than if the wine is in a bucket of ice *without* water.

Drip-Free Wine Pouring

Just as you finish pouring a glass of wine—right before you are about to lift it away from the glass—give the bottle a slight twist. The drip will roll around the bottle's lip and disappear, instead of ending up on the tablecloth or on someone's lap.

Wine Recycling

◆ Save leftover wine for recipes that call for wine. To keep the wine's flavor longer, add 1 teaspoon of vegetable oil to the bottle and put it in the refrigerator.

◆ Freeze leftover wine in ice cube trays. You can then use the cubes anytime for recipes or in wine coolers.

Cool Idea for Hot Coffee

Freeze leftover coffee in ice cube trays and use it to cool *hot-hot-hot* coffee...or to make iced coffee...or to add great flavor to eggnog.

Better Wine Storage

Remember the 2004 film that featured people who are passionate about wine? The name of the film is *Sideways*—which is the best way to store bottles of wine, especially pinot noir.

If a bottle is stored sideways, the wine is always in contact with the cork. (A wet cork expands to form a tighter seal. Exposure to air can spoil wine.)

If you keep several bottles of wine in your house, a wine rack is a wise investment.

Amount to Buy

When you're having a party and want to figure out how many bottles of wine to buy, start with the number of people who have accepted your invitation. Then consider how much your guests will drink—how many may limit themselves to 2 or 3 glasses, and how many will nurse 1 glass all evening? Once you have that number, figure on 5 glasses of wine per average bottle. OK, now you do the math...and the ordering.

Champagne/Sparkling Wine

Dom Pierre Perignon, the 17th-century Benedictine monk who is credited with the invention of champagne, was quoted as saying, "Come brothers, hurry, I am drinking stars." *Here are some tips to help you reach for those stars...*

Proper Amount of Bubbly

According to the Champagne Wines Information Bureau (*www.champagne.com*), for a champagne aperitif at cocktail hour, 1 bottle (*see* "Champagne Equivalents" on page 86) should serve 3 or 4 guests. When serving a meal, count on 1 bottle for every 2 or 3 people.

For the traditional champagne toast to the bride...or the birthday honoree...or the retiree...or the newly promoted someone—1 bottle can usually be stretched to serve 6 to 10 people.

Proper Way to Open a Bottle

Also according to the Champagne Wines Information Bureau, begin by slanting the champagne bottle at a 45° angle away from guests. Then, with a thumb on the cork, untwist and loosen the wire muzzle. Grasp the cork firmly, twist the bottle slowly and let the pressure help push out the cork. Allow a light and merry pop.

Service Preparation

Refrigerate champagne for no longer than 2 to 3 hours before serving. Overdoing it in the fridge may weaken the champagne's taste and its bouquet.

The Coolest Way to Chill

If the opportunity presents itself—and we're talking snowstorm here—chill the champagne in an ice bucket filled with snow.

Champagne Equivalents

When you serve champagne, figure there will be about 4 ounces per serving. If you're using champagne for a toast, figure on 2 ounces for each guest. *The following can help you place your champagne order...*

Split	2	4-ounce servings
(½ pint)	4	2-ounce servings for a toast
Half	4	4-ounce servings
(1 pint)	8	2-ounce servings for a toast
Bottle	8	4-ounce servings
(1 quart)	16	2-ounce servings for a toast
Magnum	16	4-ounce servings
(2 quarts)	32	2-ounce servings for a toast
Jeroboam	32	4-ounce servings
(4 quarts)	64	2-ounce servings for a toast
Rehoboam	48	4-ounce servings
(6 quarts)	96	2-ounce servings for a toast
Methuselah	64	4-ounce servings
(8 quarts)	128	2-ounce servings for a toast
Salmanazar	96	4-ounce servings
(12 quarts)	192	2-ounce servings for a toast
Balthazar	128	4-ounce servings
(16 quarts)	256	2-ounce servings for a toast
Nebuchadnezzar	160	4-ounce servings
(20 quarts)	320	2-ounce servings for a toast

Graceful Pouring

Fill each flute about ⅓ of the way, then begin again at the first glass, doubling the amount so that each glass is appropriately ⅔ full.

By pouring champagne ⅓ at a time, you allow the fizzing to subside, which prevents the bubbly from bubbling over.

Ice Cubes

Who would think there's a lot to learn about ice cubes? You just put water in a tray, and put the tray in the freezer. Ahh, but there's so much more. *See for yourself...*

Preventing Fizz Overflow

If you want a glass of soda with ice, first rinse the ice cubes with cold water before putting them in the glass. The rinsing changes the surface tension of the ice and prevents the soda from fizzing over.

Storing Ice Cubes

When you want to accumulate ice cubes in your freezer, keep the extra cubes in a brown paper bag. It helps prevent them from sticking to each other and becoming a big frozen blob.

Get Frozen Faster

Just-boiled water freezes faster than cold water. The reason is that hot water evaporates faster than cold water, so there's less water to freeze. Also, the evaporation process creates an air current over the ice cube tray, and this creates a cooling effect—similar to blowing on a spoonful of hot soup. If you don't believe us, try it and see for yourself.

Clear and Not Cloudy Cubes

Fill your ice cube trays with distilled water (available at most supermarkets and grocery stores). This will make extra-clear cubes that look like crystals dancing in your drinks.

Floral Ice Bowl

For you artsy and ambitious hosts and hostesses, this is something special—a beautiful floral ice bowl in which to serve a dessert (such as berries or ice cream), a colorful side dish (such as cranberry relish) or anything else in your recipe repertoire that needs to be served cold. If you have the time—and room in the freezer—this floral ice bowl can be a spectacular addition to your table.

To create this bowl made of ice, you'll need 2 freezer-proof glass or aluminum bowls of the same shape, but one of the bowls should be about 2" smaller than the other. You'll also need an assortment of edible flowers (*see* "Colorful Ingredients," below) or slices of citrus fruit, herbs or confetti.

Pour 1" of cold tap water into the larger bowl and stand it flat in the freezer. After a few hours, start checking to see if the water in the bowl is completely frozen. (The amount of time it takes depends on your freezer and the size of the bowl you use.)

When the water in the bowl is completely frozen, take the bowl out of the freezer. Place the smaller bowl inside the larger bowl, perfectly centered on the ice. Tape the bowls together to hold them in place—you don't want them to shift positions.

Pour water into the space between the 2 bowls, until it's halfway up the sides. Drop the flowers, herbs, citrus slices or confetti into the water, all around the perimeter of the bowl. You may want to use a pencil or chopstick to push down the decorations.

Put the bowls back in the freezer, again on level ground. When the water is frozen solid, remove the bowls from the freezer. Take off the tape and gently separate the bowls. If they won't budge, run tepid water over the outside of the larger bowl until the ice bowl is released.

Once it's dislodged, put the ice bowl back into the freezer until it's time for your party. Chill a glass plate or tray, and serve the ice bowl on it so that dripping water from the melting ice will collect on the plate.

Colorful Ingredients

Surprise your guests with pretty and tasty ice cubes in their drinks. Before you fill your ice-cube trays with water, put a single mint leaf…a strawberry…a raspberry…a maraschino cherry…or a few edible flowers—such as Johnny Jump-ups, nasturtium, violets, roses or borage (available at specialty food stores)—in each cube compartment. If you're serving alcoholic drinks to adults, you may want to prepare ice cubes that contain cocktail onions or olives.

 Substitute Ice Cube Tray

Wash the bottom half of an empty plastic egg carton, fill it with water and then put it in your freezer.

Keeping Punch Cool

The larger the ice cube, the slower it melts. A few days in advance of your party, make 2 big ice cubes. You can do this by cutting off the tops of milk or juice containers, washing them, filling them with water and putting them in the freezer.

 NOTE: The large cubes will take hours to freeze. It's a good idea to leave them overnight. If you have a hard time removing the ice from the container, run some tepid water over the bottom of the container.

When the punch is made, put 1 of the large ice cubes in a punch bowl, and then add the punch. This will keep it cool…for a long time. Use the other big ice cube for the punch bowl refill.

> **NOTE:** If you feel that a big ice cube will water down the beverage, add an extra amount of whatever ingredient makes the punch punchy.

◆ Another option is to prepare big or small ice cubes made with juice—the same juice that goes into the punch—and use them to keep punch cool without diluting it.

Other Beverages

If your tastes go beyond wine and champagne, we offer several suggestions on how to make your adult beverages even more sophisticated.

 Keep It Cold
Fans of chilled vodka know to drink it in small glasses with stems so that their hands won't warm up the vodka.

Keep Beer from Getting Flat

Whether you're drinking a bottle of beer at an outdoor barbecue or an indoor card game, place a wooden matchstick across the mouth of the bottle to keep your suds from going flat.

The next time you host a party, you may want to provide matchsticks with the beer.

Prevent Spills When Serving Drinks

If you're taking several drinks from the kitchen out to the dinner table, deck chairs or backyard picnic table, carry them in a clean muffin tin. Most glasses (such as tumblers), coffee mugs and beer bottles will fit in the muffin holders of an average-sized muffin tin.

Vodka on Ice

For those of you who have a dramatic flair, this is a creative and exciting way to serve chilled vodka...in an ice bucket made of ice. *Here's what to do...*

You will need either a metal champagne bucket, a large metal can or a plastic bucket —it should be large enough to hold the vodka bottle with some space on all sides.

Fill the bucket with water. Place a vodka bottle in the middle, and add pretty, freezable things—such as lemon, lime and orange slices...flowers and leaves...berries and grapes—to float around the sides of the bucket. This will become a decorative mold.

Place the bucket in the freezer and let it stay overnight. The next day, make sure that it's frozen solid when you take it out. Unless your freezer is exceptionally cold—we're talking cryogenics-laboratory cold—the vodka in the bottle will not freeze.

When you're ready to serve, get the decorative mold out of the container by carefully holding the bucket sideways under warm running water—but don't let the water go over the top of the bucket!

Once the mold is released from its container, put it on a rimmed plate with an absorbent towel underneath to catch the water as the ice melts. The mold is now your ice bucket!

Keep Drinks Cool at an Outdoor Party

If you're hosting a casual backyard party, a great way to keep soda, beer and bottled water cold and available to your guests is to fill a small kiddie pool with lots of ice. Then just add the drinks.

PICNICS

It's glorious to eat outside on a lovely day and get in touch with nature. *To enjoy your outing even more, here are a few ideas to perk up a picnic and have it be less messy…*

◆ When you're going on a picnic, take along a paper or cloth table covering. Picnic tables can be very unsanitary. Also bring a container of premoistened baby wipes. They make great napkins for messy kids of all ages.

◆ Bring a big plastic garbage bag with you, and use it for trash so that you leave the picnic area as clean as when you arrived.

◆ Most picnics consist of free-for-all food laid out on a blanket or table. Consider, instead, preparing individual lunches for each person at the picnic.

　　If the picnic-goers are your immediate family, then you will know exactly what each person would like in his/her picnic lunch box. This separate-lunch system frees everyone up to eat when they want to—not just because the food is out there, sweltering in the sun.

◆ If you are going to picnic in an area where there are wildflowers growing, bring along an empty coffee can. Once you get to the picnic grounds, pick some flowers, put them in the coffee can and fill the can with water…or sand…or soil…or pebbles. Then put the floral arrangement on your picnic table or blanket for all to enjoy nature's beauty.

THEME GATHERINGS

You don't have to wait until it's someone's birthday or a holiday to throw a party. Select a theme, think it through, make your plans and let the festivities begin! *Here are a few suggestions to help your creative juices begin to flow…*

◆ Have a slumber party that's just for grown-ups. Why should kids have the only fun? Eat pizza, bake cookies and stay up late watching scary movies.

◆ Invite friends over for a Clothing-Swap Party. Everyone has clothes that he/she is willing to trade for something that fits better or is more comfortable or more flattering. This is an especially good idea for women whose sizes tend to change more frequently.

◆ Have a Bring-and-Bid Party. Guests bring items that you auction off. It can be a fundraiser for charity or just for fun.

◆ Start your own Book Club or DVD Club. There are many Web sites available to help guide you. (To get started, try *www.ehow.com/how_6181_start-book-club.html*.)

◆ Anyone can celebrate New Year's Eve, Easter or Labor Day. Be innovative and find an underplayed or obscure holiday and build a theme party around it. The fourth Sunday in July is Parents Day. June 5th is World Environment Day. August 26th is Women's Equality Day. Getting inspired? September 13th is Defy Superstition Day.

　　One of the most unusual, educational and fun parties we ever attended was on November 2nd—it was a birthday celebration in honor of the 11th president of the United States, James K. Polk.

GUEST TREATMENT

It's tricky when guests visit—you want to make them feel at home, but you don't want them to stay forever. *Here are some ideas that may make their visit a happy—but not overly long—stay...*

Putting a Guest at Ease

According to the theory of *neuro-linguistic programming* (NLP), you will make a person feel accepted and interesting if you mimic (pattern) his/her body language while talking to him.

For example, if your guest sits with his legs crossed at the ankles, cross yours at the ankles. If he sips his drink with his pinky extended, you do the same thing.

Just do it in moderation, and be sure not to pattern that person's nervous twitch—or you might wind up with a punch in the nose.

Getting Rid of Dinner Guests

When your guests have outstayed their welcome around your dinner table, you can get rid of them without being rude. Simply place your hands—fingers together, palms down—on the table in front of you, as though you were about to stand up. Your guests may subconsciously pick up on that cue and assume that the party's over. This subliminal signal should have them on their feet, grabbing their coats and thanking you for a wonderful evening.

If the hand signal doesn't work, then start to yawn. Within seconds, everyone else will start yawning and realize that the party's over.

Welcome a Sleepover Guest

A lovely way to welcome an overnight guest is to leave a goody bag on the bed or dresser. Fill the bag with gender-appropriate sleepover items, such as 1 or 2 magazines (in keeping with your guest's interests), a sweet treat, some night cream, a scented candle and holder, a sleep mask, a packaged toothbrush and a little card wishing your guest "pleasant dreams."

TAKING PICTURES

Writer Eudora Welty said, "A good snapshot stops a moment from running away." Make your photographs the most treasured memories they can possibly be. *These hints may help...*

Set Up Your Shot

The day before you plan to use the camera, check the batteries. If the camera is not digital, be sure you have film. Clean the lens with a lint-free cloth. You may also want to snap a few pictures, just to test that the camera is in good working order.

If your batteries die unexpectedly, rub both ends with a clean pencil eraser—you may be able to get a few more shots.

Making Memories

If you're hosting a party, buy a few disposable cameras for your guests to use during the festivities.

Positioning the Camera

Hold the camera at the subject's eye level, even when the photos are candid and the subject is not staring into the camera lens. That eye-level angle will create a personal and inviting feeling that pulls the viewer into the picture.

Be prepared to stoop all the way down when photographing young children.

Souvenir Photos

◆ The next time you're hosting a party, use your digital camera to take a picture of every guest at your gathering. If you have a printer at home, you can give each guest a souvenir print just before he/she leaves.

◆ If the occasion calls for you to send a thank-you note, paste a fun photo on the front of a blank card and write your note inside.

◆ Take photos of your friends at a party or social gathering. The next time you invite them over for a dinner party, put their photos in little frames and use them as place cards.

HOLIDAYS

We're probably all in agreement that the holidays have gotten to be way too commercial. But when you think about it, putting aside the in-your-face marketing aspects, the holidays are a wonderful time to celebrate being with the people you hold dear.

It's a time to talk about the good old days… to eat more than you should…to exchange gifts …to play catch-up…and to promise that you'll get together more often. Holidays are a time for making happy memories.

So here are some hints to enhance a handful of national holidays, in the hope of helping you create those happy memories while you celebrate a specific time of year.

New Year's

Although the exact date may vary depending on where it's celebrated, New Year's is the most universally observed holiday in the world. It's filled with traditions, rituals and resolutions that may be in 1 year and out the next. But many believe that there is *magic* in the air on New Year's. It's a time to be with family and friends, and a time for letting go of the old and embracing the new.

For your next New Year's celebration, add some foreign flavor to the festivities by incorporating customs from other countries. *Here are some from which to choose…*

Good Luck from Around the World

According to folklore from across the globe, there are certain food and home traditions that are supposed to bring good fortune into your life for the next 365 days. These traditions come with no guarantees, just with every good wish for a most wonderful New Year.

◆ **China**—The color red is the Chinese symbol of good luck and happiness. Paint your front door with a new coat of red paint or hang a red banner.

Although Chinese families have a feast for the New Year, food is prepared on the last day of the old year. On New Year's Day, all knives are put away for 24 hours to prevent anyone from cutting himself/herself, which is believed to cut the family's good luck for the New Year.

◆ **England/Wales**—When the clock starts to strike midnight, open the back door of your house and then close it. You will be releasing the old year, along with all of its misfortune. Then, on the 12th chime of the clock, open the front door, which welcomes in the New Year with all of its good luck.

◆ **France**—Good health and good fortune will come to those who eat a stack of pancakes on New Year's Day.

- **Italy/Sicily**—Good luck will come to those who eat lasagna on New Year's Day, but Sicilians warn you to stay away from macaroni or any other type of noodle on the first day of the year.

- **Japan**—This good luck tradition comes from the Japanese practice of *feng shui,* which is the positioning of objects based on the patterns of *yin* and *yang*...this is believed to create a flow of positive and negative effects.

  Buy a yard of tiny, white tree lights to symbolize stars. Bunch the string of lights loosely in a clear glass vase. Place the vase in the southwest part of your living room.

  When it is dark outside, just before 12 midnight on New Year's Eve, light the lights. This will ensure that you invite lucky stars into your life and have a fresh start for the new year.

- **Norway**—Prepare rice pudding and hide 1 whole almond in the bowl. Dish out the pudding to family and friends on New Year's Day. The person who gets the almond is assured of major wealth.

- **Peru**—Eat 12 grapes to mark the New Year. A 13th grape must be eaten to assure good luck.

- **Puerto Rico**—At 12 midnight, children throw pails of water out of a window in the belief that doing so rids the home of evil spirits.

- **Spain**—At 12 midnight, eat 1 grape with each toll of the clock, which will assure that you have good luck each month of the year.

  If you don't have a clock that chimes, get out your grapes and follow the countdown on television.

- **Switzerland**—On New Year's Day, let a drop of cream land on the floor to make sure you have a rich New Year.

- **United States** (Southern states)—Eating a dish of hamhocks and black-eyed peas on New Year's Day is thought to bring luck and prosperity. Some people add a dime to the peas for an extra bit of luck (just try not to eat the dime).

  Salad greens—such as kale, collard greens, spinach and mustard greens—symbolize folding money, and they are often eaten along with the black-eyed peas.

St. Valentine's Day

According to the Society of American Florists, the Chocolate Manufacturers Association and the National Confectioners Association, US consumers purchase approximately 180 million roses and more than 36 million heart-shaped boxes of chocolate for Valentine's Day each year.

Sure, it's easy to go out and splurge on something nice that your loved one(s) wouldn't buy for themselves. But we think it's a better idea to top off your store-bought gift (or replace it) with a *priceless* loving-hands-at-home gift. *Here are a few ideas...*

The Gift That Keeps Giving

Prepare a booklet of coupons for your mate and/or someone you love. Decide on the number of coupons—1 for each year you've been together, 1 for each month of the year, 1 for each day of the week—and come up with doable things that will make the person happy.

The coupons could range from personal pleasures to practical chores—from a 30-minute back massage to washing the car. This gift's true test—wouldn't *you* like to get a booklet of coupons from someone special?

Love, Sweet Love

Chocolate contains *phenylethylamine* (PEA), which some scientists believe releases the same chemicals in the brain that induce the euphoria we feel when we are in love.

So bring on the chocolate! Bake some fudgy chocolate brownies, a chocolate cake or prepare chocolate pudding—whatever it is will be extra-sweet because you made it.

Easter

'Twas Easter Sunday.
The full blossomed trees
Filled all the air with fragrance and with joy.
Henry Wadsworth Longfellow used those words to express his feelings during this spring-time holiday. We hope your Easter is filled with joy. *As for the air being filled with fragrance, consider the following suggestions so you can help make it happen…*

Easter Flowers

Flowers always make a home more festive and usually more fragrant. For a colorful, Eastery way to display the daffodils, irises, tulips, lilacs and hyacinths in bloom during this season, put the flowers in an appropriate-sized vase and fill it with water. Then put that vase in a larger, clear-glass vase. Fill the space between the 2 vases with jelly beans. Colorful and Eastery, don't you think?

 Sweet Decorating Idea

If you are using artificial flowers, use only 1 clear-glass vase for the flowers—and use the jelly beans in place of water.

Easter Centerpiece

If you want a beautiful, sugar-coated fruit-and-flower centerpiece, gather the following ingredients, and then set aside some time to be your most creative self.

    Spring flowers
    About 6 pounds of fresh fruit (coordinate
        the selection of fruit with the color of
        the flowers)
    1 cup of apple jelly
    1 cup of water
    Superfine sugar
    Pastry brush
    Wax paper
    Flat basket, platter or tray
    Big doilies (optional)

1. Cover your work surface with waxed paper. Wash and dry the fruit and put it on the waxed paper.

2. Mix 1 cup of apple jelly with 1 cup of water until the jelly liquefies. You may have to zap it in the microwave for 20 to 30 seconds to get the apple jelly to dissolve completely.

(If you do heat it, let the liquid cool before continuing.)

3. Using the pastry brush, give the fruit a once-over with the apple jelly mixture.

4. Pour the superfine sugar on a small plate and roll the moist fruit around in it. If you don't want the fruit covered with the sugar, you can just sprinkle the sugar on the fruit instead of rolling it. (But we think *more* sugar looks better.)

5. Let the sugared fruit dry thoroughly. If possible, let it stand overnight, uncovered, on the counter.

To make your seasonal centerpiece, use a decorative basket, platter or tray, and build a beautiful mound of sugared fruit. Intersperse the flowers.

Optional: Line the basket, platter or tray with doilies.

 NOTE: A centerpiece like this can be created anytime throughout the year—for every occasion. Just use the loveliest seasonal fruit and flowers you can find.

Easter Place Cards

◆ Put chocolate Easter bunnies at each place setting. Attach a name tag on each bunny with a ribbon that matches your tablecloth.

◆ Use hard-boiled eggs as place cards. Cut out strips of construction paper or cardboard (about 1" x 5"), and write a different guest's name on each strip. Form a circle, overlapping 1 end of the strip on top of the other, and glue or tape it to stay that way. Use this as an egg stand and place 1 at each table setting.

Egg-stra Special Place Cards

◆ Write your guests' names on the eggs with crayon, then dye them with food coloring or egg dye.

◆ If you have extra time and the talent, you can also decorate the eggs to resemble each guest.

Independence Day (4th of July)

Independence Day, the original American holiday, was first celebrated on July 4, 1777. And we Americans have been celebrating our country's birthday ever since with parades, parties, picnics and pride.

For many, displaying the American flag is a time-honored tradition. If you want to get in on the action, the National Flag Foundation (*www.americanflags.org*), the foremost authority on US flag etiquette, offers this advice on how to do it right. *For example...*

◆ **Lapel pin**—Position the flag pin on the left side, over your heart.

◆ **Indoor flag**—If you hang the flag on a wall, do not tack down the bottom edge. A flag should hang as freely as possible.

◆ **Outdoor flag**—When it's raining, cotton or wool flags should not be left outside. Water weighs them down, preventing them from flying properly. If a flag cannot be illuminated at night with a spotlight, porch light or streetlamp, take it down at sunset.

◆ **On a car**—The flag should be firmly attached to the right bumper (this means your right side when you are behind the wheel).

All flags should be displayed upright, with the stars on the upper left side. When flags become tattered or frayed, it's respectful to remove and replace them immediately.

Decorations

Red, white and blue are the patriotic colors of the day. Decorate with streamers, banners and balloons, tablecloths, napkins and place settings, all in those colors.

◆ Get a blue vase and fill it with red flowers (roses, zinnias, scarlet salvia or dahlias) and white flowers (phlox, Queen Anne's lace, cosmos or chrysanthemums).

◆ When the sun goes down, add some atmosphere to an outdoor gathering by lighting many festive red, white and blue votive candles and placing them on tables and surrounding surfaces.

◆ Create a patriotic centerpiece. Fill a tray with things that represent to you the greatness of this country. A few things that come to mind are an apple pie, a bottle of Coca-Cola, a baseball and maybe even a DVD of "Yankee Doodle Dandy."

Once the goodies are on the tray, trim it with an American flag and red, white and blue streamers.

Food for the 4th

◆ Serve a patriotic appetizer—cherry tomatoes, a creamy white cheese and blue corn chips.

◆ Prepare red, white and blue desserts using strawberries, blueberries, vanilla ice cream and/or whipped cream in between.

◆ Hollow out half of a watermelon, leaving 1" or 2" of the red fruit. Then add scoops of vanilla ice cream and sprinkle with blueberries.

◆ Whip up white frosting and spread it on brownies or cupcakes, then top it off with red, white and blue sprinkles.

Halloween

According to the National Retail Federation (*www.nrf.com*), sales of Halloween cards, decorations, costumes and candy will be more than $4 billion this year (nearly $60 per person). It's everyone's favorite holiday!

The majority of the money is for candy, but it's not just for kids. The National Confectioners Association (*www.ecandy.com*) claims that 90% of parents admit that they sneak goodies from their children's Halloween trick-or-treat bags.

Here are some tricks to help you make this Halloween a treat…

Perfect Pumpkin Presentation

◆ Use an ice cream scoop to clean out the pumpkin's pulp. It's a fast and easy way to do it.

Then use a drywall knife (available at home improvement stores) to carve your pumpkin—it provides better control than a kitchen knife.

◆ Nobody wants a moldy jack-o'-lantern. In a spray bottle, combine 2 parts lemon juice to 1 part water, and spritz the carved pumpkin inside and outside to prevent mold.

◆ If you're putting a candle in a scooped-out pumpkin, first sprinkle in a little cinnamon and nutmeg, so that when the candle burns, the air will smell as though you're baking a scrumptious pumpkin pie.

◆ Draw or paint a face on your pumpkin instead of carving it. Then, after Halloween, you can cut it up and use the pumpkin meat for baking pies or bread.

Eerie Lights

◆ Replace some of your regular lightbulbs with black-light bulbs (available at hardware stores). White and light-colored objects will seem to have a spooky glow.

◆ To create a creepy Halloween atmosphere, replace a few of your regular lightbulbs with green bulbs.

Halloween Costumes

With just a little imagination and some stuff around the house, you (or your child) will be all dressed and ready for the holiday. You may want to use 1 of these suggestions…or perhaps they'll inspire you to come up with something even more original.

◆ **Static Cling**—Wear a gray sweat suit and use doubled-sided tape or safety pins to attach the things that usually cling when taking clothes out of the dryer—such as socks, a fabric-softener sheet, a washcloth, underwear, etc. Brush your hair so that it's a static mess, and spray it to stay that way.

◆ **Castaway**—Shred the bottoms of an old pair of khaki pants or shorts. Wear them with a seen-better-days T-shirt. If you're a man, don't shave for a few days…if you're a woman, fix your hair as though you haven't put a comb through it for weeks. Man or woman, carry a volleyball named Wilson.

◆ **Woodstock Survivor**—Wear a dirty, old tie-dyed T-shirt, your torn jeans, old sneakers, a bandanna around your head, several strands of love beads and wire sunglasses. Groovy, man!

◆ **Junk Drawer**—Wear a black sweat suit or a black leotard and tights, and pin on the stuff found in a junk drawer—odd pieces of string, a used-up tape dispenser, coin wrappers, buttons, etc.

◆ **Movie Theater Floor**—Wear a black sweat suit or black leotards and tights. With double-sided tape or safety pins, attach empty candy wrappers, chewed gum, popcorn pieces, empty soda cups, ticket stubs, straws, etc. And wear a popcorn bucket as a hat.

Halloween Party Treats

◆ Serve apple cider in a punch bowl along with floating "hands" and "eyeballs." To make the hands, fill rubber or latex gloves with water, close them tightly at the top with twist ties or rubber bands and put them in the freezer the day before Halloween. When the hands are frozen solid and you're ready to put them in the punch bowl, carefully peel off the gloves.

The eyeballs can be made from peeled red seedless grapes.

◆ For more gore, prepare popcorn and bloody it up—mix red food coloring into melted butter, and drizzle it over the popcorn.

◆ Who wouldn't want a cup of worms in soil? It's easy to prepare for a Halloween party, and you don't have to dig 'em up from your garden. *Here's what to do…*

Make chocolate pudding and refrigerate it for a few hours. Spoon out individual portions into clear plastic cups. Don't smooth it out—just sprinkle some cocoa powder or crushed chocolate cookies on top so that it really looks like soil. Then place a few gummy worms in each cup.

Put the cups in the refrigerator until it's party time.

Thanksgiving Day

The first Thanksgiving was celebrated in 1621 to commemorate the harvest that was reaped after a harsh winter. In 1789, US President George Washington declared Thanksgiving a holiday. In 1863, President Abraham Lincoln was looking for ways to unite the country during the divisive Civil War, so he declared the last Thursday in November as a day of national thanksgiving. Now it's traditionally observed on the 4th Thursday in November.

According to humorist Erma Bombeck, "What we're really talking about is a wonderful day set aside on the fourth Thursday of November when no one diets. I mean, why else would they call it *Thanksgiving*?"

Here are some tips to help make this diet-free day something extra-special…and another reason to give thanks.

Centerpiece de Résistance

Also called a "horn of plenty," a *cornucopia* is traditionally a goat's horn that is overflowing with an abundance of fruit, vegetables and flowers. This signifies the wealth of the fall harvest at Thanksgiving time.

Enjoy creating a magnificent and meaningful cornucopia basket centerpiece, overflowing with a selection of the season's harvest—such as apples, dried ears of corn, tomatoes, carrots, peppers, pumpkins, artichokes, pomegranates, gourds, mixed nuts, cranberries, leaves, pine cones and flowers. You can buy cornucopias at craft stores, or wherever big selections of baskets are sold.

You can also make and bake your own edible cornucopia (*see* below). But before you start gathering the necessary ingredients, take into consideration the size of your table, the size of the cornucopia (check the measurements)

and the available space in your freezer...especially if you plan to make this more than a few days in advance.

If we haven't scared you away by now, then forge bravely ahead. Enjoy the process—and then the praise!—as the finished product enhances your holiday table.

To fill the cornucopia, place it on a large tray, platter or flat basket. That allows you to move it easily in case you need to make room on the table for food that's being served. You can decorate the tray or basket with artificial leaves.

Cornucopia Centerpiece

3 11-ounce containers of soft breadstick
   dough
1 egg, beaten with 1 tablespoon of water
pastry brush
heavy-duty aluminum foil
standard aluminum foil
wire-mesh cornucopia (optional, available
   at crafts stores and some florists)

1. Preheat your oven to 350°F. Lightly spray a cookie sheet with nonstick cooking spray.

2. If you have a wire-mesh cornucopia, cover it with heavy-duty aluminum foil, skip the next step and go directly to step 3.

If you don't have a wire cornucopia, tear off a 30" x 18" sheet of heavy-duty foil. Fold it in half so that it's 15" x 18". Roll it diagonally to form a hollow cone about 18" long, with a diameter of 5" at its widest (the cornucopia's opening). Fasten the end with clear tape. Stuff the cone with crumpled regular foil until the form is solid. Bend the tail of the cone up and then down at the very end.

3. Spray the outside of the cone with the nonstick cooking spray and place it on the cookie sheet.

4. On a work surface, open and unroll the first container of breadstick dough. Separate

the breadsticks. Begin the wrapping process with 1 breadstick around the tip of the cone.

5. The beaten egg with the tablespoon of water is the glaze that acts as glue. Brush the end of the second breadstick with glaze and attach it by pressing it to the end of the first breadstick.

Continue spiral-wrapping the cone with the breadsticks from all 3 containers, slightly overlapping the dough. Stop when there are 6 breadsticks left.

6. Pinch 3 breadsticks together at 1 end and then braid them. Then pinch the other 3 breadsticks together at 1 end and braid them.

7. Brush the glaze around the opening of the cornucopia and gently press on the braid. Brush the entire cornucopia with the glaze.

Optional: Sprinkle on sesame seeds.

8. Bake for 45 minutes or until the bread is a rich brown. (If you notice that a part of it is darkening too much, carefully cover that part with a piece of foil.)

When it's done and you take it out of the oven, leave it on the cookie sheet. Put the cookie sheet on a wire rack to help it cool. When the cornucopia is completely cool to the touch, gently remove the foil.

Consider using straw, excelsior or raffia—artsy stuffing that is available at crafts stores and florists—as filler for the cornucopia. They will support the fruits and vegetables you put inside (also, you won't have to use as much produce if you have filler). Keep in mind that waxy-skinned fruits and vegetables (eggplant, cucumbers, apples, pomegranates, turnips and bell peppers) last longest without refrigeration.

This cornucopia is edible, but chances are, your harvest arrangement is going to be so beautiful that nobody would dare take a bite out of your horn of plenty. In fact, you may want to preserve it and use it again next Thanksgiving, or throughout the year. In that case, spray it with shellac or clear enamel, or a spray acrylic lacquer (available at art-supply, hardware and paint stores).

If you choose not to preserve the cornucopia with shellac, you can bake and freeze it up to a month before the big day. Just make sure that the baked cornucopia is completely cool, leave the foil inside it and then wrap the outside airtight with foil. Now it's ready for the freezer.

 NOTE: If you haven't given the cornucopia enough time to fully defrost, you can still decorate the table with it...even if it's partially frozen.

Thanksgiving Place Cards

◆ Use the fall harvest or foliage to hold place cards—for example, cut a slit on top of an apple or a miniature pumpkin, and stand a name card in the slit...write each guest's name on a leaf using a paint pen...wedge a place card into a pinecone or hot-glue it on.

◆ Here's a more schmaltzy way of saying, "sit here"—get a few small paper bags, and use a magic marker to write something on the bag that shows your appreciation of the guest.

Include his/her name so that the bag also serves as a place card.

For example, you could write—"I'm thankful for you, (guest's name)"...or, "You're a blessing, (guest's name)"...or, "You grace my table, (guest's name)." When you're done with the writing, add a few pieces of candy to the bag, tie it up with some colorful ribbon and place it on your table.

Thanksgiving During-Dinner Amusement

You and your guests can talk about your gratitude in a fun way around the table. Have the person whose name is first alphabetically begin telling something that he/she is thankful for, starting with the letter "A." The next person at the table continues by telling what he/she is thankful for, starting with the letter "B." And so on around the table and through the alphabet.

Keep it going through the alphabet—twice or more if your guests are enjoying it. When you do stop, tell everyone that this will give them some idea of the countless blessings in our lives for which we should all be thankful.

Thanksgiving End-of-Dinner Game

Here is a fun memory game to play around the table. The mental exercise may help keep people awake at the end of a high-carbohydrate, sleep-inducing meal.

Have the first player start by saying, "At the first Thanksgiving dinner, the Pilgrims ate turkey." Go around the table—the next player must repeat the sentence and add another dish. For example, the second player might say, "At the first Thanksgiving dinner, the Pilgrims ate turkey and cranberry sauce." The game continues with each player repeating the Pilgrims' menu and adding a new item to it.

When a player makes a mistake, he/she is eliminated. The game continues until there is only 1 player left. Give the winner a chocolate turkey…and a nap.

Thanksgiving After-Dinner Turkey Trot (for children)

◆ Play some lively music, get out the camera and ask the children to move like different types of turkey—for example, happy turkey, scared turkey, adorable turkey, goofy turkey, sad turkey, big turkey, jerky turkey, tough turkey, baby turkey, tired turkey, etc.

◆ Hold an "Act Like a Turkey" contest. Each participant has to go through the motions and sounds of a turkey. Be prepared with prizes for all, for fun distinctions including "loudest turkey," "cutest turkey," "most authentic turkey," "turkey most likely to be kept as a pet," "most outrageous turkey," and any other turkey title that comes to mind.

Chanukah

No matter how you spell it—Chanuka, Channukah, Hanukah, Hannukah, Hanika, Kaneka or Khanukkah—this happy Jewish holiday is the "Festival of Lights." It is celebrated for 8 days beginning at sundown on the 25th day of Kislev, a month in the Hebrew calendar. Chanukah

---

■ Recipe ■

The most traditional oil-laden Chanukah dish is potato latkes (*latkes* is the Yiddish word for *pancakes*). Our mother's latkes were the greatest. Mom never measured the ingredients she used—it was as though she was divinely guided. Through trial and error, we did our best to re-create our mother's recipe.

Lilly's Luscious Latkes

> *Yield:* About 12 latkes
>
> 2 pounds (about 6 medium-sized) potatoes
> 1 medium onion
> 1 large egg, beaten
> salt and pepper to taste
> vegetable oil for frying

1. Peel each potato and then put it in a bowl of cold water.

2. Coarsely grate the potatoes and onion using a grater or a food processor.

3. Place the grated potatoes and onion in a fine-mesh strainer or clean dish towel and squeeze out all of the water over a bowl that is big enough for the whole latke mixture. The potato starch will settle on the bottom of the bowl. Carefully pour out the water, leaving the starch, and then mix in the grated potatoes as well as the onion and the egg. Add salt and pepper to taste.

4. Coat a griddle or nonstick pan with a thin layer of vegetable oil and warm it over medium heat.

5. Flatten about 2 tablespoons of the potato mixture in the palm of your hand and then place it on the griddle. Use a spatula to flatten it even more. Let it fry for a few minutes until it's golden. Flip the pancake over and brown the other side.

6. Remove and let each latke drain on paper towels, or use a cut-open brown paper bag (which is what our mom used).

Serve as soon as possible with sour cream or apple sauce. Latkes are great as an appetizer, side dish, dessert or snack.

usually falls sometime during November or December.

Chanukah is meant to be an uplifting holiday of renewed dedication and faith. Although it commemorates a victory and celebrates a miracle, the loud-and-clear message of Chanukah is "never lose hope."

Traditional Food

The ancient miracle of Chanukah occurred in 165 BCE. It had to do with a little bit of oil—there was not enough to burn for more than 1 day, yet it *miraculously* burned for 8 days and nights. So an important part of the Chanukah celebration is eating foods cooked in oil.

Latke Cooking Hints

◆ Several latke mavens we know recommend using Yukon gold potatoes for a more buttery batch. But ordinary baking potatoes are fine—russets, Idaho or Oregon. However, NEVER use red-skinned bliss potatoes. They will make the latkes gummy.

◆ Press the water out of the grated potatoes and onion before you mix in other ingredients—doing so makes for a firmer, crispier latke.

◆ Put the potato starch back into the mixture to add real potato flavor.

◆ For frying, use canola, peanut or another vegetable oil. These lighter-tasting oils will ensure that the full flavor of the latkes won't be overpowered by the taste of oil.

◆ You can freeze the latkes, then crisp them in a preheated 350°F oven for about 10 minutes.

Chanukah Party Ideas

Chanukah is a great time to spend with people who *light up your life*. Hey, that's an appropriate phrase to use when sending out e-mail (or snail-mail) Chanukah party invitations.

In addition to lighting Chanukah candles and serving food (and plenty of it), you may want to plan some entertainment before and after the meal, or anytime during the festivities. *Here are a few suggestions…*

◆ In some families, gift giving is a part of the Chanukah holiday. If it is in yours, have a grab bag. Ask your guests to bring 2 gifts—1 for a child (if children are going to be at your gathering) and 1 for an adult. You may want to set limits on price. Or tell your guests that the gifts must be homemade…or have a Jewish theme…or they must be made of paper. Be sure to have a big basket or box in which to collect the wrapped gifts. You also may want to prepare some extra gifts in case some people didn't bring any.

Game Time with Gelt

After dinner, ask everyone to open his/her sack of gelt, and take out the chocolate coins. Then challenge all of your guests to a game of "Go Know!"

You go first. Start the game by saying "I have never _____" (fill in the blank). *Some examples…*

◆ I have never gone horseback riding.

◆ I have never had a pedicure.

◆ I have never talked into a microphone.

◆ I have never had a passport.

Anyone who *has* done what you have *never* done has to give you a gelt coin. After everyone has had a turn saying "I have never ____," the person with the most coins wins. Or, you can keep going, eliminating players as they run out of gelt coins. The player who ends up with all the coins wins.

When you feel the time is right, pass around the container with the gifts and give everyone a chance to take something.

◆ If you and your guests are musically inclined, make copies of various song sheets and have a sing-along.

◆ Decorate the dinner table with Chanukah *gelt* (money)—the chocolate-wrapped-in-gold-foil candy that comes in gold net sacks (available at some supermarkets, card, candy and kosher stores). Attach a name tag on each bag, and use them as place cards on your table.

Christmas

Some popular holiday traditions—such as the yule log, carolers singing from house to house, parades, the giving of gifts, church processions and holiday feasts—can trace their origins back thousands of years to Mesopotamia, an ancient region of southwest Asia. Over the years, those traditions have evolved into the holiday we know as Christmas.

In the words of clergyman and positive thinker Norman Vincent Peale—"Christmas waves a magic wand over this world, and behold, everything is softer and more beautiful."

Here, to help you perform your own kind of magic, are some tips to brighten up this special holiday season.

Christmas Tree Care

Christmas trees are grown in all 50 states, and an average-sized tree (7 to 8 feet tall) takes 7 to 10 years to mature. More than 100,000 people are employed in the Christmas-tree industry, making it possible for you to have a tree for the holiday.

Your job is to select a wonderful tree, take care of it and enjoy it.

Fireproofing Your Tree

◆ The Department of Risk Management and Safety at the University of Arizona (*http://risk.arizona.edu/healthandsafety/holidaydecorations.shtml*) strongly recommends that cut Christmas trees should be treated with a flame-retardant solution (the trees can be either sprayed or dipped).

The recipe is 9 ounces of borax powder, 4 ounces of boric acid, 1 gallon of water and ½ teaspoon of low-sudsing laundry detergent.

 CAUTION: Keep borax powder and boric acid away from children and pets. Both are harmful when ingested.

◆ The most important fire-retardant is water. Give your tree plenty of water daily. The first time you water it, make it hot water—about 80°F. The warm temperature helps open up the tree's circulatory system, enabling it to draw up the water more easily. After that, use lukewarm water.

The average tree will consume up to 1 gallon of water per day.

Quick Freshness Test

If you're buying a balsam fir, gently bend a needle between your thumb and forefinger. If the tree is fresh, the needle will break.

If you're buying a pine tree, the needle should not break if the tree is fresh.

For any species, if the tree is fresh, the needles will stay on the branch and not fall off if you touch them.

Treats for the Tree

◆ The first time you water your tree, use hot water—about 80°F. After you're done watering, add 2 ounces of antibacterial mouthwash to the water to prevent the growth of any unwanted bacteria.

◆ Give the tree a pick-me-up by adding 1 ounce of maple syrup to the water. The syrup's sugar feeds the tree. It seems to make the pine needles a more vibrant green, and they may last longer, too.

Tree Decorations

Whether you use all, some or none of the same ornaments each year on your tree, the following tips and suggestions may inspire you...

◆ Use a used fabric-softener sheet to wipe glass Christmas ornaments. They will get clean and also repel dust while on the tree.

◆ If you want to decorate your tree with strings of popcorn, air-pop the corn a few days before the stringing. Stale popcorn is a lot easier to work with than fresh popcorn—it's tougher and holds together better. Besides, fresh popcorn is too tempting to eat.

Christmas "Family" Tree

Decorate a tabletop Christmas tree with photo ornaments. Make small color copies of your favorite family photos. Mat them with red and green construction paper. You may want to put photos in the center of stars or other shapes. Punch a hole in each mat and thread a red, green or gold ribbon through it and attach each one to the tree...the "family" tree.

Write Down a Christmas Tradition

Write out note cards that say wonderful things. Place them in small red envelopes (in some Asian countries, red is believed to be the color of good fortune and happiness). Then, attach them around the Christmas tree with paper clips, small clothespins or clamps.

Tell every guest that comes into your home to select a red envelope. The uplifting message will make the person feel hopeful, happy and glad he/she stopped by.

Here are some examples of what the cards could say...

◆ All of your dreams will come true in the New Year.

◆ Your dazzling personality makes the sun shine brighter.

◆ Many memorable adventures are in store for you.

◆ Your creative ideas will soon pay off.

◆ Expect the best because you are the best.

◆ Your kindness will soon be rewarded.

House Decorations

At the risk of sounding like a Christmas card— let the spirit of the holiday season bring you joy outside and inside your home. Start by surrounding yourself with festive decorations. *Here are some suggestions...*

◆ As soon as you hang your holiday wreath outdoors, spray the ribbons and bows with super-hold hairspray. It will help keep the wreath clean and crisp. Just be sure to hang the wreath in a place where it cannot be rained on, OK?

◆ This is a great way to decorate windows— first, mix equal amounts of Epsom salt (available at drugstores) with stale beer. A little

Proof That Santa Claus Was Here!

This idea requires stencils of a pair of men's boots and flour in a sifter. Are you getting the picture? Place each boot on a big enough piece of cardboard—you can use the thin cardboard that comes from the cleaners in a man's shirt, or use a manila file folder. Then outline a right boot and a left boot, and cut out the insides of the outlines. You will now have cardboard stencils of a pair of boots.

Once the wee ones have visions of sugar-plums dancing in their heads, figure out the path Santa would take from his entrance into the house (a fireplace is, of course, ideal) to the Christmas tree. Place both stencils on the floor, creating Santa's first 2 footsteps inside your home, and sift the flour over each (it should look like snow from his boots).

Gently and slowly lift each stencil, and dump the excess flour into a paper bag. Now you're ready to create Santa's next 2 footsteps. Keep repeating the footstep process all the way to the tree, then back again to the fireplace (or other point of entry/exit).

The flour will vacuum up in seconds the next morning. If you have a rug or carpeting, you may want to use baking soda instead of flour. The baking soda will actually help clean the rug!

> **NOTE:** This suggestion may not be a practical Christmas surprise if you have pets roaming around the house.

goes a long way, so start with ¼ cup of each. Then use a clean sponge to apply the mixture to a small area of the window you want to decorate.

As you work with it, you'll get a feel for the frost-and-snow effects you can create.

Give the small section a chance to dry. Then you'll be able to complete the job…knowing what to expect, what you want and how to achieve it.

When the holiday season is over, wipe off the faux frost with warm, soapy water. A vacuum cleaner will be helpful to clean up the powdery residue.

◆ In the middle of your dining room table, make an arrangement of small, gift-wrapped packages nestled in holiday greenery—such as fir sprays or holly. Coordinate the colors of the wrapping paper and ribbon to match the tablecloth and napkins. The packages may or may not be real gifts for people seated at the table. If they are, you may want to hand them out after dessert.

The Best Christmas Gifts

Oren Arnold—novelist, journalist and humorist—provides this advice…"To your enemy, forgiveness. To an opponent, tolerance. To a friend, your heart. To a customer, service. To all, charity. To every child, a good example. To yourself, respect."

And, according to writer Burton Hillis—"The best of all gifts around any Christmas tree [is] the presence of a happy family all wrapped up in each other."

Kwanzaa

If you think that Kwanzaa is an ancient African celebration—think again. The holiday was first established in 1966 for the African-American community as a way to celebrate their heritage and to reinforce positive community values.

Kwanzaa is the Swahili word for "the first," referring to "the first fruits of the harvest." The holiday lasts from December 26th through January 1st.

Meaning of the Kwanzaa Candles

The 7 candles that are used in the holiday *kinara* represent the *Nguzo Saba*, which means "7 principles" in Swahili. These values are central to the celebration of Kwanzaa—they help to build and reinforce family, community and culture among African-Americans as well as Africans throughout the world.

1. *Umoja oja* (Unity)—fostering togetherness for the family and the community.

2. *Kujichagulia* (Self-Determination)—building our lives in our own images and interests.

3. *Ujima* (Collective Work and Responsibility)—being responsible for our failures as well as our victories and achievements.

4. *Ujamaa* (Cooperative Economics)—sharing wealth and resources and building financial security.

5. *Nia* (Purpose)—discovering each person's ability to put his/her skill or talent to use.

6. *Kuumba* (Creativity)—building and developing our creative potential in order to improve the world.

7. *Imani* (Faith)—believing in ourselves, developing the family and the community, and controlling our own destiny.

For more information on the traditions and celebration of this wonderful holiday, visit the official Kwanzaa Web site at *www. officialkwanzaawebsite.org/index.shtml.*

Traditions

This is a new and evolving holiday, which means it's an opportunity for you to create traditions. *Here are a few suggestions to start you thinking about how you can participate and celebrate...*

◆ Prepare a fun video with the people around you, and send copies to relatives and friends who can't be with all of you for the holiday.

■ Recipe ■

If you want to bring something special to your Kwanzaa Feast, consider tossing together this colorful dish we created...

Confetti Salad

> 2 15-ounce cans whole-kernel corn, drained
> 1 15-ounce can black beans, rinsed and drained
> 12 scallions, chopped
> 1 small red onion, chopped
> 1 green bell pepper, chopped
> 1 red bell pepper, chopped
> 1 avocado, peeled, pitted and cut in small chunks
> 1 4-ounce jar pimentos, chopped
> 12 black olives, pitted and chopped
> 4 medium tomatoes, seeded and chopped
> 1 cup fresh cilantro, chopped
> 3 cloves garlic, peeled and finely minced
> ½ teaspoon salt
> ¾ cup Italian salad dressing (or any other dressing you prefer)

1. In a big salad bowl, combine all of the ingredients except the Italian dressing.

2. Mix about ½ cup of the dressing into the salad, then taste the salad. Continue adding more dressing, a little at a time, until the salad tastes great. If you need more than ¾ cup, add more.

3. Chill until ready to serve.

◆ Make resolutions and set goals. Then during next year's Kwanzaa, take out the list and see how many resolutions you've kept and how many goals you've reached.

◆ Ask your holiday guests to bring some form of African culture—such as a book, a poster, a statue—and have "show and tell."

Decorations

Use an African motif to decorate your home for the holiday. The Kwanzaa colors are black, red and green. Trim your home with balloons, streamers and flowers in those colors, and include them in the traditional holiday candleholder (called a *kinara*) with 1 black, 3 red and 3 green candles (*see* page 104 for an explanation of the candles' meaning). Also, use African-design fabrics as a tablecloth and napkins.

The Kwanzaa Feast (Karamu)

The purpose of this special event, held on December 31st, is to bring the celebrants closer to their African roots. It's a time for culture, tradition, food and festivities. It is usually held at a church or community center. ■

■ Products ■

Vacuum Wine Saver

Save money and save wine with this fantastic product...it has a re-usable rubber stopper to reseal the bottle, ensuring that the wine stays fresh and flavorful. It works by slowing down the oxidation process—so you don't have to polish off the entire bottle in one evening. The bottle can be opened and resealed as many times as it takes to finish the wine. The Vacuum Wine Saver is made from stainless steel and is sold throughout the country.

Rapid Ice Cooler for Wine

Keep this ice jacket in the freezer until you are ready to chill a bottle of wine. Put the jacket over the bottle and the wine will go from room temperature to chill in just 5 minutes—and it will stay chilled for hours. The jackets are available in different sizes and designs. They are also unbreakable, reusable and don't take up much room in the freezer. (Separate chillers are also available for champagne, cans, beer and water.)

Wine Server Crystal

Lets you pour wine easily without spilling a drop. Not only does this special device prevent dripping, it also returns any excess wine back into the bottle. The high gloss transparent material gives the server a crystal appearance. Fits most wine bottles.

Source: Vacu Vin Inc., 415-382-1241, *www.vacu vin.com.*

Chocolove

Linking *chocolate* with its natural companion *love,* each Chocolove bar resembles a love letter, addressed and affixed with a stamp that declares its cocoa content. Waiting on the inside of the wrapper is a romantic love poem.

Chocolove was the first US company to specify its chocolate's cocoa content on the front of its bars (that was in 1995). Bars range from 77% cocoa content in the Extra-Strong Dark Chocolate bars to 33% in the Milk Chocolate bars. Premium Belgium chocolate is used, but Chocolove bars are made in the US—produced in small batches to ensure quality and freshness.

Chocolove is available nationwide at select specialty retailers, gourmet grocers and natural food stores as well as online.

Source: Chocolove, 888-CHOCOLOVE (246-2656), *www.chocolove.com.*

Judaica

Looking for a special gift for Chanukah, a wedding or other celebration? The Jewish Museum in New York City has 2 shops that offer a great variety of items in a wide price range that make perfect gifts for family, friends—and for yourself.

The Cooper Shop at The Jewish Museum

1109 Fifth Avenue at 92nd Street
New York, NY 10128
212-423-3211

Find Museum reproductions, ceremonial objects for every Jewish holiday, an extraordinary selection of menorahs for Chanukah, books, music, jewelry, stationery and a lot more.

Celebrations—The Jewish Museum Design Shop

1 East 92nd Street (next door to the Museum)
New York, NY 10128
212-423-3260

This store specializes in finely crafted ceremonial objects to commemorate the holidays and other joyous occasions. *http://shop.thejewish museum.org.*

CHAPTER 5

Our Favorite Folk Remedies

You may wonder—what's a health chapter doing in a book of household hints? Well, we believe that the most important part of any home is the people who live there. You can't take care of your house and physical surroundings if you haven't taken care of yourself—and the people you love—first.

We're providing a collection of practical, safe and effective health remedies that are easy and simple enough to use every day—and many of the necessary ingredients can be found in your kitchen. In this section, we've included old and new ways to help you feel better physically and emotionally, organized by condition in alphabetical order.

We've been collecting folk remedies for more than 2 decades. And where do we get them? From *folks*, of course! Can you trust that they're safe? All of the remedies we share with our readers have been reviewed (for safety) by a medical doctor. Do we know that these remedies work? Well, they worked for the people who shared them with us—so we're hoping they'll work for you, too.

We do, however, caution you to heed the CAUTION at right…really!

CAUTION: Before you use any of these remedies to treat yourself or somebody else, please check with your health care professional. This is *extremely important* if you have ANY existing health problems, including—but not limited to—cancer, liver or kidney disease, diabetes, high blood pressure, ulcers, bleeding disorders or a compromised immune system.

Even natural remedies can have side effects, so if you notice a reaction after trying a particular treatment, stop using it immediately and consult your doctor. If you have allergies, be very careful about ingesting any of the foods and/or herbs that are recommended, or applying certain topical treatments—for example, ingesting royal jelly or applying honey can cause a serious reaction if you are allergic to bee venom.

Also, if you are taking any medications —including prescription and/or over-the-counter drugs, vitamins or other homeopathic remedies—be aware that certain herbs or natural treatments may interact with them. If you notice any kind of reaction, stop using the remedy immediately.

So, if we haven't stressed it enough— just to be on the super-safe side, be careful and *consult your doctor before trying any of these treatments.*

CONDITIONS A TO Z

Acne

At least 3 out of every 4 people in the US have had acne at some point in their lives, making it the most common skin disease. The myth is that it's caused by dirt. In fact, acne is a disorder caused by the action of hormones on the skin's oil glands (sebaceous glands), which leads to plugged pores and outbreaks of lesions (pimples).

According to the American Academy of Dermatology (*www.aad.org*), frequent washing does nothing to prevent these outbreaks. Over-washing is actually irritating, and excess irritation can worsen acne. A washcloth can aggravate this situation further. So use your bare hands to wash gently, and only wash twice a day.

Here are some suggestions to help clear up the condition...

◆ First, wash your face with a mild soap—as it removes dirt, oil, makeup, sunscreen and/or moisturizer, it will not remove your skin's natural *acid mantle*—the protective layer on your skin's surface.

Mix the juice of an average-sized lemon (about 2½ tablespoons) with 1 teaspoon of dark brown sugar. Then gently apply the mixture all over your face. Let it stay that way for 20 minutes. Rinse with lukewarm water and pat dry. Do this twice a day for at least 2 weeks, and you should see the acne clear up.

◆ To speed the healing along, mix 1 tablespoon of honey with 1 tablespoon of unfiltered apple cider vinegar (available at health-food stores) in 1 cup of hot water. It may be tough to do, but try to drink this solution 2 to 3 times a day.

 Powerful Pimple Prevention

To prevent acne, moisten a cotton ball with some unfiltered apple cider vinegar (available at health-food stores) and dab it on. Do this after a shower or washing your face with mild soap or another gentle cleanser. *Be careful not to get any of the vinegar in your eyes!*

Excessive cleansing can destroy your skin's acid mantle—the oily layer on the skin's surface that protects the skin from bacteria and other environmental impurities. Vinegar helps restore the skin's natural pH balance (the acid mantle) while it acts as an astringent to help tighten your skin's connective tissues.

In just a few days, your complexion should look healthier.

Allergies

If you have a runny nose, sore throat and/or itchy eyes, you may be suffering from seasonal allergies. These allergies generally occur when your body overreacts to the pollen from trees, weeds, flowers or crops.

When the pollen count is sky-high and you dread going outside, dab the inside of your nostrils with a little sesame oil. It can help stop the irritation and allergic reaction that is caused by breathing in environmental or seasonal allergens.

Arthritis

According to the US Centers for Disease Control and Prevention in Atlanta (*www.cdc.gov*), arthritis is among the leading diseases in the United States. Approximately 70 million Americans are affected by arthritis—which has over 100 different forms. *Arthritis* is actually a catchall term that refers to many types of inflammation of (and pain in) the joints.

Here are some remedies that could help spell *r-e-l-i-e-f*...

◆ Eat a serving of gelatin daily, either sugar or sugar-free. The amino acids are believed to help restore cartilage and make a difference in the flexibility of your joints. It takes time—about 3 months—to notice an improvement, so try to stick with it.

◆ Check your jars of mustard and curry and you will see that turmeric is 1 of the ingredients. Turmeric has been used for centuries in India for its healing properties. The herb's inflammation-fighting compounds are now recognized and being researched.

For joint pain, the recommended dosage is 400 to 600 milligrams (mg) of turmeric capsules (containing 95% curcumin), taken 3 times a day. Or you can take ½ to 1 teaspoon of turmeric liquid extract, mixed into ½ cup of water, 3 times a day. You should feel better within a week.

If there is no improvement after a week, then it may not help relieve your joint pain. Take comfort in knowing that turmeric has excellent antioxidant, disease-fighting properties and is good for your digestion.

◆ Bruce Fife, ND, director of the Coconut Research Center in Colorado Springs, Colorado (*www.coconutresearchcenter.org*) and author of *Coconut Cures* (Piccadilly Books), uses turmeric in the following ginger-tea recipe to restore health to joints affected by rheumatoid arthritis. Use as much fresh ginger (available in the produce section of most supermarkets and grocery stores) as you like. In fact, the more ginger, the better—it helps to reduce inflammation.

Bring ½ cup of water to a boil. Cut the ginger into thin slices, add them to the hot water and simmer for 5 minutes. Remove the pan from the heat and discard the ginger. Stir ¼ teaspoon of powdered turmeric and 1 tablespoon of unflavored gelatin into the water. Add 1 tablespoon of coconut oil, and continue to stir until the gelatin is dissolved. Then add ½ to 1 cup of calcium-enriched orange juice. Drink this tea once or twice a day.

◆ Mix 1 tablespoon of unfiltered apple cider vinegar (available at health-food stores) in an 8-ounce glass of water, and drink it 2 or 3 times a day. Give it a fair chance to work—at least a week or so.

As a bonus, the apple cider vinegar may also help you lose weight, but be careful because too much vinegar can cause gastritis or heartburn.

According to the Johns Hopkins Arthritis Center in Baltimore, joint pain from is strongly associated with body weight. Being just 10 pounds overweight increases the force on the knee by 30 to 60 pounds with each step.

Go to the "Weight Control" section on pages 142–146—you'll find suggestions for taking a load off your feet, your knees, your back...you get the picture.

 FYI: Lighten Arthritis Pain
The results of a recent study suggest that losing weight, even just 1 pound, can slow the progression of arthritis. When participants in the study lost weight, it made walking a lot less painful. For each pound they lost, they enjoyed a 4-pound reduction in the force on their knees.

Asthma

During an asthma attack, bronchial tubes narrow and secrete an excess of mucus, making it very hard to breathe. Asthma in certain people may be attributed to exercise, allergies or emotional problems—or possibly a combination of all of these factors.

 CAUTION: Asthma is a serious condition, and it can be fatal if left untreated. If someone is having an asthma attack and cannot breathe, DO NOT try these remedies—call 911 and get him/her to the emergency room.

But there are encouraging words from Isaac Eliaz, MD, director of the Amitabha Medical Clinic in Sebastopol, California (*www.amit abhaclinic.com*). He says that at least 99% of the more than 17 million Americans with asthma can lead symptom-free lives without taking a ton of medication. *To help you do that, here are the doctor's recommendations…*

◆ *Pycnogenol* is a pine-tree extract that contains a potent anti-inflammatory, which can help prevent airway-narrowing inflammation. In a clinical trial, subjects who used pycnogenol showed improvement in how easily they could breathe. The dose used in the study was 250 milligrams (mg), 3 times a day. Pycnogenol is available in health-food stores.

◆ Eat an apple a day—with the skin—and you will get the fruit's rich supply of lung-nourishing *flavonoids*. According to British research, eating an apple daily could reduce the risk of an asthma attack by 20%.

◆ If you drink soy milk, stop for a few weeks and see if your asthma flare-ups subside. The results of an Australian study showed that soy-milk drinkers had more wheezing and full-blown asthma attacks than those who did not drink soy milk.

Genetically modified soy milk that has a high sugar content may increase inflammation in airways, causing spasms when exposed to irritants, such as pollen and mold.

◆ For just 20 minutes a day, meditate, visualize, do yoga or another relaxing activity—anything that will have you breathing slowly and deeply.

According to Dr. Eliaz, breathing this way helps when asthma attacks strike. Deep breathing calms the nervous system, preventing the airway spasms that trigger asthma attacks in the first place.

For a helpful breathing exercise, *see* "Deep-Breathing Exercise for Hypertension" on page 129.

Back Pain

It is estimated that 8 out of 10 people have, at some point in their lives, experienced disabling back pain. Also estimated is the amount spent for the diagnosis and treatment of back pain—more than $5 billion annually.

A simple acupressure massage can relieve stress-induced back pain instantly by triggering the reflexology point that is linked to the spine. Apply firm pressure from the big toe of your left foot, along the inner sole, all the way down to the heel. Then do the same thing on your right foot. There now…feel better?

 CAUTION: It's extremely important that any back pain be evaluated by a medical professional to rule out serious illness or injury. If your back pain is chronic, persistent or severe, see a doctor.

Bad Breath, Gum Disease And Toothaches

Natural remedies can help ease the pain of a toothache and, in some cases, alleviate problems caused by nervous tension and low-grade infections. But since it is difficult to know what is causing mouth problems, make an appointment to see your dentist as soon as possible. More important, have the dentist see your teeth and gums.

◆ Coconut oil kills germs that cause bad breath, tooth decay and gum disease, according to Bruce Fife, ND, director of the Coconut Research Center in Colorado Springs, Colorado (*www.coconutresearchcenter.org*) and author of several books, including *The Coconut Oil Miracle* (Avery).

Brush your teeth daily using a mixture of ⅛ teaspoon of baking soda and ½ teaspoon of organic extra-virgin coconut oil (available at health-food stores).

◆ If your gums feel sore, massaging them with coconut oil should bring relief.

Bladder Infection

Also *see* "Urinary Problems" on page 141.

The most common *symptoms* of a bladder infection or urinary tract infection (UTI) are...

◆ Frequent urination

◆ Strong, painful urge to urinate

◆ Pain or burning when urinating

◆ Foul-smelling or bloody urine

◆ Fever (with a moderate to severe bladder infection)

The most common *causes* of bladder infections are...

◆ Holding in urine

◆ Constipation

◆ Improper wiping

◆ Exposure to irritating substances, such as soap and bubble baths

 CAUTION: If you think you have a bladder infection or UTI, it's very important to check with your health care professional before trying any of the following remedies.

◆ Put 1 teaspoon of olive oil and 1 teaspoon of finely minced garlic into a glass of warm water and drink it 3 times a day, before meals. These three glasses a day should help destroy the bacteria that's causing the bladder infection.

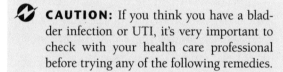

◆ Chop 1 large onion. Put the onion in a pot with 2 cups of regular milk, and boil it down

to 1 cup. Strain out the onion pieces and drink ½ cup of the onion milk. Four hours later, drink the other ½ cup.

 NOTE: When you have a bladder infection, *do not* drink carbonated beverages and stay away from salty and rich foods. Keep it simple—broth, salad, fruit. Also, drinking 100% cranberry juice can help relieve and prevent bladder infections.

★ **Blueberries Help Bladders**

A study conducted at Rutgers University in New Jersey found that eating a handful of blueberries daily may help prevent bladder infections. This is because blueberries contain a polymeric compound that keeps bacteria from sticking to the bladder wall.

Blisters

A blister is a local swelling of the skin that contains watery fluid. Resist the urge to pop it because you run the risk of infection.

If the blister is open and oozing, that means there is an infection present. Apply antibiotic ointment and—if it gets worse—get professional medical attention as soon as you possibly can.

◆ If the blister is open and *not* infected, cover it with a bandage during the day and take off the bandage when you go to bed. Let the blister dry out.

◆ If the blister is intact, but it's still painful, soak your foot in regular cold milk to reduce the pain and swelling. You can also apply a cold compress (for 10 minutes at a time) to relieve the inflammation.

★ **Keep Things Slick**

To prevent blisters, apply any type of antiperspirant to the bottom of your feet before you go jogging or hiking. The antiperspirant should prevent the friction that causes blisters.

You can also use other types of lubricants to prevent blisters, such as petroleum jelly (available at drug stores) and BodyGlide (available at sporting goods stores).

Blood Cleanser

Ben Kim, DC, a chiropractor in practice in Barrie, Ontario (*www.drbenkim.com*), promotes the benefits of seaweed as an excellent blood cleanser, believed to support optimal brain function.

■ Recipe ■

Here is Dr. Kim's family recipe for a traditional Korean seaweed soup...

Mi-Yuk Gook

> 1 package of dried seaweed* (1 ounce is enough for 4 servings)
>
> 6 cups of vegetable broth or organic chicken broth
>
> 2 teaspoons of sesame oil
>
> naturally brewed soy sauce or sea salt, to taste
>
> 1 teaspoon of garlic, minced (optional)

1. Soak the seaweed in water for 2 hours or until soft. Drain and rinse really well, as dried seaweed can come with a lot of dirt, just like spinach.

2. Put all ingredients, including seaweed, into a large pot and bring to a boil, then simmer for 5 minutes to allow all the flavors to come together.

Koreans traditionally enjoy this seaweed soup with a bowl of white or brown rice—sometimes together in the same bowl.

*If you buy the seaweed in a Korean market, ask for 1 package of seaweed for soup. If you shop at a health-food store, buy 1 package of nori seaweed.

Brain Boosters

The adult human brain is about the size of 2 clenched, average-sized adult fists...it weighs approximately 3 pounds...and has about 1 million individual neurons or nerve cells—give or take a few.

The brain is an incredible organ with an almost infinite capacity for storing information. Recalling that information is another story, though. *Here are some suggestions to banish brain-fog moments, sharpen your focus and be on high alert when you need to be...*

◆ Jump-start your day *hydrotherapeutically.* That's a fancy way of saying—take a shower! Begin with warm water, then make it hotter for 10 seconds (not *burning* hot), then cold again for another 10 seconds, then hot again for another 10 seconds. (Do you notice a pattern forming here?) Repeat the hot/cold cycles 5 times.

Hot water dilates blood vessels for a circulation surge...cold water constricts blood vessels for a slowdown in circulation. This switching act revs up the morning's sluggish blood flow, sending oxygen to the brain, which should make you more alert and focused for the rest of the day.

◆ If you are right-handed, brush your teeth with your left hand, and if you're left-handed...well, you know. This challenging little exercise stimulates the nondominant side of your brain and encourages it to develop new nerve-cell connections.

If you really want to pack on those new nerve-cell connections, do a crossword puzzle with your nondominant hand. In no time, you'll be wanting to know when *Jeopardy!* will be holding auditions in your area.

◆ Breakfast is the most important meal of the day when it comes to being your sharpest for work, school, a meeting, an interview—or as a contestant on *Jeopardy!* Researchers find that people score higher on thinking tests when they eat the right breakfast foods.

A study conducted at Tufts University in Boston proved that children who ate instant oatmeal for breakfast the day of testing performed significantly better on tests of short-term memory, spatial memory and listening skills than those who ate either cold cereal or no breakfast.

The Tufts' scientists believe that the high fiber and protein content in oatmeal helps to slow down digestion, which promotes a slower and more sustained release of *glucose* (a simple sugar that is the body's main source of energy) into the bloodstream.

The controlled release of glucose seems to influence the way the brain uses it, especially when it comes to memory performance. So, maximize mental function starting with breakfast—preferably oatmeal.

◆ People who take a daily B-complex supplement tend to be more alert and less affected by stress throughout the day. Be sure to follow the recommended dosage on the label. *Consider the contents and value of the B-complex components...*

◆ Vitamin B-1 (thiamine) is used by the brain to help convert glucose (blood sugar) into fuel. Without it, the brain rapidly runs out of energy.

◆ Vitamin B-3 (niacin) deficiency can produce agitation as well as anxiety, as well as mental and physical slowness.

◆ Vitamin B-5 (pantothenic acid) is needed for hormone formation as well as the uptake of amino acids plus the brain chemical acetylcholine, which combine to prevent certain types of depression.

◆ Vitamin B-6 (pyridoxine) is needed for the manufacture of serotonin, melatonin and dopamine—hormones that promote a sense of well-being.

◆ Vitamin B-12 is important in the formation of red blood cells. A deficiency may lead to an oxygen-transport problem known as *pernicious anemia*. This disorder can cause

mood swings, paranoia, irritability, confusion, dementia, hallucinations or mania, eventually followed by appetite loss, dizziness, weakness, shortage of breath, heart palpitations, diarrhea and tingling sensations in the extremities.

◆ Folic acid is necessary for the production of SAMe (S-adenosyl methionine), a powerful nutrient that helps prevent depression.

◆ When you learn something new, go to sleep for several hours right afterward, instead of staying awake and practicing or studying whatever you learned. Researchers at the Harvard Medical School in Boston found that you will remember your new facts better after you awaken.

◆ When you need on-the-spot smarts, put your index finger on the *Renzhong* (the acupressure point in the middle of your *philtrum*, which is the spot between your nose and upper lip). Press in and try to stay that way for 30 seconds.

◆ Maybe allergies or smog or too little sleep is making you feel as though you're struggling to think straight. If so, put a golf ball between your palms and roll it around, massaging your *adrenal reflex areas*—they are located halfway down the long first metacarpal bones of the hands below the thumbs.

Reflexologists believe that there are reflexes on the hands (and feet) that correspond to all parts of the body. Stimulation of the appropriate reflexes can activate the body's own natural healing system. This reflexology exercise ought to clear out the cobwebs.

◆ Hold your breath as long as you can without turning blue. Studies show that taking in extra oxygen, like when you're preparing to hold your breath, gives you a burst of energy and will boost your alertness by 60%.

◆ Alan R. Hirsch, MD, director of The Smell and Taste Treatment and Research Foundation in Chicago (*www.smellandtaste.org*), says that the distinctive smell and taste of butterscotch instantly switches the brain back to the moment it first absorbed new information, making it easier to recall facts.

So, eat butterscotch candy when you're learning new information and when you need to get the data from the "tip of your tongue."

◆ Snack on walnuts, a super brain food. They are rich in omega-3 fatty acids...and great for heart health, too.

◆ If you have to think on your feet, grab a handful of raw pumpkin seeds. *Tyrosine*, an amino acid found in pumpkin seeds, helps your mind work like a well-oiled machine.

◆ If accuracy counts, surround yourself with a citrus scent. Suck on a lemon drop, or put a couple of drops of lemon oil on a cotton ball and put it in your work space. Studies have shown that workers exposed to the smell of lemon made 50% fewer errors.

◆ Eat blueberries to keep your memory sharp. Researchers at Tufts University in Boston found that *anthocyanin*, the chemical in blueberries that gives them their beautiful blue color, also encourages the growth of new brain cells.

◆ Color consultant Leatrice Eiseman (*www.colorexpert.com*) suggests keeping purple in your line of sight. If you use a computer, make the color purple part of your desktop, wallpaper or screen saver. Accessorize any work area with shades of purple.

The regal color combines the energy and excitement of red with the confidence and serenity of blue. The result is a calming influence and an alert, active mind.

◆ Eating certain fatty fish—such as salmon, tuna, halibut, mackerel, herring or sardines—is believed to keep your mind agile. It will improve memory, hand–eye coordination and high-level problem solving. Fish is also said to lessen anger, hostility, cynicism and mistrust. Eat fish 2 or more times a week to get those brain-boosting omega-3 fatty acids.

 CAUTION: Some types of fish contain dangerous levels of mercury or other contaminants that can be toxic when consumed in high quantities. With this in mind, the Food and Drug Administration (FDA) and the Environmental Protection Agency (EPA) have issued guidelines for consumption—especially for women who are pregnant (or who may become pregnant), nursing mothers and young children.

The FDA suggests that women and young children eat no more than 12 ounces (2 average meals) per week of a variety of fish and shellfish that are lower in mercury.

Certain fish—including shrimp, tilapia, salmon, pollock and catfish—generally contain low levels of mercury. Fish such as shark, swordfish, king mackerel and tilefish tend to have higher levels, and should not be consumed as often.

For more information, visit the FDA food safety Web site at *www.cfsan.fda.gov/~frf/sea-mehg.html* or the EPA Web site at *www.epa.gov/ost/fish/.*

◆ Make exercise more fun by working out to music—you'll also make it easier to organize your thoughts and heighten your alertness.

According to a study conducted by Charles Emery, PhD, associate professor of psychology at Ohio State University in Columbus, subjects who worked out on a treadmill while listening to music (such as Vivaldi's *The Four Seasons*) scored significantly higher on a test of verbal fluency. It was shown that an exercise/music combination stimulates the brain's *cortical region*, the seat of logic and analytical thinking.

Breast-feeding

Breast-feeding helps to protect your baby from developing gastrointestinal trouble, respiratory problems, ear infections and allergies. Nursing your baby for at least 6 months may also boost your child's intelligence, and protect him/her against obesity later in life.

You may know all of that already, but do you know that breast-feeding also benefits *you* in many ways? It helps the nursing mother lose weight, lower her stress levels and reduce postpartum bleeding, may reduce her risk of developing some types of cancer and may protect her against osteoporosis later in life. *If you are breast-feeding, here is valuable information…*

According to Ben Kim, DC, a chiropractor in practice in Barrie, Ontario (*www.drben kim.com*), "Seaweed is amazingly effective at stimulating healthy breast-milk production in nursing moms." Dr. Kim advises women to eat seaweed soup during pregnancy and the nursing period as a virtual guarantee of healthy breast-milk production.

See "Blood Cleanser" on page 112 of this chapter for Dr. Kim's family recipe for the traditional Korean seaweed soup, *Mi-Yuk Gook.*

Bronchitis

Bronchitis is an inflammation of the bronchial tubes and can be caused by bacteria, viruses, breathing in certain chemicals or smoking.

In fact, 80% to 90% of emphysema and chronic bronchitis cases are caused by smoking. So if you smoke—whether you have chronic bronchitis or want to avoid getting it—STOP SMOKING!

 CAUTION: If you have *chronic* bronchitis—or any serious lung condition that is marked by a productive cough (with sputum) and/or shortness of breath (especially with asthma or chronic obstructive pulmonary disease)—you must work with a health care professional to reduce your risk of lung damage.

If you have been diagnosed with *acute* bronchitis—the kind that lasts a week or so and is generally caused by a viral infection (which may begin while you have a cold or sore throat)—consider the following treatment for your inflamed bronchial tubes…

Put 1 quart of filtered or springwater in a pot, then add 3 tablespoons of dried oregano and 3 average-size cloves of garlic that have been chopped *with the skins on.* Let it boil for 10 minutes, then take the pot off the fire and let the mixture steep for 5 minutes. Next, put a towel over your head and neck and bend over the steaming pot. Breathe deeply and exhale. Keep doing that for 5 minutes.

 CAUTION: Be extremely careful not to get too close to the hot pot—you could get a steam burn.

Warm up the liquid and repeat the steam treatment every few hours, especially before bedtime. It should help you sleep through the night. (Again, *please* be careful not to get too close to the steam.)

Make another pot of oregano-and-garlic water and drink it throughout the day—½ cup at a time. You may want to add honey and lime juice to make it more palatable.

Bruises

Bruises generally appear when the skin has undergone some form of trauma (minor or not) that caused little blood vessels to break. This can happen from bumping into the edge of a table or from something more serious like a car accident.

Most minor bruises will go away on their own with time (usually after going through a rainbow of colors), but these remedies may speed up the healing process…

◆ A popular Mayan remedy to reduce swelling and promote the healing of a bruise is to cut a lemon in half and rub the pulp over the bruise. Do this every hour until you go to bed, and there should be a big improvement by the time you wake up.

 CAUTION: If there is broken skin along with the bruise, be warned that applying lemon juice will *sting*!

◆ Before you go to bed, soak a washcloth in a mixture made from equal parts water and apple cider vinegar. Wring out the cloth and wrap it around the bruised and swollen area—be sure it's not too tight, or you can cut off your circulation.

Then put a layer of plastic wrap on the washcloth (to protect your bedsheets) and cover the plastic wrap with a towel. Hold it in place with a large bandage or medical tape, and let it stay that way overnight. In the morning, there should be a tremendous improvement—hopefully, no swelling and just a minimal amount of bruising.

◆ Increase your intake of vitamin C. Taking up to 2,000 milligrams a day can help reduce the pain and inflammation from a bruise.

Carpal Tunnel Syndrome

This condition results from swollen tendons that compress the median nerve within the carpal tunnel canal in the wrist. It's usually accompanied by numbness, swelling, soreness, stiffness, weakness, tingling, discomfort and pain…*a lot* of pain. It tends to be caused by continual, rapid use of your fingers, wrists and/or arms.

At the first sign of carpal tunnel–type pain, warm about ¼ cup of olive oil. Take it off the heat before it starts to boil. When the oil is cool enough to touch, massage it into your skin from your elbow to your wrist.

Even though you may hit some very sore and painful spots, keep massaging and try to dissolve the pain. Every couple of minutes, stop and manipulate the fleshy webbed acupressure area between your thumb and forefinger, then go back to massaging.

Stop after a reasonable amount of time—or when your hand is too tired to continue. Just let your wrist rest until the next day. And, even though it may feel fine the next day, do the wrist-to-elbow olive oil massage once a day for a full week. If there is someone else who can do it for you, that's even better.

The recommended dosage for carpal tunnel inflammation is the same as for arthritis joint pain—400 to 600 milligrams (mg) of turmeric capsules (containing 95% curcumin), taken 3 times a day. Or take ½ to 1 teaspoon of turmeric liquid extract mixed into ½ cup of water, 3 times a day. You will know the turmeric is working if you feel relief within a week.

Cholesterol

In 2004, the US government revised the guidelines for what is considered a dangerous level of cholesterol. Previous levels were a maximum of 100 milligrams per deciliter (mg/dL) of low-density lipoprotein (LDL or "bad") cholesterol, and the new recommendation is to have LDLs no higher than 70 mg/dL.

These guidelines are for very high-risk people with heart disease as well as multiple, poorly controlled risk factors (such as diabetes, high blood pressure and smoking), and who are being treated with medication. But even people with moderately high risk (for example, those who have already had a heart attack) should keep their LDL levels well below 100 mg/dL.

We have always believed (and our research proves) that certain foods—such as apples, avocados, fenugreek, garlic, kiwi, flaxseed, beans and, of course, oatmeal—can help lower cholesterol. While continuing our research, we heard about a woman who was advised by a

Heart-Healthy Treats

How many times have you thought, "If only candy were good for me!" Well, in fact, researchers have found that dark chocolate (when eaten in moderation) can be good for your heart. The *stearic acid* in dark chocolate is converted in the body to *oleic acid*, which is the main fatty acid in olive oil…and we all know how heart-healthy olive oil is.

Also, dark chocolate is chock full of antioxidant-rich compounds known as *flavonoids*. Flavonoids may help to increase HDL ("good") cholesterol levels by as much as 10%, according to Penny Kris-Etherton, PhD, professor of nutrition at Pennsylvania State University in University Park.

The results of a long clinical trial conducted by Mary Engler, PhD, RN, and her colleagues at the University of California in San Francisco, showed improvement in subjects' blood vessel function after they consumed small daily doses (about 1.6 ounces) of flavonoid-rich dark chocolate over an extended period of time.

Dr. Engler concluded that eating a small amount of dark chocolate every day is good for most people. The higher the cocoa content, the better. Some manufacturers, such as Lindt and Chocolove, list the cocoa content on the label of the chocolate bar.

 Personal Preference

I've been a milk chocolate person most of my life, and I always found dark chocolate to be bitter. But now I eat Lindt's 85% cocoa, which is very bitter, and I love it. The secret is to break off a small piece and let it dissolve in your mouth (rather than chew it). It tastes great, lasts a long time and I'm satisfied eating less.—*Lydia*

 CAUTION: Keep in mind that, while flavonoids are great for your blood vessels, they don't cancel out fat and calories. It's important to stick to the recommended amount (about 1.6 ounces) of dark chocolate daily.

In addition, it's not true that the more chocolate you eat, the healthier you'll be. So if you are on a sugar-free diet, even a small daily dose of chocolate may do you more harm than good. Talk to your doctor.

Also, don't try this remedy if you are allergic to chocolate.

Butter Replacement

Pour extra-virgin olive oil in a wide-mouth jar with a tight-fitting lid, and refrigerate it. It will solidify and then you can use it as a healthy spread on bread or toast, in place of butter.

doctor at the Mayo Clinic in Rochester, Minnesota, to eat a handful of walnuts daily.

The Mayo Clinic reviewed the results of some small studies, which showed that walnuts can significantly reduce blood cholesterol levels. Rich in polyunsaturated fatty acids, walnuts may also help keep blood vessels more healthy and elastic.

All nuts are high in fat calories, and many doctors would advise you to add walnuts to your diet ONLY as a substitute for other foods that contain high levels of saturated fats, such as cheese, butter and fatty meats.

We start the day by eating ½ cup of cooked oatmeal, which is high in fiber and provides 20% of our daily vitamin A. We add cinnamon and some raisins for iron and potassium…or blueberries for antioxidants and vitamin C…as well as walnuts for omega-3 fatty acids. We sweeten it all with a natural sweetener called stevia (available at health-food stores).

Colds and Flu

The common cold can wipe you out, and the influenza virus—which is characterized by inflammation of the respiratory tract and fever, chills and muscular pains—can really knock you down for the count. *If you're feeling run down, have a red, runny nose, chest congestion and that achy-all-over feeling, this remedy may help…*

Pour 1 cup of Epsom salt (available at drugstores) into the bathtub and fill it with hot water. Then add 2 cups of 3% hydrogen peroxide (the inexpensive kind that you get at the drugstore). When the bath is still warm, but cool enough to not burn you, get in and soak for 30 minutes. Then dry off quickly, put on cotton bedclothes and get under the covers.

The bath should help relieve the achiness that comes with a cold and it should also promote a good night's sleep, which will help you get over your cold more quickly.

Cold Sores

About 85% of all Americans are prone to getting cold sores. This unsightly blemish is caused by the *herpes simplex* virus, which bursts into bloom when you least want it—usually, it's when your resistance is low because of a cold, the flu, pregnancy, sunburn, your wedding day or some other stressful factor.

Cold sores generally take about 2 weeks to clear up. *Here are a few suggestions that may speed up the healing process…*

◆ Dab a cold sore with a swab that's been dipped in a little vodka—the alcohol will help dry it out. But be warned that the alcohol will also sting.

 The Ears Have It!

The second you get that tingly feeling on your lip and know that it's the start of a cold sore, rub your finger against the back of your ear.

Then, with that same part of your finger, rub the spot the cold sore is starting to emerge. This should make it disappear. (We can't help but wonder HOW someone discovered this remedy!)

Be sure to wash your hands thoroughly after touching the cold sore—the virus is contagious and can be spread to other people (and body parts) very easily.

◆ Puncture a vitamin E gel capsule—400 international units (IU)—then squeeze out the oil and cover the cold sore with it. Do this 3 times a day. By the third application, the pain should be gone. By the end of the next day (the sixth application), the cold sore should be healed.

 Go for the Gold!

Rubbing a gold ring over a tingly cold sore spot may also put the sore into remission. Hey, it's worth a try.

Colic

Doctors aren't sure what causes a baby to get colic (it could be an allergy or indigestion—or just the child's disposition). But whatever the cause, it's hard to listen to a baby cry from such discomfort. *This remedy may bring relief…*

Put a clean, soft towel on your bed and place the baby on the towel. Then pour a little castor oil on your hand and gently rub the baby's tummy with it. It may take about 10 minutes for the castor oil to kick in and the colicky episode to abate, so be patient.

Constipation

If you are constipated more often than every once in a blue moon, you might want to limit your intake of certain foods that are known to cause constipation. They include milk, cheese, ice cream, unripe bananas, heavily salted and spiced foods, chocolate, alcoholic beverages and products made with white flour.

Foods that help keep you regular are very ripe bananas, figs, dried plums/prunes (of course), flaxseed, avocados, cooked cabbage, apples, oatmeal and salads. Try to vary these foods in your daily diet, and remember—natural inexpensive constipation relievers should not present any side effects if used in moderation.

 NOTE: Constipation is a common problem that may be a symptom of disease or lead to more serious ailments. It is important to consult a medical professional before starting any self-help treatment.

This saline laxative for the relief of occasional constipation generally produces results in 1 to 6 hours. For adults (12 years of age or older), dissolve 1 to 2 teaspoons of Epsom salt (available at drugstores) in 4 ounces of water and drink it. Take no more than 2 doses per day.

 CAUTION: Epsom salt is made with magnesium and *shouldn't* adversely affect anyone on a salt-restricted diet, but we urge you to check with your health care professional before trying the previous solution.

In addition, people with kidney disease or renal failure should NOT use this remedy under any circumstances.

Contact Lenses

New technology and materials have made contact lenses more comfortable and more convenient than ever. *If you have lenses—or are thinking about getting them—here's another thing to cross off your concerned list…*

If you're among the people who think it's possible to lose your contact lens in the back of your head, there's no need to worry. The *conjunctiva*, a clear lining that covers the inner lid and connects to the eyeball, makes it impossible for a lens to slip into your head.

If your contact lens gets stuck, retrieve it by flushing your eye with a sterile saline solution (available at drugstores).

Cough

The cough center in your brain is generally motivated by an irritation in the respiratory tract. In other words, a cough is nature's way of helping you loosen and get rid of mucus that's congesting your system.

If you want to get rid of a nagging cough, follow the recommendation of Jane Guiltinan, ND, faculty member at Bastyr University Center for Natural Health in Seattle…in a large glass, combine the juice from ½ lemon (about 4 teaspoons) with ½ cup of warm water. Then stir in 1 tablespoon of table salt and ¼ teaspoon of cayenne pepper.

Gargle with this solution for as long as possible and as deeply as you can tolerate it. Then spit it out. *DO NOT SWALLOW IT.*

Dandruff

As dead cells fall off the scalp, new cells form beneath them. We all lose skin cells this way, but with dandruff this process is faster…a greater number of cells are shed in clumps, often big enough to be seen. If you have dandruff, wear light-colored clothes so that it's not as noticeable. *Then check out the remedies below to help dandruff disappear…*

◆ Are you sure that you have dandruff and not just a buildup of hair spray, styling gel or mousse? Cut back on the products that can cause flakiness, and see what happens. But if you still have dandruff, then it's time to try thyme.

Bring 1 cup of water to a boil, add 2 heaping tablespoons of dried thyme and let it simmer for 7 to 10 minutes. Strain out the thyme and let the water cool. Meanwhile, shampoo your hair as usual. Once the brew is cool, and while your hair is still damp, gently massage the thyme water into your scalp. *Do not rinse it out.*

◆ Get an aloe vera plant. The night before you're going to shampoo your hair, cut off a piece of the lowest leaf of the plant. Peel off the skin of the leaf, and squeeze the gel on your hair and into your scalp. Cover your hair with a bandanna or scarf and sleep that way.

The next morning, when you wash your hair, do not use shampoo. Instead, foam up the aloe gel. This treatment is good for your hair and can, surprisingly, help you get rid of dandruff quickly.

Depression (The Blues)

According to a survey, the average person spends 3 days every month feeling a little sad. There are a variety of things that might make you feel mildly down—from the weather to pressures at the office and/or problems with your partner. *Perk up during those occasional down days with these suggestions…*

 CAUTION: If you are having trouble coping or feel sad and deeply depressed for more than a few days at a time, seek professional assistance to help pinpoint the cause and recommend treatment. Severe depression can lead to suicide, so seek help immediately.

◆ Don't stop reading just because you see the word *exercise*. Because, according to a study from the University of Texas Southwestern Medical Center and the Cooper Institute (both in Dallas) performing 30 to 40 minutes of moderate aerobic exercise—a brisk walk, a few laps in the pool or pedaling a bike—3 to 5 times a week, could help to alleviate many of the symptoms of mild depression.

You may have to push yourself to do it, but give exercise a try for a few weeks—when you start to feel a whole lot better, it will have been worth it.

 NOTE: Do not start any exercise program without permission from your doctor. Trying to do too much too soon can lead to injury—which can make you more depressed. Consult your health care professional for a physical evaluation and instructions on how to start an exercise routine.

Positive Affirmations

Words have power—great power. Our subconscious acts on our words and thoughts without discrimination. And so we should be careful about what we think and say.

That's why affirmations are wonderful. They are positive programming for the subconscious and, as a bonus, they also make us feel better consciously.

Start by assigning an appropriate affirmation to yourself. Write it down on an index card and read it over and over—at least 7 times in a row, out loud if possible—time and time again throughout the day. Think about the meaning of it, and when you say it—mean it. Even if you memorize it and say it by rote, it will impact your subconscious, and your subconscious will act on it.

Louise L. Hay, Science of Mind minister, metaphysical lecturer and author of *Power Thoughts* (Hay House, *www.hayhouse.com*), says that an affirmation is like planting a seed. *She graciously provided us with a few of those seeds…*

◆ I now choose to release every negative, destructive, fearful idea and thought from my mind and my life.

◆ My body is always working toward optimal health. I am happy and healthy.

◆ I trust life to be wonderful. I see only good ahead of me.

At some point in time, you may want to create your own appropriate, meaningful affirmation by pinpointing whatever is your physical or emotional challenge, its possible underlying cause and the outcome you want. When that time comes, keep it simple, strong and personal.

One of our favorite affirmations is a classic that was created by Émile Coué (and altered by José Silva)…*every day in every way I'm getting better, better and better!*

◆ When you sing out loud, you produce brain vibrations that trigger the release of *endorphins*—chemicals in the brain that can elevate mood and help kill pain. Find a song that you like to sing and then personalize it with happy and positive lyrics that will lift your spirits.

◆ Restore calm and contentment by using the Chinese art of *qigong*. While lying down or standing up, use your palm to rub the area around your belly-button in a clockwise motion. After doing it for 3 minutes, hold your hand over the area (not touching your skin) for 5 seconds.

This process is believed to unclog energy blockages so that your *chi* (life energy) can flow freely, which should put you back into happy balance.

◆ Chase away the blues by petting a friendly dog. Scientists at the University of Missouri in Columbia found that petting a dog increases levels of the get-happy hormone *serotonin*. (Interacting with a *robotic* dog caused a dip in serotonin levels.)

◆ You know how having a *bad-hair day* (BHD) makes you feel totally unattractive? Marianne LaFrance, PhD, professor of psychology at Yale University in New Haven, Connecticut, conducted a study and found that having a BHD can make both men and women feel almost worthless. Restore your happiness-inducing self-confidence by doing whatever it takes to make your hair look its best.

◆ Psychologists and color consultants agree that the color pink conveys calm and helps to soothe. So think pink! It's an attractive and flattering color when worn by men as well as women.

In addition to wearing it, put a vase of pink flowers on your table or desk. Put pink accents around your work space and/or house. Be in the pink. The more, the merrier!

Diarrhea

Diarrhea is a common condition that is often caused by overeating…a bacterial, viral or parasitic infection…mild food poisoning or intolerance…an adverse reaction to medication…or emotional anxiety. It's important to drink clear fluids during and after a bout in order to avoid electrolyte depletion and dehydration.

 CAUTION: If diarrhea persists, it may be a symptom of a more serious ailment. Get professional medical attention.

Having diarrhea is no fun. Apple cider vinegar (preferably unfiltered, available at health-food stores) will let nature take its course, and will lessen the intensity and get you back in control in a relatively short time.

Take 1 teaspoon of apple cider vinegar mixed in 8 ounces of water, both before meals and in between. That means 6 glasses a day. But it's worth it for all the good it does. Also, the *pectin* (a natural fruit enzyme) in the vinegar will add bulk to the stools and help destroy some types of bacteria that cause diarrhea.

Dry Eye Syndrome

Tear ducts that do not produce enough fluid to keep the eyes moist can result in an uncomfortable dry-eye condition that is characterized by irritation, burning and a gravelly feeling. You may be more at risk for dry eye if you're a long-term contact-lens wearer…or you have had LASIK vision-correction surgery…or you have high blood pressure or rheumatoid arthritis…or if you're getting on in years, especially if you're a woman.

Researchers at Brigham and Women's Hospital and Schepens Eye Research Institute in Boston conducted a Women's Health Study. They found, based on 37,000 women who were enrolled in this landmark study, that women who reported eating at least 5 servings of tuna per week had a 68% reduced risk of dry eye syndrome compared with women who ate only 1 serving per week.

In addition to tuna, it's a good idea to eat foods that are rich in omega-3 fatty acids—such as salmon, halibut, mackerel, herring, sardines, walnuts and pumpkin seeds—ideally, at least 3 times a week.

 NOTE: See the CAUTION on page 114 for more information about mercury and other toxic contaminants that are found in fish, and also the US government's guidelines on limiting fish consumption.

Also, dry eyes may be relieved by eating ground flaxseed and/or flaxseed oil daily (follow the recommended dosage on label), both available at health-food stores. You can also take omega-3 supplements. Follow the dosage on the bottle.

Eczema (*Atopic Dermatitis*)

Eczema is a chronic skin disease that is very uncomfortable, but not contagious. It tends to show up most often on elbows, knees and wrists, and may be triggered by allergies.

 CAUTION: Persistent or chronic eczema is best treated by a health care professional.

◆ A Japanese study reported that drinking oolong tea reduced itching and inflammation in people suffering from eczema. Drink 34 ounces (about 1 liter) of oolong tea (available at supermarkets and health-food stores) throughout the day, after meals and between lunch and dinner. Its antioxidant properties relieve itching, redness and swelling.

 NOTE: Oolong tea is NOT caffeine-free, so you should not have it close to bedtime if you're sensitive to caffeine.

◆ To help reduce inflammation from eczema, take 1 tablespoon of flaxseed oil daily.

◆ A popular European treatment is evening primrose oil. The usual dose of this omega-6 fatty acid is 2 to 4 grams a day, taken with food. To soothe cracked skin, you can also use evening primrose oil externally.

◆ We recently heard about an eczema remedy that worked when nothing else did—it is Crisco, the vegetable shortening our grandmother used for cooking and baking (available at supermarkets).

The woman we heard about applied Crisco to her flared-up areas of eczema 2 to 3 times a day until the eczema was gone.

 NOTE: Applying Crisco is neither easy nor practical, especially if you go to work. Then again, having eczema is not easy. If you can give this remedy a try, do so for at least 1 or 2 weeks. If the symptoms start to disappear, continue with the Crisco until the eczema is all gone. (Petroleum jelly may also work.)

Edema

Occasional swelling of the legs, ankles or feet may be due to water retention from getting too much salt in your diet. But whatever the cause, it's important to talk to your health care professional to determine *exactly* why it's happening—underlying causes of edema can be heart failure, kidney disease, lymphoma, *deep vein thrombosis* (DVT), bone fracture or some other injury.

And while you're talking to your doctor, be sure to ask him/her about the following herbal remedies to make sure that it's OK for you to take them...

◆ For decades, the herbal preparation horse chestnut (capsules are available at health-food stores) has been used to relieve the swelling and pain of a variety of vein conditions, including varicose veins and chronic venous insufficiency.

Horse chestnut helps reduce inflammation, facilitate blood flow, reinforce the strength of the vein walls and promote their elasticity. Follow the dosage instructions on the bottle.

 NOTE: Horse chestnut should be used *only* for chronic venous insufficiency—not for any other type of edema.

◆ Butcher's broom (capsules are available at health-food stores) has been a traditional medicine for treating vein disorders for more than 50 years. In addition to relieving leg pain and swelling, it can help with itching, numbness and cramping. Follow the dosage instructions on the bottle.

Energy Boosters

Dale Carnegie—public speaker and motivational pioneer—believed that "our fatigue is often caused not by work, but by worry, frustration and resentment."

Author Eric Hoffer contends, "Men weary as much of not doing the things they want to do as of doing the things they do not want to do."

Those are important words that may give you food for thought. If you're always tired, take a look at your life and chances are, you'll be able to figure out what's causing your fatigue. Then figure out how to make some positive changes.

While you're figuring that out, here are some picker-uppers for a quick energy boost...

◆ Grab a food that's rich in the essential mineral *selenium*—such as brazil nuts, celery, broccoli, yogurt, cottage cheese, mushrooms, fish and cabbage. Studies show that selenium can help bolster your mood as well as your energy levels.

◆ Singing out loud brings extra oxygen into your body and releases feel-good endorphins, which should give you a right-then-and-there burst of energy.

◆ If you just can't carry a tune, take a deep breath. As you exhale, slowly say the vowels *A-E-I-O-U.*

According to John M. Ortiz, PhD, of the Institute of Applied Musicology in Dillsburg, Pennsylvania (*www.soundpsych.com*) and author of *The Tao of Music* (Weiser), the vibrations produced while making those sounds radiate through your body. They actually function as an internal massage that soothes and revives your entire system.

◆ After standing all day, or sitting for long periods of time, your circulation is diminished and blood pools in your legs and feet. Your energy decreases because blood is not being reoxygenated quickly enough by your heart. Reverse the situation by elevating your feet and letting the pooled blood become recirculated with more oxygen. Your energy level will also be elevated.

Walk Away DVT

To help prevent *deep vein thrombosis* (DVT, the formation of a blood clot that can be extremely dangerous—and even fatal), it's important to exercise the legs on a regular basis. Just take a brisk 30-minute walk every day.

And, do not sit or lie down for extended periods of time without moving your legs—if possible, get up and move around every 30 to 60 minutes to help prevent clots.

◆ If sitting with your feet up isn't practical, slip off your shoes, reach down and rub your feet. Massage the acupressure point in the webbed area between the first and second toes of each foot for 2 minutes. The stimulation will give you an energy surge.

◆ If you're among other people (such as at a long meeting or presentation) and you feel as though you're going to nod off instead of being alert, press your elbows against your sides and press your knees together for a few seconds. Exerting a lot of pressure this way will increase your blood circulation, and you should feel more awake and responsive.

◆ Alan R. Hirsch, MD, director of The Smell and Taste Treatment and Research Foundation in Chicago, has found that scents can influence our energy levels. Dr. Hirsch's studies show that wearing perfume or cologne that you love improves your self-esteem as well as your energy level.

In addition, the scent of cinnamon stimulates the *trigeminal nerve*, the area of the brain that governs wakefulness and raises energy levels. Have cinnamon at breakfasttime—sprinkle it on toast, hot oatmeal, cold cereal or even coffee. Or, during the day, put a drop of cinnamon oil on the inside of your wrist and sniff the invigorating scent.

Erectile Dysfunction

Male impotence or *erectile dysfunction* can be caused by certain psychological problems, such as stress, anxiety, depression, fear or guilt… high blood pressure or cholesterol…hormonal abnormalities, such as low testosterone levels… and prescription and over-the-counter medications. (Incidentally, cigarette smokers are more likely to suffer from erectile dysfunction than nonsmokers—cigarettes decrease the blood flow through veins and arteries.)

If any of these things have been interfering with your ability to perform, you should take appropriate measures to correct the situation.

First and foremost, talk to your doctor —especially if you think your performance problems may be related to medication. Erectile dysfunction can also be a symptom of a more serious condition, such as hypertension, diabetes or vascular disease, so it's best to get checked by your physician.

Meanwhile, to help *boost* your efforts, here's an interesting Native American remedy you may want to try...

Cornsilk tea helps to prevent impotence, and it's also said to enhance a man's sexual performance. Take the silken hairs from 6 ears of corn, and boil them in 3 cups of water for 10 minutes. Strain out the silk, let the tea cool and drink the 3 cups throughout the day. Do the same thing the next day and the day after that—for a total of 3 days in a row. You will then be ready to test this remedy.

Cornsilk tea is a mild diuretic, which is the reason it's believed to make a man ready and "good to go."

Fertility

There are some persistent myths out there that many people believe about fertility. But we feel it's important to dispel these mis-*conceptions*. *Here's the full truth...*

◆ Overall good health doesn't necessarily mean that a person is fertile.

◆ Weight (either overweight or underweight) can affect a person's ability to conceive.

◆ Sexual positions do NOT play a part in the success of conception.

◆ The results of some recent studies concluded that a man's underwear—no matter how brief or tight—does NOT cause a decrease in sperm count.

◆ Ovulation day is the *last* day on which to conceive. Having sex on the 2 days prior to ovulation offers the greatest chance of conception.

This fact is so important that we repeat it below...along with other suggestions that may help stack the deck in your favor.

◆ Ladies, just say "no" to champagne and wine. One study showed that downing 1 alcoholic beverage a day will cut your odds of conceiving by half. Not so for men. No matter how much alcohol they drink, their fertility remains the same. (That said, smoking can significantly reduce a man's potency.)

◆ Men, take royal jelly—up to 1,000 milligrams (mg) a day—to increase your sperm count and make those little swimmers more aggressive.

For an ovulation calculator, visit *www.baby hopes.com/ovulation-calendar,* or consider a trip to your drugstore to check out the following...

◆ **Fertility monitor and test strips**—Based solely on hormone monitoring, the monitor and test strips display a woman's personal level of fertility (low, high or peak) and her chance of conceiving.

◆ **Digital basal thermometer**—Used to monitor body temperature. A temperature increase near the middle of a woman's menstrual cycle can indicate when ovulation is occurring.

◆ **Ovulation test kit**—This tests for the *luteinizing hormone* (LH) surge, which lets a woman know when she is about to ovulate. Having sex 2 days prior to ovulation generally gives the best chance of conception.

Fever

The average human body temperature is 98.6°F. *Fever* is a term that refers to a temperature that is higher...typically above 100°F in adults. Fever is a *symptom* of illness—not a disease itself. It is the body's response to an outside stimulus, usually an infection.

There are 2 schools of thought with regard to treating adults' fever—either let it run its course, or bring it down. In general, a fever below 104°F can be allowed to run its course…but if it's any higher than that—or if the fever persists for more than a day or so—contact your physician. You may need emergency medical attention.

In the meantime, you can cool a fever by pouring a little bit of rubbing alcohol on a soft cloth and massaging it on the insides of your elbows, in back of your knees and also on your forehead and neck.

 CAUTION: DO NOT use rubbing alcohol on a child. Rubbing alcohol applied externally can be toxic to a child.

Food Poisoning

According to Medline Plus (*www.nlm.nih.gov/medlineplus*), a service of the US National Library of Medicine and the National Institutes of Health, food poisoning affects between 60 and 80 million people worldwide each year.

Food poisoning tends to occur at picnics, large social functions and in school cafeterias. These are situations where food may be improperly refrigerated, or food-preparation techniques may not be sanitary.

The most common causes of food poisoning are undercooked meats and eggs, improperly refrigerated dairy products (like mayonnaise mixed in coleslaw or potato salad) and unwashed produce. *The next time you're in charge of the coleslaw and burgers, here's a preventive measure…*

When added to food, spices like garlic, cloves, cinnamon, oregano and sage may help to prevent food-related *pathogens* (the living microorganisms in food, including *E. coli* and *Staph aureus*) from proliferating in improperly prepared foods.

Daniel Y. C. Fung, PhD, professor of food science and an internationally acclaimed microbiologist, and his team of researchers at Kansas State University in Manhattan, discovered that moderate amounts of spices—that is, enough to actually taste the garlic, cloves or cinnamon, etc.—will help prevent raw or undercooked food from making eaters sick.

That said, the best way to prevent food poisoning is to practice meticulous food preparation—wash your hands and all cooking/preparation surfaces thoroughly and cook foods to the recommended safe temperature. (For more information, *see* "Thermometers/Cooking Temperatures" on pages 64–65 of Chapter 2, "The Best-Ever Food Secrets.")

Gout

Gout tends to come on suddenly—but you'll know when you have it. Caused by a buildup of uric acid in the joints, it usually settles in a person's big toe or knee. Gout can be extremely painful, but is also extremely treatable.

Your gout symptoms should subside if you can avoid consuming mushrooms, oatmeal, shellfish, salmon, sardines, anchovies, asparagus, legumes, meat (especially organ meat, such as liver), meat gravies, yeast products (including bread and beer), alcoholic beverages, soda, fried foods, rich desserts, pastries and spices. *In addition, these remedies should help…*

◆ Drink celery-seed, dandelion or yarrow tea after meals. If the tea is loose rather than in tea bags, follow the brewing instructions on the box. (All of these teas are available at health-food stores.)

◆ If it's corn season, simmer 3 fresh corncobs in 1 quart of water for 15 minutes. Discard the cobs, and pour the water in a jar and refrigerate it. After each meal, heat up and drink 1 cup of the corncob tea.

◆ Eating 4 ounces of fresh bing cherries a day is the best way to treat gout. You can also flush the excess uric acid out of your system by drinking 6 ounces of cherry juice 2 or 3 times a day, or taking 1 tablespoon of cherry concentrate 3 times a day.

◆ *Quercetin* (available in health-food stores) is a flavonoid* that inhibits uric acid production —in the same way that prescription drugs do.

The recommended dosage is 1,000 milligrams (mg) of quercetin taken along with 1,000 to 1,500 mg of *bromelain* (an enzyme that enhances the absorption of quercetin), 2 to 3 times daily between meals. Bromelain can also help reduce the inflammation that is caused by gout.

 CAUTION: Do not take aspirin for gout pain. Doing so can raise levels of uric acid in your system.

*Flavonoids are plant substances that act as antioxidants and anti-inflammatories in the body.

 Sensual Gout Prevention

To prevent gout, have sex! Yes, sexual activity (specifically ejaculation) helps to reduce uric acid levels in fertile men. So, that should give you something to think about...or something to do in the name of preventive medicine.

Guilt

Is something nagging at you? Something that you regret or feel remorseful about? Follow the findings of Los Angeles–based psychologist Yvonne Thomas, PhD (*www.yvonnethomasphd.com*), and get your mind to release the buildup of this negative, guilty feeling. (And if that's all there is to it, then you may not even need the following exercise.)

Before doing the "good-bye guilt" exercise, ponder this—is it possible that the thing about which you feel guilty has been forgotten by everyone except you? Depending on your answer to that question, all you may need to do is forgive yourself.

Otherwise, just take a pen and paper and write down whatever it is that's bothering you. Then tear the paper into tiny pieces and throw it away, along with the guilt or regret. Gone! We hope you start to feel lighter and better, right then and there.

Gum Disease

See "Bad Breath, Gum Disease and Toothaches" on pages 110–111.

Hair

Spraying, teasing, blow-drying, setting, volumizing, coloring, perming—all are forms of hair torture. No wonder your mane is dry and damaged! *Never fear, my dear—help is here...*

In a small bowl, thoroughly whisk together ⅛ cup of your favorite shampoo along with 1 teaspoon of avocado oil (we use high-quality Maranatha oil, available at health-food stores) and ½ tablespoon of coconut milk (available at supermarkets). Shampoo as usual, then rinse. This doctored-up shampoo should nourish your hair and leave it with a wonderful shine.

 NOTE: If you have very long hair, double the amounts in the avocado/coconut/shampoo formula.

Headache

There are about 150 different categories of headache, and nearly everybody suffers from an occasional bout. But 45 million Americans endure regular headaches several times a week—most typically, the so-called *tension headaches*, which can be brought on by fatigue, hunger, stress or overexertion.

Some 28 million people suffer from *migraine headaches*, which scientists now believe result from inherited abnormalities in certain areas of the brain and are triggered by changes in weather or sleep patterns, fatigue, food sensitivity, stress and other factors.

Other types of headaches are generally caused by sinus problems, hormonal changes... even eating ice cream too fast.

> ⚡ **CAUTION:** Regularly recurring headaches might be caused by eyestrain or allergies—or something more serious. Seek professional medical attention immediately if the headache comes on suddenly, is very painful or is accompanied by a fever.

Whatever the reason for your aching head, here are some remedies that should help the pain go away...

◆ Prepare a cup of green tea with sprigs of fresh mint, or combine a green tea bag and a peppermint tea bag to make a big, strong cup of headache-relieving tea. Drink the minty tea and your headache should fade away in about 15 minutes. (Drinking 1 or 2 cups of regular coffee at the onset of a tension headache—NOT a migraine—can help prevent it from getting worse.)

◆ If you feel a headache starting, peel a small piece of fresh ginger (available in the produce section of most supermarkets) and chew it. It's strong and may be hard to get used to, but it beats having the headache.

◆ Migraines—especially morning migraines—can be related to biorhythm disturbances. These problems may be caused by low levels of *melatonin*—a naturally occurring hormone that regulates the body's biological rhythms, such as sleep cycles.

A small but significant study was conducted at the Hospital Israelita Albert Einstein in São Paulo, Brazil—it gave 40 test subjects 3 milligrams of melatonin 30 minutes before bedtime, every night for 3 months.

At the end of the study, more than ⅔ of the patients said that the frequency of their migraines was reduced by 50% or better. Some patients had no subsequent migraines. And, of the subjects who continued to develop migraines, the melatonin helped to decrease their frequency, intensity and duration.

> **NOTE:** If you would like to take melatonin to help prevent migraines, discuss the appropriate dosage with your health professional. Melatonin may eventually lose its effect if high doses are taken for too long.

◆ To prevent migraines, mix 2 teaspoons of unfiltered apple cider vinegar (available at health-food stores) and 2 teaspoons of honey in an 8-ounce glass of water. Drink it once or twice a day.

This remedy works like magic for some (former) migraine sufferers. So, if you're not allergic to honey, and you're not on a sugar-restricted diet, it's worth a try.

Hiccups

A hiccup is a spastic contraction of the diaphragm—the large circular muscle that separates the chest from the abdomen.

A movement of some kind—or a disruption in your breathing pattern—can put an end to the spastic contractions. There are dozens of ways to do that.

And we thought we had heard them all, but then we came across this great cure for the hiccups—stand up straight with your arms reaching for the sky, and wiggle your fingers. (Try it—what have you got to lose?)

Hypertension (High Blood Pressure)

More than 65 million Americans have been diagnosed with *hypertension* (high blood pressure). If you're among those people, obviously you're not alone. We urge you to discuss your lifestyle with your doctor and, once and for all, do something to change whatever is causing the problem. *These remedies may also help…*

◆ Blood pressure readings can vary by as much as 40%, depending on the time of day you do the testing. At a recent annual meeting of the American Society of Hypertension (*www.ash-us.org*), it was reported that the best time to check your blood pressure is during the morning through midday—blood pressures tend to be higher at the end of the day. Also, blood pressure is generally higher in winter than in summer.

◆ Taking your blood pressure at home is a good way to monitor the success of your efforts between doctor visits. It also gets you used to having your blood pressure taken so that you won't be nervous when you're cuffed in the doctor's office.

◆ Some research studies have shown that eating dark chocolate daily helps decrease blood pressure. Before you make a dash for the candy counter, check out "Heart-Healthy Treats" on page 117. But check with your health care professional before indulging, especially if you are on a special diet.

Deep-Breathing Exercise for Hypertension

If you are among the millions of Americans who have been diagnosed with high blood pressure, consider doing a simple breathing exercise to help get your numbers down.

Once a day, lie on your back and put a book on your stomach, right over your bellybutton—sure, go ahead and use this book—and gently inhale to the count of 7 and exhale to the count of 10, moving the book up and down. Do this for 10 minutes.

Deep-breathing exercises like this calm the muscles surrounding the small blood vessels and allow blood to flow more freely. This helps lower blood pressure.

Indigestion

Mild indigestion usually produces 1 or a combination of symptoms—stomachache, heartburn, nausea and vomiting or gas (flatulence). *If you are suffering from a minor tummyache, here are some remedies that might help…*

 CAUTION: Severe indigestion or chronic stomach pain may be a symptom of something more serious than you think, such as a heart attack or pulmonary embolism—seek medical attention immediately.

◆ Grate the peel of an organic grapefruit. Spread out the tiny grated bits on paper towels and let them dry overnight. Then store them in a jar with a lid and label it clearly. Keep it in your medicine cabinet…then, whenever you have an upset stomach, take ½ to 1 teaspoon of the grapefruit bits. Chew them thoroughly before swallowing.

◆ If you're traveling, bring along all-natural peppermint toothpaste. As soon as you have that upset stomach feeling, swallow ½ teaspoon of the toothpaste. (Check the label first to make sure it's safe to swallow.)

◆ If you're in a restaurant, order peppermint tea, or carry strong peppermint candies with you. (There are always a few Ricolas or Altoids in each of our purses.)

Insect Bites/Stings

For an insect bite or sting, home treatment is often all that is needed. The problem is, you may not be at home when you're bitten or stung. *Here are a few remedies that should be appropriate for the great outdoors...*

 CAUTION: If you have a history of being allergic to stinging insects, keep an antihistamine or a physician-prescribed emergency sting kit with you at all times.

   If any insect bite gets very swollen or seems out of the ordinary, get professional medical attention immediately.

◆ As soon as you know you've been bitten by a bug, take 3 leaves from 3 different kinds of trees, and mash them with your fingers (unless you happen have a mortar and pestle outside with you).

   When the juice of the leaves comes out, apply it to the bite. In minutes, the pain should be gone as the bite starts to heal.

 NOTE: Make sure that you get the leaves from *trees*, and not plants growing on the ground—rubbing poison ivy or poison oak on your skin would be much worse than an insect bite!

◆ If you're at a picnic and you get an insect bite or sting, apply mustard to the area to help relieve the pain, itch and redness. You can also use ice cubes or a paste made from the table salt and water to bring down the swelling.

 FYI: The Great Greek Way

In the 6th century, BC, Greek scientist Pythagoras (he of the famous mathematical theorem) used mustard to treat scorpion stings. We don't know exactly why it works, but mustard is very healing.

Insomnia

Trouble falling asleep...waking up too early and not being able to fall back asleep...frequent awakenings...and waking up feeling unrefreshed—each of these problems is a symptom of insomnia.

   In a survey conducted by the National Sleep Foundation (*www.sleepfoundation.org*), 58% —more than half—of American adults reported having insomnia at least a few nights a week. More women than men are insomniacs, in part because of hormonal changes, such as premenstrual syndrome (PMS), menstruation, pregnancy and menopause.

   Male or female, if you consistently can't get a good night's sleep, take a look at your life. Once you figure out what may be keeping you awake, talk to your doctor (it's always a good idea to discuss sleep problems with a health care professional). Then you can make the necessary changes to get more restful sleep. *Until then, these remedies might help...*

◆ Do you exercise at night and then have trouble falling asleep? *A-ha!* Exercising right before getting into bed will energize you and boost your alertness, making it harder to fall asleep. Instead, exercise at least 3 to 6 hours prior to bedtime—this will help you fall asleep and stay asleep.

◆ When you go to bed, say a prayer and, as studies confirm, you should fall asleep easier and wake up fewer times during the night. The act of praying relaxes the body and mind, and may contribute to your well-being.

◆ In a glass jar with a lid, combine 2 tablespoons of unfiltered apple cider vinegar (available at health-food stores) with 1 cup of honey. Keep the closed jar next to your bed. When you have trouble sleeping, take 2 teaspoons of the mixture, close the jar again, and expect to be asleep within 20 minutes.

◆ In terms of melatonin (a naturally occurring hormone that regulates biological rhythms, such as sleep cycles)…more is definitely *not* better. In fact, Richard Wurtman, MD, director of MIT's Clinical Research Center in Cambridge, Massachusetts, believes that taking too much melatonin will eventually cause it to have no effect at all.

After analyzing several studies, Dr. Wurtman and his research team learned that even just 300 micrograms (mcg) is all that's needed for restful sleep. Most people take 10 times that amount, and then they lie awake, wondering why the melatonin isn't working.

Intestinal Parasites

There are 3 major groups of intestinal parasites that can wreak havoc with a person's gastrointestinal tract—*protozoans* (organisms having only 1 cell), *nematodes* (roundworms) and *cestodes* (tapeworms).

Parasites can make their way into a person's intestine orally via uncooked or unwashed food, contaminated water and/or hands, as well as through skin contact with larva-infected soil or contact with animals. People can also become infected if they kiss or have oral sex with a partner who is infected.

 CAUTION: Infection from parasites can be serious and debilitating. It's important to work with a health professional who is experienced in treating parasites—most people will need to take an antibiotic.

While you're waiting for your doctor's appointment, you may want to brace yourself and try the following drink…

◆ Licensed naturopathic physician Nancy Caruso, ND, based in St. Charles, Michigan, suggests adding 1 smashed clove of garlic to ¼ cup of extra-virgin olive oil—drink this concoction 3 times a week for 5 weeks. Your excessive gas and bloating should disappear, along with the parasites.

 NOTE: Although extra-virgin olive oil is a healthy monounsaturated fat, keep in mind that ¼ cup (4 tablespoons) contains a whopping 480 calories and about 56 grams of fat (enough fat for an entire day).

We recommend that if you drink Dr. Caruso's tonic, you try to reduce your overall calorie and fat intake for that day.

◆ If you're traveling in countries where papaya is readily available, you should eat this fruit every day. It will help digestion and prevent intestinal parasites, especially if you're eating foods that you're not used to eating.

More important than the papaya meat are the seeds inside the papaya. Eat 1 teaspoon of the raw seeds daily. They have a surprisingly peppery taste. They also contain *papain*, a protein-digesting enzyme that breaks down the cell walls of the parasites.

 Don't Drink the Water!

The best way to prevent parasitic infection is to avoid consuming local water (and ice cubes) when you travel—many local water systems are untreated and unsanitary. Be sure to wash all raw fruits and vegetables with clean bottled water, and wash your hands thoroughly after handling them.

Itchy Skin

Dry skin is the most common cause of minor itches...but if you keep scratching it, it could turn into a rash. Other itches are caused by more serious conditions, like eczema or poison ivy. If the itch or rash is persistent, see a doctor.

◆ For generalized itching, take stinging nettle capsules (available at health-food stores...follow the recommended dosage on the label).

◆ Colloidal oatmeal—oatmeal that is finely ground or pulverized—is great for therapeutic baths. Use tepid water in the bath—hot water will further inflame the itchy area, and dehydrate your skin rather than lubricate it. Add several cups of the oatmeal to the bath as it's filling up. Then soak in it for 10 minutes. Pat your skin dry—do not rub it.

 CAUTION: If your skin is severely inflamed, do *not* take an oatmeal bath. It can be irritating.

 FYI: Slippery When Wet!
When colloidal oatmeal mixes with water, it becomes slightly milky and gives the water a slimy consistency. That's good because it coats the skin...moisturizing, softening and protecting it. The bad part is that the bathtub will become very slippery.

Please be *extremely careful* getting out of the tub or have someone help you out. And be sure to clean the tub thoroughly when you're done, so that whoever uses it next does not slip and fall.

Also *see* "Eczema" on pages 122–123—the oolong tea remedy has been known to suppress the allergic reaction that causes itchiness and skin inflammation.

Jellyfish Sting

With more than an estimated 2,000 species of jellyfish, only about 70 are toxic to humans. But *only* doesn't help when you want to swim, sail or surf in unfamiliar waters. To be safe, ask the lifeguards or other locals what to be aware of with regard to jellyfish and other sea urchins in the water.

And remember—even detached tentacles found on the beach pose a hazard to humans. They can still sting if touched.

Use the following remedies to treat the sting as soon as possible, and it should go away in a day or so. In the meantime, it might be a good idea to see a doctor—just to make sure that the bite isn't serious.

 CAUTION: If you're stung by a jellyfish or any kind of sea urchin, and you develop muscle spasms and find it hard to breathe, get medical treatment immediately.

◆ Most jellyfish are not dangerously poisonous, but their sting can be painful. It can burn, and you may break out in a puffy rash that may blister. Do not rub the stung area. It will spread the venom.

If you—or someone helping you—need to touch the stung area, wear gloves, if possible. Jellyfish venom can be easily spread to exposed hands and then to other body parts.

◆ Putting fresh water on the sting will cause the release of more venom. Put saltwater or ice on the area instead—this will neutralize the venom and cool the heat. Applying distilled white vinegar will also help to deactivate the toxins.

◆ If you're stung on a hairy part of your body, shave it. You'll remove the stingers and some of the venom that's embedded in the hair.

◆ If you have access to some adhesive tape, apply it to the stung area. When the sticky tape is pulled off, it should take some of the stingers with it.

◆ For quick relief from a painful jellyfish sting, pour saltwater (saline), beer, vodka or wine on the stung area. These liquids help to dry out the stingers, which will relieve the pain from the venom. (And—although it's a less savory option—urine works, too.)

 NOTE: If you are stung by a stingray, hot water works best to get out the barbs.

If you are stung by a Portuguese man-of-war, DO NOT apply alcohol or urine—both can cause the release of more venom.

Liver Cleansers

The average adult human liver weighs about 3 pounds and is roughly the size of a football. It's located in the upper-right-hand part of the abdomen, behind the lower ribs.

The liver has more than 200 functions—including converting food into chemicals that the body needs to stay healthy…eliminating toxic substances from the blood…controlling the production and excretion of cholesterol…producing bile (which is essential for digestion)…and at least another 196 other jobs. Gosh—and you thought *you* were busy!

 CAUTION: If you have hepatitis (inflammation of the liver) or any other problem with your liver, be sure to talk to a health professional before trying any of these remedies.

Needless to say, it's important to take care of your liver. *According to Mayan folk medicine, the best liver cleansers are…*

◆ **Lemon and water**—Add the juice of 1 lemon (about 2½ tablespoons) to an 8-ounce glass of lukewarm water. Have this drink before you even eat breakfast. It's a fantastic way to start your day.

◆ **Parsley**—Eat fresh parsley in salads, or juice ½ cup of the leaves along with ½ beet and 1 carrot for a sweet, healthy drink.

◆ **Radish leaves**—The most nutritious part of the plant are the dark green leaves, which are packed with minerals and vitamins. Wash them thoroughly and add to salads or soups.

◆ **Onions**—Ancient Mayan healers believed that eating cooked and/or raw onions will keep the liver clean, healthy and working well.

Menopause

The North American Menopause Society (*www.menopause.org*) sponsored a Gallup survey that revealed that more than half (51%) of the respondents (American women between the ages of 50 and 65 who had reached menopause) said they were the happiest and the most fulfilled now, compared to how they felt when they were in their 20s, 30s or 40s.

If you are suffering from menopause-related depression, that Gallup survey should help cheer you up and give you hope. *And so should the following remedy…*

Boil 1 tablespoon of dried rosemary in 1 pint of water for 5 minutes. Let it steep for 10 minutes. Then strain out the herb and drink the tea—1 cup between breakfast and lunch…another cup between lunch and dinner.

Rosemary, an herb that was among the Mayans' most important spiritual healing plants, acts as an antidepressant for many menopausal women. It is rich in vitamins A and C as well as the minerals phosphorus, iron, magnesium and zinc. The herb is a wonderful tonic for the nervous system.

Menstrual Cramps (*Dysmenorrhea*)

Most cases of *dysmenorrhea* (severe menstrual cramps) are caused by very strong uterine contractions. More than half the women who menstruate experience these severe cramps.

And, according to the American College of Obstetricians and Gynecologists (*www.acog.org*), approximately 1 out of every 10 women experience menstrual pain that is so severe that she is unable to perform her normal routine for several days each month.

Well, help is finally here for those women who are mildly to intensely affected during that time of month...

◆ Yarrow tea (available at health-food stores) is extremely effective when it comes to easing menstrual cramps (and both of us speak from experience!).

Put 1 teaspoon of yarrow or 1 tea bag in a cup of just-boiled water. Let it steep for about 7 minutes. If it's loose tea, strain and drink. If it's a tea bag, remove it and drink.

Drink 3 cups throughout the day if cramps persist. One cup daily would usually do it for each of us.

◆ If you've run out of yarrow tea, and you're doubled over with cramps, drink a few ounces of pickle juice from the jar in your refrigerator. (For some reason, this saying comes to mind—"What doesn't kill you, makes you stronger.")

 NOTE: In some cases, painful cramps may be caused by a deficiency in *acetylcholine*, the neurotransmitter that stimulates your muscles to work. Pickle juice contains acetic acid, which helps the body make the much-needed acetylcholine. So drink a little pickle juice—it's worth a try until you get some yarrow tea.

Muscle and Joint Pain

If you're experiencing muscle and/or joint pain, see your health care professional for a diagnosis—it's a good idea to get a checkup to find out *exactly* what's causing that pain.

Also, take a look at your daily routine. Do you carry a heavy shoulder bag or briefcase? Are you a mom, dad or child-care worker who's constantly lifting and carrying small children? Does your job require some type of movement that may be causing this discomfort? If you figure out that the pain is due to a repeated physical pattern of activity, break the pattern and the pain will probably go away.

Whether the pain is recurring, or a 1-shot deal, the following remedy should help...

Add 2 cups of Epsom salt (available at drugstores) to a warm bath, and relax in it for 20 minutes or more. The salt's natural mineral —magnesium sulfate—relieves and soothes aches, pains, soreness, stiffness and stress.

 CAUTION: Keep Epsom salt away from your mouth, nose and eyes. The delicate tissues can become irritated.

Nail Fungus

Nail fungus is usually caused by a mild trauma that makes the nail—usually the big or little toenail—vulnerable to a fungal infection. And you don't have to walk around barefoot on a shower floor or in a locker room to get an infection. Fungi are everywhere—in the air, in the dust and even in the soil.

To help prevent a fungal infection, wear comfortable shoes and hosiery that allows your feet some breathing space. Wash your feet daily and dry them thoroughly.

Also, keep your toenails trimmed and, before using pedicure tools, be sure to thoroughly disinfect them with rubbing alcohol.

If you already have an infection, use the following remedy every day to help eliminate fungus and make your nails more resistant to developing future infections...

Combine 1 quart of warm water and ½ cup of apple cider vinegar (available at health-food stores) in an appropriate-sized basin or bowl (a sturdy plastic shoebox also works well for soaking either a hand or a foot).

Soak the affected toenails or fingernails in the vinegar solution for 15 minutes, then towel-dry your foot or hand. Follow that with a hair dryer set on *warm* for 1 or 2 minutes.

As the final step of this treatment, prepare a mixture of equal parts tea tree oil (a powerful fungus fighter) and lavender essential oil (a strong antimicrobial agent), and dab the solution on the infected nails.

 NOTE: Nails take a long time to grow out completely—about 3 months for fingernails and 6 months for toenails. So be aware that, if you try this remedy, you may have to stick with it for a while.

Nausea

Nausea is an uneasiness in the stomach that may lead to vomiting—which can be a great relief. But it's not always convenient to relieve yourself if you're not at home.

Here are a few suggestions to relieve nausea, whether you're at home, at someone else's home, at a restaurant—or anyplace else, for that matter...

◆ Both of us carry either peppermint Altoids or Ricola cough drops at all times. These strong peppermint candies help make the nausea disappear as they settle the stomach.

◆ When you're feeling nauseous, sniff a piece of lemon or orange peel. To intensify the peel's scent, keep squeezing it as you sniff.

◆ Smelling the printer's ink from a black-and-white newspaper can relieve queasiness.

 CAUTION: Severe indigestion or nausea may be a symptom of a more serious ailment, such as a heart attack or pulmonary embolism. If the nausea persists, seek medical attention immediately.

Nosebleed

Nosebleeds tend to be quite minor and can be brought on by several things—allergies, cold weather, sinus infection and other illnesses. When your nasal passages are irritated by rubbing, picking or blowing, the tiny blood vessels break...and the blood flows.

 CAUTION: Nasal hemorrhaging—blood flowing copiously from both nostrils—requires immediate medical attention. Call 911 and get to the nearest hospital emergency department.

Also, recurrent nosebleeds may be a symptom of an underlying ailment. Seek appropriate medical attention.

◆ For an *occasional* nosebleed, the first thing to do is to gently blow your nose. Then pinch the fleshy part of your nostrils closed for 10 minutes. (If the nosebleed hasn't stopped after 10 full minutes, you should go to the emergency department.)

◆ You can also stop the nosebleed with lavender oil. Apply the oil with your finger, a cotton swab or a cotton ball. The oil should be soothing to your nasal membranes as it stops the bleeding.

 CAUTION: Licensed naturopathic physician Nancy Caruso, ND, based in St. Charles, Michigan, recommends using only *therapeutic grade* essential oil (available at health-food stores or through naturopathic doctors) to treat nosebleeds.

If you use an adulterated essential oil (oil that's cut with alcohol or other chemicals), it will burn the inside of your nose.

Poison Ivy/Oak/Sumac

Poison weeds—such as ivy, oak and sumac—grow in just about every part of the United States. And these weeds all produce the same sort of uncomfortable reactions. Chances are, if you're allergic to 1 weed, you're allergic to them all. It's estimated that as many as 10 million Americans are affected by these plants.

 NOTE: Poison oak is to the West Coast of the US what poison ivy is to the Eastern part of the country. So the poison ivy remedies here should also be effective for treating poison oak.

◆ If you know that you brushed up against poison ivy, rinse off the area as soon as possible—within 3 to 5 minutes. Any cool liquid will work—water, soda, beer...the trick is to wash it off *quickly*.

The fast washing will help to neutralize or deactivate the poison ivy's *urushiol oil*—the nasty stuff that causes the itchy blisters.

It's important to use cool/cold water only—either warm or hot water will open the skin's pores and let in the urushiol oil.

◆ If you don't have time to wash away the oil—and you already have itchy blisters—then put ½ cup of baking soda in a bowl and add cold, black, brewed coffee...keep adding until it's the consistency of thick paste.

Apply the paste and leave it on until it flakes off by itself. This paste should take away the itch and help dry out the blisters. Keep reapplying it until the itching stops.

◆ If you don't brew your own coffee, then make a baking soda paste—mix 1 tablespoon of baking soda with 1 teaspoon of water. Glop it on the affected areas, let it dry and eventually flake off. This paste should take away the itch and help dry out the blisters.

◆ Truth be told—neither of us has had personal experience with the following whiskey remedy. We heard about it from several reliable sources, but we urge you to proceed with caution. And you should always be aware of your surroundings in areas that have poison ivy.

To help prevent poison ivy infections, moisten a washcloth with whiskey, and rub your exposed body parts with it before going into areas that might have poison ivy.

 CAUTION: Do not use whiskey on broken skin—the alcohol can sting! And NEVER apply alcohol to children's skin—it can be toxic.

◆ Another way to prevent poison ivy infections is to spray exposed skin with a deodorant that contains *aluminum chlorohydrate* (such as Right Guard). This active ingredient prevents the urushiol oil from sticking to skin.

◆ You have to *really* want to immunize yourself to try this remedy...first, get a goat and let it graze in a patch of poison ivy (this will not harm the goat).

Once the goat has eaten the poison ivy, put on gloves, cover up the rest of your body, and then milk the goat. Throw away that first milking. The *second* milking is the one to drink. Drink at least 2 cups of goat milk, and it will immunize you for a year. We *kid* you not.

Sinus Problems

Sinus conditions can be caused by changes in the weather, by a room that's overheated, by air-conditioning, by dust, by...gosh, by anything that collects in a person's mustache.

Symptoms of a sinus condition include a runny nose, nasal congestion, headache, neck ache, teary eyes, swollen eyelids—and then some. To discover your sinus trigger, pay attention to when and where symptoms begin.

And to help alleviate the symptoms, try the following elixir…

You can clear up sinus congestion with a "brace-yourself" cocktail. In a pot, combine 1 cup of tomato juice, 1 teaspoon of finely minced fresh garlic, ¼ to ½ teaspoon of cayenne pepper (depending on your hot-spice tolerance) and 1 teaspoon of lemon juice.

Heat the mixture until it's warm, but not too hot to drink. Pour it in a 10-ounce glass and brace yourself—then drink it. Expect good results quickly.

Sore Throat

A sore throat is a mild inflammation and should go away in about 3 days. But if it lasts longer, see your health care professional and get tested for strep throat—this bacterial infection of the throat and tonsils *must* be treated with antibiotics.

But mild sore throat pain can be alleviated with this soothing drink…

In a mug, mix ¼ teaspoon of cayenne pepper, ½ teaspoon of ginger powder and 1 rounded tablespoon of honey. Add 8 ounces of just-boiled water and stir. When the mixture is cool enough to drink, stir it some more and take a big sip. While the mixture is in your mouth, lean your head back, then lean your head to the right and then to the left, and finally, swallow.

Continue doing this with the rest of the drink. When you get down to the bottom of the mug, discard the residue. If your throat is still sore a few hours later, have another mug.

Swab Away Sore Throats

To prevent sore throats, gently and carefully give your ears a once-over with a cotton swab dipped in 3% hydrogen peroxide—every day. Doing this should help prevent a sore throat.

Stress and Anxiety

There are as many symptoms and outward manifestations of anxiety as there are reasons for it. According to the National Health Interview Survey—reported by the Health Resource Network (a national nonprofit health education organization, *www.stresscure.com*)—75% of the general population experiences at least some stress every 2 weeks. Tranquilizers, antidepressants and antianxiety medications account for about 25% of all prescriptions that are written in the US each year.

We're hoping that you'll find positive, natural ways to cope and won't need a prescription. *Here are some ways to help you calm down, chill out, hang loose and feel happy—or at least feel happier…*

◆ Turn up the music—literally. According to a report in *Athletic Insight, The Online Journal of Sport Psychology* (*www.athleticinsight.com*), it's hard to hold on to or focus on negative thoughts while listening to loud music.

 CAUTION: Be careful not to listen to music that is so loud that it can cause hearing loss or other damage to your ears.

Extended exposure to any noise above 90 decibels may injure your hearing—as a guideline, normal conversation is about 50 to 60 decibels, and most "loud music" is around 100 decibels.

◆ According to neurologist David Perlmutter, MD, founder of the Perlmutter Health Center in Naples, Florida, people who supplement with 1 or 2 grams of fish oil daily tend to have lower levels of stress hormones during anxiety-producing situations. The fish oil's DHA (a healthful fatty acid) helps regulate *serotonin*, the brain's feel-good chemical.

◆ Soothe your tension by stimulating the acupressure point (*Yingtan*), which is ¼" above the midpoint of your eyebrows. Once you've located it, use your middle finger to tap on it lightly for 10 seconds. Hey, just by stopping you'll feel better.

◆ Add magnesium, the antistress mineral, to your daily supplement regime. Nan Kathryn Fuchs, PhD, a nutritionist practicing in Sebastopol, California, and editor of the Women's Health Letter (*www.womenshealthletter.com*), says that when under stress, the body uses more magnesium than normal, and it takes it from anywhere it can—like your vital organs and bones.

Supply your body with 300 milligrams (mg) of magnesium daily to help cope with stress, and not at the expense of your organs and bones.

◆ Breathing easy is a key to relaxation, especially in stressful situations, such as having a job interview or speaking in public. Wearing too-tight clothes may be keeping you from breathing freely from the abdomen. Men, loosen your belts and ties. Ladies, loosen your belts and wear larger pantyhose that do not constrict your waistlines.

Wearing more comfortable clothes will allow you to expand your stomach as you take a few deep breaths. Those deep breaths will help you feel relaxed and less stressed, plus the inhaled oxygen will give you a boost of energy.

◆ Calm down with a very simple and effective eye exercise from clinical psychologist Fred Friedberg, PhD, author of *Do-It-Yourself Eye Movement Techniques for Emotional Healing* (New Harbinger). *Follow these instructions...*

Select 2 objects in front of you—something in the extreme right of your field of vision, and the other in the extreme left. Then, as you think about how stressed you are, move your eyes from 1 object to the other as fast as you can, 25 times.

Pause for a moment, then repeat the eye movement another 25 times...then pause and repeat for a third time. This repetitive side-to-side action slows your heart rate, blood pressure and breathing, which should make you feel a lot calmer.

◆ Soak a washcloth in ice-cold water and put it on the nape of your neck. Keep it there for about 10 minutes...enough time for the cold to constrict blood vessels and slow circulation to the head. That decreases activity in the brain's stress-storing region (the *hippocampus*), making it easier to shut down your anxiety-causing thoughts.

◆ Aromatherapy may make your drive time a lot more pleasant. Use 1 or 2 drops of essential oil (available at health-food stores) on a cotton ball, and tape it to your dashboard or wherever the scent will waft to your nostrils.

Need a picker-upper? Use peppermint oil for alertness, and cinnamon oil to increase blood flow. Have a problem with road rage? Calm down with some lavender or jasmine oil. Does traffic cause you anxiety? Orange oil will help to quell those nerves.

◆ Summer seems to be the most stressful season for women, according to Amy Niles, former president and CEO of the National Women's Health Resource Center in Red Bank, New Jersey (*www.healthywomen.org*). We wonder—could it simply be the mere thought of putting on a bathing suit?

Whatever the reason, chill out by walking barefoot and activating reflexology points in the soles of your feet. Doing this should have an immediate soothing effect from head to toe. Just be sure that wherever you walk barefoot—in your home, out on the patio, around the pool, on the lawn or at the beach—it's clean and free of stuff you don't want to be stepping on.

Walking barefoot is also a good idea for men who suffer from summer stress.

◆ Mitchell L. Gaynor, MD, senior medical oncology consultant at The Strang Cancer Prevention Center in New York City and author of *Sounds of Healing* (Broadway Books), said, "I've never found anything more powerful than sound and voice and music to begin to heal and transform every aspect of people's lives."

And so, to prevent stress, *sing...sing a song.* The breathing patterns used for singing are said to create chemical changes in the body that lower levels of the stress hormone *cortisol.* This helps to prevent stressful, anxious feelings. We know from experience that singing is an upper—it really does make you feel happier.

 Stress-Busting Advice

David J. Schwartz, PhD, author of *The Magic of Thinking Big* (Fireside) and an authority on motivation, gave great advice when he said, "To fight fear—act. To increase fear—wait, put off, postpone."

Both work. It's up to you—and only you—to dispel your fear by plunging in and doing whatever needs to be done, or to do nothing except let that fear fester and grow.

Skin Blemishes/Stretch Marks

Skin is among the human body's largest and heaviest organs. The average adult's skin measures 19 square feet and weighs about 9 pounds. The thinnest sections of skin are on your eyelids...the thickest are on your palms and the soles of your feet. Stretch marks occur when the skin gets stretched (obviously) and suffers small micro-traumas under the outer layer.

To help prevent stretch marks—or to speed the healing of them or any scars or blemishes on your 19 square feet of skin—you should know about coconut oil. *And we're here to tell you about it...*

Bruce Fife, ND, director of the Coconut Research Center in Colorado Springs, Colorado (*www.coconutresearchcenter.org*)—and the man we refer to as "The Coconut King"—recommends the daily use of extra-virgin coconut oil (available at health-food stores or on-line at *www.simplycoconut.com*) to help prevent stretch marks. It's especially appropriate for pregnant women and body builders, who are prone to developing stretch marks.

If you already have stretch marks or scars or blemishes of any kind—such as cuts, burns, insect bites, warts, moles—they will heal faster and with less scarring (if any) when treated with coconut oil.

Fife says to put the container of coconut oil in hot water until the oil is very warm—that way, it will be absorbed more efficiently and penetrate deeper into the skin. Massaging the oil into your skin also increases absorption.

The secret to getting the best and fastest results is to keep the coconut oil on the injured skin continually until it's healed. Apply the oil as often as is practical throughout the day.

It also helps to cover the oil with a bandage made from a piece of clean, white cloth or gauze, then put a piece of plastic wrap over the gauze and keep it all in place with medical tape. (Adhesive bandages like Band-Aids don't work well because the oil tends to dissolve the adhesive, causing them to slip off.)

Sties

If you develop a painful red bump on your eyelid, then you probably have a sty. A sty occurs when the oil glands around the eyelid get infected and inflamed. The classic remedy for when you feel a sty coming on (you know, that annoying little twinge each time you blink) is to rub a gold ring across it. *But when it's too late to "go for the gold" because the sty has already blossomed, try this remedy...*

Cut a potato in half and, with the edge of a spoon, scrape out about 3 tablespoons of raw potato. (Be sure to scoop—using a grater will make the potato too watery.)

Then roll up the glob of potato in a clean white handkerchief...or a triple layer of cheesecloth...or unbleached muslin, then lie down and place the poultice over your closed eye. Keep it there for about 40 minutes. When you take off the poultice, gently clean the area around your eye with a damp cloth.

If that annoying twinge doesn't ease off by bedtime, then apply a fresh poultice again before you go to sleep. Expect the sty to keep getting better until it completely disappears within a few days.

 CAUTION: If the sty doesn't improve after 2 days, contact your doctor. You may have an eye infection or other serious problem that needs to be treated with a topical or oral antibiotic.

Sun Damage

Studies show that 80% of sun damage is from "incidental exposure"—such as waiting outside for a bus, walking to your car or sitting in a restaurant with the sun shining in. So, even though the average person may not be basking on the beach, he/she is exposed to the sun for about 18 hours a week...enough to cause skin damage if protective measures aren't taken. *So, listen up—for the sake of your skin...*

A moisturizing lotion can put a barrier between damaging sunlight and your skin. Choose a lotion with a *sun protection factor* (SPF) of at least 30—this means that, if you begin to burn after 10 minutes, SPF 30 extends your protection about 30 times longer, depending on your complexion and/or skin type, the strength of the sunlight, and the brand and amount of sunscreen you apply.

Most products are good at screening out the sun's UVB rays—the type of ultraviolet rays that cause sunburn and skin cancers. But you want a product that also offers protection against UVA rays—the kind that put wrinkles in your skin. Any of these ingredients—*oxybenzone* or *titanium dioxide* or *parsol 1789*—will help block out some of the UVA rays. Use the lotion daily—women, before applying makeup...men, after shaving.

Toothaches

See "Bad Breath, Gum Disease and Toothaches" on pages 110–111.

Tongue Burn

Which muscle of the body, proportional to size, is the strongest? Yes, it's the tongue! Well, with all the talking we do, it's no surprise that it gets lots of exercise.

Aside from helping us form words, whistle and blow bubbles with gum, the tongue makes it possible for us to enjoy food. Taste buds are located in different areas of the tongue, mostly around the edges. They are sensitive to 5 specific tastes—bitter, sour, salty, sweet and *umami* (the taste that is associated with monosodium glutamate—MSG).

It was probably 1 of those tasty foods that caused you to burn your tongue. *Here are a couple of soothing suggestions...*

◆ If you've just eaten spicy-hot food and you feel as though your tongue is on fire, swish whole or 2% milk, sour cream or yogurt around in your mouth. (Indian restaurants, which tend to serve very spicy food, always have yogurt in the kitchen.)

◆ When you eat something made with chili peppers or cayenne pepper and you burn your tongue, quickly eat a piece of chocolate. *Casein*, a protein in chocolate, seems to attach to and remove the *capsaicin*—the *hot-hot-hot* chemical compound found in chili peppers—from the tongue's nerve receptors. In any case, it's a good excuse to eat a piece of chocolate!

Urinary Problems

Also *see* "Bladder Infection" on page 111.

The urinary system includes the kidneys, ureters, bladder and urethra—organs and ducts that are involved in the body's release and elimination of urine.

The average adult bladder holds about 24 ounces of urine. When the walls of the bladder are stretched, nerve impulses trigger the urge to urinate. That usually happens when the bladder contains 10 to 16 ounces of urine.

The kidneys, which are located in the back of the abdomen, 1 on each side of the spine, are the principal organs of the urinary system. They filter the blood—all of it—once every hour.

Yes, the urinary system is extremely complex and, when something goes wrong, it needs to be properly diagnosed and cared for.

> **CAUTION:** Any problem with the urinary system is a serious condition that should be evaluated and treated by a health care professional. Talk to your doctor before trying any natural remedy.

◆ A recent study conducted by Robert Levin, PhD, director of research at the Albany College of Pharmacy in Albany, New York, showed that eating ¾ cup of fresh grapes daily can prevent problematic urination urgency and frequency in men who have enlarged prostates.

Why? Because an enlarged prostate can compress the urethra, which reduces blood flow to the bladder and may cause muscle damage. That muscle damage can be responsible for increasing the urgency and frequency of urination. The grapes' antioxidants help protect against possible muscle damage.

> **CAUTION:** An enlarged prostate can be a sign of cancer. If you are having difficulty with urination, it's important to consult your physician.
>
> In addition, some prostate problems can be a symptom of a more serious condition—see your doctor for a thorough checkup.

◆ If you have a urinary tract infection (UTI), consider the following advice from Bruce Fife, ND, director of the Coconut Research Center in Colorado Springs, Colorado (*www.coconut researchcenter.org*) and author of *Coconut Cures* (Picadilly Books).

He says to drink 6 to 8 glasses of water and consume at least 3½ tablespoons of organic extra-virgin coconut oil (available at health-food stores) every day. Divide the oil into equal doses and take them throughout the day.

Start doing this the moment you suspect an infection is coming on. The earlier you start treatment, the quicker the problem will be resolved.

> **CAUTION:** If you think you have a bladder infection or UTI, it's very important to check with your health care professional before trying any natural remedies. You may need to take an antibiotic.

◆ Drink 100% unsweetened cranberry juice (not juice blends) or take cranberry supplements to get the powerful antioxidants called *proanthocyanidins*. Look for grapeseed extract (also called *pycnogenol* or PCO) and follow the dosage instructions on the label.

Warts

The medical term for the common wart is *Verruca vulgaris*. (Don't you think a wart looks like a *Verruca vulgaris*?) Most warts appear on the hands and face—warts that appear on the sole of the foot are known as *plantar warts*. Warts are generally thought to be caused by some type of virus.

No other ailment is as rich in handed-down, ridiculous remedies as warts. For example—rub the wart with a stolen egg, then wrap the egg in brown paper and leave it at a cross-roads. When a stranger picks up the package and breaks the egg, the wart will be transferred from you to that stranger.

The most incredible thing about some of the outrageous remedies we've heard is that they actually work for some people! Here are a couple of *sensible* remedies that should work… and you don't even have to steal an egg.

◆ For plantar warts, mix 1 teaspoon of baking soda with 1 tablespoon of castor oil to create a paste. Put it on the plantar warts and cover with a small, square bandage. Apply a fresh mixture of the paste every morning and evening until the warts are gone. It could take anywhere from 1 week to 1 month.

◆ Dab some tea tree oil (available at health-food stores) on the warts with a cotton swab or cotton ball, and cover them with a bandage. Do this twice a day. Be consistent and patient.

 CAUTION: Genital warts are a symptom of a sexually transmitted disease which *must* be treated by a health care professional.

Weight Control

We won't bore you with talk about eating sensibly and exercising to lose weight—we're sure you've heard it all before.

But what you may not know are some suggestions that can help you stick to that sensible eating plan, speed up your metabolism and expand your healthful menu with interesting foods and beverages, as well as promote behavior modification, which will help you make healthier choices. *Read through the hints below with an open mind, then go to the supermarket with an adventurous spirit…*

◆ Bored with celery and carrot snacks? Enjoy the fresh, licorice-like taste of fennel stems and fronds, either raw or cooked. Fennel (available at most supermarkets and grocery stores) is a good digestive aid and may even help to lower blood pressure. There are only 12 calories in 3½ ounces.

◆ Have a *mochaccino* without the cost and without the calories. Mix 1 packet of sugar-free hot cocoa mix with 1 teaspoon of instant coffee. Add hot water (according to package directions) and stir. As a special treat, add a dollop of Cool Whip Lite (2 tablespoons contain 20 calories and 1 gram of fat).

◆ In a study, people who suppressed their mid-morning hunger pangs by eating 1 tablespoon of peanut butter every day lost nearly twice as much weight as those people who didn't eat the nutty spread.

Additional research reveals that daily peanut-butter eaters (limited to only 1 tablespoon a day) tend to eat 333 fewer calories a day on average.

 Go Nuts for This Spread!
Try to eat all-natural peanut butter rather than commercial brands, which may have a lot of added sugar. We eat Maranatha Organic Peanut Butter (available at health-food stores). It has no sugar, no salt, no hydrogenated oils, no trans fats…nothing but dry-roasted peanuts and incredibly good taste.

◆ At your next meal, compare your serving sizes (*see* page 143) to the "correct" serving sizes that we should all be eating. Then gradually work your way down to the proper size portion.

One serving...	*Is the size of...*
1 cup of cereal flakes	a closed fist
3 ounces of cooked meat	a deck of cards
3–4 ounces of grilled or baked fish	a checkbook
½ cup of pasta	an ice cream scoop
½ cup of fruit	a tennis ball
1 serving of bread	a cassette tape
½ cup of vegetables	a light bulb
1½ ounces of cheese	4 dice
1 teaspoon of butter	a thumb tip
2 tablespoons of peanut butter	a ping pong ball

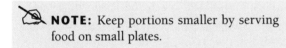

NOTE: Keep portions smaller by serving food on small plates.

◆ There is a Zen Buddhist technique called "mindful eating," which is also known as "conscious eating." It means to pay attention to the smell, taste and texture of your food, and try to enjoy every mouthful.

    Also be aware of your honest feeling of satisfaction. Keep asking yourself how hungry you are. Then establish a rating system from 1 to 5, with 1 being very hungry and 5 being very full. Learn to stop yourself when you reach 3 or 4.

◆ A study that was reported in the *Journal of Clinical Endocrinology & Metabolism* revealed that drinking 2 liters (½ gallon) of water over the course of the day will burn up to 100 calories total. Based on the findings of that study, bodybuilding.com concluded that by drinking cold water, most people will burn even more calories because the body has to work harder to bring the water up to 98.6°F.

NOTE: For more information on the *Water-Induced Thermogenesis* study, visit the Web site for the *Journal of Clinical Endocrinology & Metabolism—http://jcem.endojournals.org.*

◆ And now, from Japan, there's Enova. It's a cooking and salad oil—light and tasteless—that can be used for baking, sautéing and frying or as an ingredient in salad dressings and marinades. It contains natural soy and canola oils that have been processed to contain a higher concentration of *diacylglycerols* (DAG).

    Studies demonstrate that DAG has many health benefits, including reducing levels of post-meal blood triglycerides (LDL, the "bad" cholesterol), and it is quickly flushed out of the body before it can feed fat cells.

    In preliminary studies, scientists at the Chicago Center for Clinical Research report that having 2 tablespoons of Enova daily can help you lose 50% more weight and burn 30% more fat.

    Enova is cholesterol free, has lower saturated fat levels than conventional oils and has 0 grams of trans fat. It's available in supermarkets or on-line at *www.enovaoil.com.*

◆ There's a lot of talk about the many benefits of green tea, including its ability to increase the amount of calories the body burns. The credit is not due to the small amount of caffeine it contains, but to a powerful antioxidant called *epigallocatechin gallate* (EGCG).

NOTE: As a bonus, drinking green tea may help lower your cholesterol.

    When you shop for green tea, check the label—it should say that the tea used is standardized for caffeine and EGCG. Also make sure it's unsweetened and/or sugar-free. Drink up to 8 cups of green tea a day, along with

Use Your Nose to Lose Weight

"The stronger the flavor of the food, the stronger its power to satisfy and reduce hunger," says Alan R. Hirsch, MD, neurologist, psychiatrist and director of The Smell and Taste Treatment and Research Foundation in Chicago. *Based on his extensive research, Dr. Hirsch offers the following suggestions…*

◆ Sniff each bite of food quickly 5 times before eating. Fast sniffs signal food messages to the brain—this decreases hunger and works to satisfy the appetite without consuming excess calories.

◆ The odor molecules of fresh-cut strawberries travel directly to the *limbic system* of the brain (which is involved in emotional behavior). From there, the molecules activate the *hypothalamus* (the brain's satiety center) and trick it into believing that you've eaten more than you have.

So, if you want to feel full faster, put some fresh-cut strawberries on your plate and *sniff-sniff-sniff-sniff-sniff*.

◆ Choose to eat hot foods. The heat and steam from the food send flavor molecules up the back of the throat and into the brain's satiety center faster than cold foods.

◆ Keep a bar of chocolate with you (we suggest dark chocolate). When the snack urge takes hold, sniff the candy—but don't eat it.

Just the smell of food can trick your body into thinking you've already eaten it.

eating a healthy, balanced diet. And (sorry to have to remind you) exercise regularly.

◆ If you are a couch potato, then laugh off the pounds by watching humorous television programs. In a study conducted at Vanderbilt University in Nashville, researchers found that subjects who watched TV shows that made them laugh burned up 20% more calories than non-laughers. The researchers calculated that laughing for 10 to 15 minutes a day could burn about 50 extra calories. And that's no joke!

◆ In restaurants, at home or at other people's dinner parties, eat the amount of food that's right for you, then place your eating utensils

(probably a knife and fork) crisscrossed to form an X on top of the remaining food. As the plate sits there in front of you, the X will signal *NO MORE*.

And if that's not enough to stop you from mindlessly munching on the rest of the food, you'll think twice about picking up soiled silverware.

◆ A great way to sneak in exercise is by walking a dog. If you don't want to get your own, walk your neighbor's pooch or volunteer at a local animal shelter.

According to researchers at the College of Veterinary Medicine's Research Center for Human–Animal Interaction at the University of Missouri–Columbia, subjects in their study group averaged a weight loss of 14 pounds during a 1-year walking program.

◆ If you walk on a chilly day (with or without a dog), you can boost your metabolic rate by up to 4 times, due to muscle tensing when you shiver. That means you're burning off a lot of extra calories. Just don't stop off at the

Compounding Pharmacy

A compounding pharmacy customizes medication to meet individual patient needs, based on the specifications set by the prescribing physician. Compounding pharmacists have studied chemical interactions and compatibilities more thoroughly than all other health care professionals, plus they have the ability to prepare various dosage forms.

Scott Berliner, RPh, a natural pharmacist and nutritional educator practicing in Monroe, New York, explained to us that there are situations where compounding use becomes a necessity. *He cites these examples…*

◆ When medications are not available commercially and an alternate chemical or dosage form is required. Another scenario may be that a patient is allergic to a preservative in a prescription medication.

◆ When medications are not stable, small quantities can be prepared more frequently to ensure stability.

◆ When commercial medications need alteration. A patient may need a different dosage form

(lozenge instead of capsule…liquid instead of tablet), flavor (especially for children) or strength (seniors often require doses lower or higher than others).

Example: Mr. Berliner makes an anti-inflammatory that is 5 times as strong as ibuprofen, yet it does not upset the stomach and can be applied directly to the inflamed site to bring down swelling. His pain medications are made without Tylenol and can be time-released for extended action.

Mr. Berliner is owner and president of Life Science Pharmacy, Life Science Nutrition and VetRxLife Science Pharmacy. In his practice at Life Science Pharmacy (845-781-7613, *www.life sciencepharmacy.com*), all medications are made in a sterile laboratory from raw material using Food and Drug Administration (FDA)-approved, United States Pharmacopoeia (USP)-approved and National Formulary (NF)-approved products.

To find a compounding pharmacist in your area, contact the International Academy of Compounding Pharmacists' referral service at 800-927-4227 or *www.iacprx.org*.

corner coffee shop for a calorie-laden caramel latte to warm you up.

◆ If you feel a food binge coming on, take a walk…a brisk walk. Your urge to binge will cool down as your body heats up.

◆ Two short exercise sessions a day will stimulate the metabolism more than 1 longer session. Take a brisk 15-minute walk in the morning and another in the afternoon. Do this 5 days a week for a full month, and see if it makes a big difference on the scale.

◆ Sit at the edge of a chair with your spine straight and stay that way for 10 minutes. Do this while you're in front of your computer and again when you're in front of the TV.

Sitting erect, unsupported, for 10 minutes twice a day will help tone your core (midsection) muscles. You should see a difference within 2 weeks.

◆ Daily prayer or meditation stimulates the *amygdala* (the part of the brain that controls emotional behavior) and activates the release

 NOTE: Do not start any exercise program without permission from your doctor. Trying to do too much too soon can sometimes lead to injury.

Consult your health care professional for a physical evaluation and instructions on how to start an exercise routine.

of *serotonin*, a neurotransmitter that helps curb cravings.

In some studies, subjects prayed daily and lost weight without dieting or exercising. Of course, prayer *plus* a sensible diet and exercise routine is ideal and most advisable for good health as well as weight loss.

◆ Colorado–based nutritional expert Marc David, former workshop leader at Kripalu Center for Yoga and Health in Lenox, Massachusetts, and author of *The Slow Down Diet: Eating for Pleasure, Energy, and Weight Loss* (Healing Arts Press), said that the practice of praying before eating a meal—and by this, he meant heartfelt praying, not just rattling off a few words of thanks for the food—puts the body into a relaxation response. The effect of regular prayer before meals is that you can completely change your digestive metabolism in less than 1 minute.

Changing your metabolism through prayer means you can absorb nutrients better, have greater blood flow and oxygen to the stomach and manufacture more digestive enzymes. We *pray* it works for you. ■

■ Products ■

RESPeRATE

This is a medical device for lowering blood pressure. It is not a drug and has no side effects, and has been cleared by the Food and Drug Administration (FDA).

The relaxing treatment takes only 15 minutes a day (at least 3 days a week…more often is better). With earphones and a portable CD player, the simple and pleasant 15-minute sessions guide your breathing to therapeutic levels.

Source: InterCure, Inc., 877-988-9388, *www.resperate. com.*

 CAUTION: If you take blood pressure medication, continue to take it as directed under your doctor's supervision, even while you are using the RESPeRATE system.

Automatic Blood Pressure Monitor with Comfit Cuff

Have you heard about "white coat syndrome"? That happens when your blood pressure rises because you're nervous when seeing your doctor. You can keep track of your blood pressure at home, and here's an easy-to-use home test that remembers and stores your blood pressure history—and may even detect an irregular heartbeat. According to the manufacturer, this technology is particularly important for people with certain forms of arrhythmia or heart disorders.

The Cuff fits arms that are 9" to 17" around. (Ask a salesperson for another size if this does not fit.) Comes with an illustrated instruction manual, a brochure explaining blood pressure, 4 AA batteries, an AC adapter and a storage case.

 NOTE: Omron also has a Wrist Blood Pressure Monitor that only weighs about 9 ounces and is great for travel.

This monitor is available all over the country at retail and drugstores.

Source: Omron Healthcare, Inc., 800-634-4350 for customer service, *www.omronhealthcare.com.*

Purebrush Antibacterial Toothbrush Purifier

We never want to be without this product! We think it's an important way to help maintain good health. Why? This purifier eliminates the dark, moist environment that allows microbes to thrive and multiply in a toothbrush holder.

We don't even like to think about germs or bacteria that can spread from 1 toothbrush to another, making family members sick. You can even reinfect yourself with your own toothbrush.

Purebrush self-starts with each use, holds up to 4 toothbrushes at a time, bathes the toothbrush(es) in warm disinfecting germicidal ultraviolet light for 1 hour, and turns off automatically.

This purifier has been clinically proven to eliminate 99.9% of all yeast, molds, viruses, bacteria and illness-causing microorganisms from your toothbrush.

Source: Murdock Laboratories, Inc., 650-579-1352, *www.purebrush.com.*

Innerscan Body Composition Monitor

This high-tech scale is a sleek addition to the bathroom. And it's a great gift for any health-conscious person.

An easy-to-read LCD screen displays your weight, calculates your body fat percentage, body water percentage and bone mass.

This machine can estimate how many calories you can consume within the next 24 hours to maintain your current weight, which is helpful for dieters.

The monitor can store personal details for up to 4 people between the ages of 7 to 99. There's also a Guest Mode for anyone who wants a reading just once. Four AA batteries are included.

 CAUTION: Do not use the body composition feature if you are pregnant, or have a pacemaker or any other electronic implanted medical device.

Source: Tanita Corporation of America, Inc. To find a store, call 800-9-TANITA (982-6482) or visit *www.tanita.com.*

Cholesterol Monitor

In the comfort and convenience of your own home, find out between doctor's visits whether your diet, exercise and medication are affecting your cholesterol numbers.

The CardioChek® Cholesterol Monitor gives a reliable total cholesterol reading within 1 minute using just 1 drop of blood. It also includes information on your triglycerides, ketone and glucose levels. The monitor is compact, portable and the batteries are included.

Source: Polymer Technology Systems, 715-235-1464, *www.polymertechnology.com.*

 NOTE: A test strip is required for each cholesterol test. These strips must be purchased separately because they have an expiration date.

CHAPTER 6

Head-to-Toe Magic

In the wise words of Parisian designer Coco Chanel—an influential fashion icon in the early part of the 20th century—"I don't understand how a woman can leave the house without fixing herself up a little—if only out of politeness. And then, you never know, maybe that's the day she has a date with destiny. And it's best to be as pretty as possible for destiny."

If you're concerned with *destiny*, or you just want to know how to take care of yourself and your belongings, you're on the right path and page. There are lots of useful suggestions here—for men as well as for women—that will help to make you even more perfect than you already are.

SKIN CARE FOR YOUR BODY

Skin is the human body's largest organ. The average adult's skin measures 19 square feet and weighs about 9 pounds. The thinnest sections of skin are on your eyelids...the thickest are on your palms and the soles of your feet.

The average person sheds about 1½ pounds of skin particles every year. That means, by the time you're 70 years old, you will have lost a little over 100 pounds of outer skin! Those shed skin particles get replaced with another coat of skin about once a month.

That may be more than you need to know. So let's move along to all that you may want to know about taking care of your skin.

Bumps Remover

Do you have lots of tiny bumps on the backs of your arms? They are clogged pores. To unclog them, mix together 2 tablespoons of sugar, 1 teaspoon of lemon juice and 5 drops of vegetable oil. Rub the blended mixture on your bumpy skin in a circular motion for about 1 minute on each arm. Rinse off with warm water.

The citric acid in the lemon unclogs the pores as the abrasiveness of the sugar sweeps away dry skin and the oil moisturizes the area, making your arms nice and smooth.

Soften Dry Elbows

Cut a lemon in half and drizzle a few drops of baby oil on each half. Stand over the sink and put an oily lemon half over each elbow (1 at a time!)—then squeeze and twist the lemon like you are juicing it. Put the lemon halves on a table and place your elbows in them. Stay that way (if you can) for 30 minutes. Then rinse and dry your newly cleaned and smoother elbows.

All-Natural Underarm Deodorant

Fill a clean, empty face-powder container with baking soda, and apply evenly under your arms using a powder puff or blush brush. The alkaline nature of baking soda balances pH levels to neutralize odor.

✳ Power Up Your Deodorant
If you have a real perspiration problem and feel more secure using a commercial deodorant, you can boost its power by applying baking soda over it to absorb additional moisture.

◆ If you've run out of deodorant, you can use antiseptic mouthwash or apple cider vinegar to neutralize odor. Just dampen a washcloth, and pat it on your armpits.

Underarm Stain Prevention

If you are wearing a light-colored shirt or blouse—and you don't want to let 'em see you sweat—stick a self-adhesive mini-pad (panty liner) on the inside armpits of your garment.

If profuse perspiring is a major problem for you, ask your doctor about Botox injections. They are now the standard treatment to help reduce sweat production.

Prevent Body Odor

Baths made with apple cider vinegar help fight off unfriendly bacteria and fungal overgrowth that may cause body odor.

A couple of times a week, pour 2 to 4 cups of apple cider vinegar in with your hot bathwater and take a nice soak for at least 10 minutes. Then either rinse off under the shower or just dry off…and trust that the smell of vinegar will disappear within 30 minutes.

For body odor prevention, it's best to use pure, unprocessed apple cider vinegar, which is available at health-food stores.

Temporary Varicose Vein Treatment

After taking a warm bath or shower, soak a few washcloths in witch hazel and wrap them around your legs, covering the veins. Sit with the towels on—with your legs extended—for 5 minutes.

Witch hazel has astringent and vasoconstrictive properties, which will temporarily lighten the appearance of varicose veins and help reduce inflammation.

SKIN CARE FOR YOUR FACE

According to writer Cynthia Ozick—"After a certain number of years, our faces become our biographies." How true it is. *Here are some hints to help make your face a best-seller…*

Firming Facial

Chocolate is rich in copper, an essential nutrient for the skin-firming connective tissues.

Mix 1 heaping tablespoon of unsweetened cocoa powder with enough heavy cream to form a paste. Apply it to your clean, dry skin and leave it there for 15 minutes. Then lick it off…*just kidding!* Rinse it off with lukewarm water and a washcloth, then pat dry.

Skin Beautifying Mask

Peel a ripe peach, remove the pit and pulse the fruit in a blender with 1 tablespoon of brandy. When it's a purée consistency, smooth it on your damp face. Relax and leave it on for 20 minutes. Then rinse it off with lukewarm water and pat dry. (Throw away any leftover purée.) This mask should unmask a radiant complexion.

DID YOU KNOW?

Peaches are rich in vitamin A and, when applied topically, the fruit helps protect skin against bacteria that causes pimples and blemishes. Vitamin A also builds *collagen* (the elastic fibers in skin), which helps to improve your skin's elasticity, tone and texture.

Cleansing Mask

Want to look pretty in pink? Apply a thin layer of Pepto-Bismol to your face. Leave on until it dries completely, then rinse it off with warm water and pat dry. The claylike mineral in Pepto-Bismol (and similar products) is *bismuth subsalicylate*, which acts as a cleansing agent and helps draw out the skin's impurities.

Unclog Pores

Boil 2 cups of water in a pot, then add 2 chamomile teabags. Cover the pot and let the teabags steep for 7 to 10 minutes. Put a towel over your head and hold your face about 12" above the uncovered, steaming tea. Stay that way for about 7 minutes. Then rinse your face with cool water and pat dry.

Chamomile has properties that help unclog pores, making them look smaller and your complexion look better.

Face and Neck Toner

Each time you yawn, use the opportunity to tone your face and neck muscles. Inhale deeply as you yawn and open your mouth as wide as it will go. As you exhale, stick out your tongue and roll your eyes upward.

Oily Skin Balancer

Use witch hazel as a balancing agent. Dab it on your face with a cotton ball first thing in the morning, last thing at night and anytime you feel your face is feeling oily.

Exfoliation Scrub

Mix 1 teaspoon of sugar with a few drops of champagne—enough to form a paste. In circular motions, apply the mixture all over your face and neck, then rinse it off with lukewarm water and a washcloth, then pat dry.

The enzymes that are in champagne's tartaric acid, along with the abrasive quality of the sugar, should do a super job of exfoliating your skin.

Make Pimples Disappear

◆ Dab the blemish with regular (non-gel) toothpaste...or lemon juice...or milk of magnesia. Leave it on overnight to dry out the eruption.

◆ Zap the pimple with eyedrop solution—dab it on throughout the day to make the pimple less noticeable as it heals. Eyedrops contain the capillary constrictor *tetrahydrozoline*, which makes redness disappear.

◆ Apple cider vinegar dabbed on with a cotton ball several times during the day will also dry out an oily pimple and should make it disappear within a day or so.

◆ Make a paste using equal amounts of cornstarch and rubbing alcohol—½ teaspoon of each should be enough—and put it on the pimple to dry it out.

Combating Age Spots and Freckles

Grate half of a medium-sized onion onto a piece of cheesecloth, then squeeze the juice into a small bowl. Mix in 2 teaspoons of distilled white vinegar and 1 tablespoon of 3% hydrogen peroxide. Using a cotton swab or cotton pad, lightly dab the solution on your spotty skin and let it dry. Do this in the morning and evening.

If you don't see results in 1 or 2 weeks, then you may have to learn to love your age spots and freckles.

 CAUTION: Keep hydrogen peroxide away from your eyes. Also, be aware that hydrogen peroxide tends to lighten any body hair with which it comes in contact.

Skin Slougher for Dry, Chapped Lips

◆ Mash 2 fresh strawberries with ½ teaspoon of honey. (If you have lips like Angelina Jolie, you might want to double the recipe.) Spread the goo on your lips and wait 5 minutes for the strawberries' fruit acids and the honey's healing enzymes to do their thing. Then wet a washcloth with warm water and clean off your lips.

◆ Form a paste by combining 3 drops of lemon juice with 1½ teaspoons of baking soda. Use a soft, dry toothbrush to brush the paste across your lips.

Once all of the dead skin cells have been scrubbed away, rinse and dry your lips, and then smooth on some castor oil or petroleum jelly.

◆ Puncture a vitamin E gel capsule, squeeze out the oil and mix it with ¼ teaspoon of sugar and a few drops of vanilla extract. Work it into your lips and let it stay on for 5 minutes. Then clean it off with a clean, wet washcloth.

MAKEUP

 Retired fashion designer Calvin Klein spent many of his workdays dressing the world's most beautiful women. According to Mr. Klein—based on his years of experience working with supermodels—"The best thing is to look natural…but it takes makeup to look natural." Here are some makeup tips that will help you look your best, naturally.

Lipstick

After applying lipstick, glide an ice cube over your lips. The ice will set the color and prevent it from bleeding, melting or smudging.

 Find Your Perfect Color
Before you apply lipstick, purse your lips together for about 30 seconds. When you stop, look at the color of your lips. That's the shade to match for your most natural lipstick color.

Do-It-Yourself Lip Gloss

Dig out the clump that remains from your favorite tube of lipstick, and put it in a small microwave-safe glass bowl along with an equal amount of petroleum jelly. Zap the bowl on *high* for 10 seconds at a time, until the mixture is melted. In between zappings, stir it with a toothpick. While it's still warm, transfer your new lip gloss to an empty gloss container (available at drugstores).

Prevent Eye Shadow Buildup

Brush translucent powder on your eyelids before applying powder eye shadow. If you use cream-based shadow, apply a bit of translucent powder over it. The translucent powder will set the eye shadow so that it won't collect in the crease of your lid, and the color will last a lot longer.

Eyeliner Protection

Typically, eyeliner pencil lead is soft and breaks easily. And when you sharpen it, there goes half the pencil.

Try this—put the pencil in the freezer for about 10 minutes, and sharpen it right before using it. The cold temperature hardens the pencil, which prevents the tip from breaking off in the sharpener and makes it easier to apply.

Keep Eyelashes Curled Longer

If you are used to using an eyelash curler—they can be tricky, you know—follow up by applying waterproof mascara. The waterproof formula contains synthethic components that will lock the curl in place.

Babyish Makeup Removers

- To remove eye makeup, just lather up a couple of drops of tear-free, hypoallergenic baby shampoo in a wet washcloth and softly dab each of your eyes. Then gently rinse the eye area with water. No mess. No sting. No liner. No mascara.

- Just as baby shampoo works for removing eye makeup, so do baby wipes for removing face makeup…even if it's waterproof. Baby wipes are especially good to use if you have sensitive skin.

- Mix 1 teaspoon of nonfat dry milk powder in 1 cup of warm water. Use the mixture on a washcloth to remove makeup. Then rinse and dry.

Makeup Touchups

- If you carry a small purse and don't have room for a makeup case, dip a cotton swab into whatever makeup you may need to refresh your face—eye shadow, concealer, lip gloss, blush, etc.—and place each swab in its own little resealable plastic bag. A few little plastic bags will take up very little space, and will help you look your best day and night.

- You want to wear that sleeveless gown to a special occasion, but you have a big black-and-blue bruise on your arm. If you have Caucasian skin, you can cover up the mark with the right color makeup—yellow!

  Yellow counteracts blue tones, so it becomes an effective bruise concealer. Use your finger to pat a yellow-based stick foundation (Wet 'n' Wild is a brand to try) over the mark, then put some face powder on a makeup sponge and gently press it over the spot to set it.

Eyebrow Taming

Take an old, clean toothbrush, give it a spritz of hairspray, then brush it over your brows. The brush will put the hairs in place, and the spray will keep them there.

After each use, clean your brow toothbrush with hot water.

HAIR

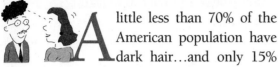

A little less than 70% of the American population have dark hair...and only 15% have blond. About 65% of us have straight hair, while 25% have wavy hair, leaving only 10% with hair that's curly.

On average, hair grows ½" each month—a little less in February, of course. Your hair grows fastest when you're in love...probably because your hormones are jumping for joy.

The average person loses about 70 hairs a day—more if you are sick, anemic, malnourished...or the love of your life leaves you.

Statistics like these are interesting, but they aren't going to help you take care of your hair. *However, these suggestions may...*

Hair Color and Dye

◆ Joseph Caron, color director at the Mark Garrison Salon in New York City, adds 2 packets of Sweet 'N Low to hair dye. The artificial sweetener neutralizes the acidity of the dye's ammonia, which helps prevent scalp irritation.

The sweetener can also be used with any at-home dye as long as it contains ammonia—read the label carefully.

◆ The standard advice to prevent hair coloring from getting on your face is to apply petroleum jelly near your hairline. Our experience is that the jelly gets in your hair. So while it prevents the dye from staining your skin, it may also prevent the dye from coloring some of your strands.

So forgo the jelly. If dye gets on your skin, wipe it off immediately with a moist paper towel. For hard-to-remove dye stains, rub a little non-gel toothpaste on the spot, then wash with soap and water.

The Color Boosters...

To boost your hair color, try an all-natural, homemade enhancer. First, boil 1 quart of water. Fold over a piece of cheesecloth—it should be large enough for you to add the ingredient that matches your hair color—and tie the cheesecloth closed with the ingredient inside. Remove the boiled water from the fire, add the cheesecloth and let it steep for 10 minutes.

Blondes: 3 tablespoons of dried chamomile

Brunettes: 3 tablespoons of fresh, bruised rosemary sprigs (bruise them by crumpling in your hand)

Auburn redheads: 1 chopped beet

Orange redheads: 1 chopped carrot

While the cheesecloth is steeping (and cooling), shampoo and rinse your hair as usual. Discard the cheesecloth bag and use the warm, color-enhancing liquid as a next-to-last rinse over your hair. The last rinse should be 1 quart of cool water.

Use this treatment once a month to add vibrancy to your hair color in a healthy, non-chemical way.

Redhead and Brunette Luster

After shampooing, rinse your hair with 1 cup of cool, brewed black coffee, then rinse with plain water. It should make your red or brown hair more lustrous.

Solutions for Chlorine-Damaged Hair

Try these remedies *after* you hit the pool…

◆ If your blond hair tends to turn green after swimming in a chlorinated pool, wash the chemicals out of your hair with club soda… lots of it.

◆ Dissolve 1 adult aspirin (325 milligrams) in 1 cup of warm water and massage it into your hair. Let it sit for 5 minutes, then shampoo. Rinse thoroughly.

Fresh Water Protection

Before you expose your lovely locks to the harsh chemicals in a pool, saturate your hair with fresh water from a shower, hose or faucet. Drenching your hair with plain water helps to block the absorption of chlorine.

Dry Shampoo

Sprinkle talcum or baby powder in your hair, massage it into your scalp and then brush it out thoroughly and completely. Your hair will be cleaner than it was, and it will smell nice, too.

Hair Volumizers

Use a hair volumizer *after* shampooing and towel-drying your hair…

◆ In a spray bottle, dissolve 1 teaspoon of table salt in 8 ounces of warm water. When the water is room temperature, spray your entire head of hair. The salty water adheres to hair strands and increase their diameter, making your hair fuller and ready to be styled.

◆ Combine ¾ cup of water with ¼ cup of beer. Dip a cotton ball into the mixture and dab it on your hair, starting at the roots. The yeast in the beer is said to expand each strand, giving the appearance of a fuller head of hair.

◆ Mix equal amounts of Epsom salt (available at drugstores) and deep hair conditioner in a pan and warm it. Then when the mixture is still warm but cool enough to touch, work it into your hair. Let it stay that way for 15 minutes, then rinse.

Hair Thickener

A deficiency in mineral salts is believed to be a common cause of thinning hair. Studies show that mineral-rich apple cider vinegar improves the overall health and volume of hair.

Drink 3 teaspoons of apple cider vinegar in a glass of water right before a meal or first thing in the morning. Do this daily for a few months, and you should see your hair thicken up.

Thicker Hair Bonus

In addition to thicker hair, don't be surprised if weight control or even weight loss seems easier while using the vinegar remedy.

Freeze Frizz

◆ If you wake up with out-of-control frizz and have no gel to tame it, take an ice cube and run it over your hair. It's a *cool* way to calm down frizz.

◆ Buy great-smelling fabric-softener sheets to run over your hair from top to bottom. *Cationics*, the softening ingredients in the sheets, lubricate hair and counteract the static that causes flyaways and the frizzies.

A Nutty Way to Care for Hair

Coconut oil (available at health-food stores) contains *lauric acid*, which helps do wonderful things for hair—it moisturizes, detangles, deflects the sun's damaging UV rays and prevents color-treated hair from fading.

Rub a dab of coconut oil between the palms of your hands, then smooth it over your hair. It's been used by women in tropical areas throughout the world for ages.

Shine On

Add 1 tablespoon of baking soda to your regular portion of shampoo—your hair will have a natural-looking shine and bounce.

Combat Oily Hair

◆ Add 2 tablespoons of Epsom salt to a bottle of your regular shampoo. Shake it thoroughly to dissolve the salts. Then, *every other time* you shampoo, massage your roots and scalp (the oiliest areas) with the Epsom-salted shampoo. (Yes, this means you'll need to rotate between 2 bottles of shampoo—1 plain and 1 salted.)

◆ Bend your head over the sink, and massage a handful of coarse (kosher) salt into your scalp. Let it stay there for about 5 minutes, then stand on newspaper or in the bathtub or shower, and shake or brush the salt out of your hair. The salt absorbs excess oil and destroys bacteria.

◆ Combine equal parts of plain water and apple cider vinegar in a spray bottle and keep it in the shower. After shampooing, spray the solution on your hair and comb it through. Wait 2 minutes, then rinse.

Vinegar's acetic acid is said to boost your hair's ability to stay oil free, plus it will restore fullness and shine.

Soften and Moisturize Dry Hair

◆ Put a dollop of sunscreen on your palm, rub your hands together, evenly distributing the lotion, and then massage it into your hair. The lotion in the sunscreen will moisturize and soften your hair and, as a bonus, the sun protection factor (SPF) will protect your hair against the sun's damaging UV rays.

◆ Cut a leg off an old pair of clean pantyhose, and turn it into a cap. Pull it over your head with your hair tucked in, and knot the top of the hose to stop it from dangling around.

Leave the cap on for about 30 minutes …enough time for the nylon to smooth the waves and for your body heat to tame the dry ends. When you remove the cap, your hair should be calmer and softer looking.

Herbal Dandruff Remover

Dandruff may be caused by an overgrowth of yeast on the scalp. Tea tree oil has antiseptic properties that can neutralize that yeast, doing away with the dandruff.

Add 5 drops of tea tree oil (available at health-food stores) to your regular amount of shampoo—but not dandruff shampoo. (Dandruff shampoo may actually remove protective oils from your hair and skin.) Some prepared shampoos made with tea tree oil are also available.

 NOTE: Tea tree oil has a pungent antiseptic scent that may take getting used to. When you open the bottle and take your first whiff, keep in mind that it will be diluted in your pleasant-smelling shampoo. And, after shampooing with it, you should rinse thoroughly.

 Mouthwash Stops Dandruff!
Twice a month, rinse your hair with antiseptic mouthwash to help prevent mild cases of dandruff.

Do not use this remedy if you have cuts or abrasions on your scalp—it may be irritating.

Combat an Itchy Scalp

Before you shower, work ¾ cup of lemon juice into your scalp. Wait 5 minutes, then rinse and shampoo as usual.

The lemon's citric acid helps slough off dead skin cells and kill the bacteria that clogs sebaceous (oil) glands, allowing the release of moisturizing scalp oils that will put an end to the itching.

Homemade Conditioners

◆ A classic conditioner is real mayonnaise—about ½ cup—massaged or combed into damp hair. Wrap your head in a towel and stay that way for 20 minutes. Then shampoo your hair as usual and wash the towel.

◆ If your hair seems damaged from commercial products…or the sun…or just neglect, you may want to try this deep conditioner—mash ½ avocado (which is rich in vitamins A and E) into ½ cup of real mayonnaise, and massage or comb the mixture into your damp hair.

Cover your hair with plastic wrap and stay that way for 20 minutes. Then shampoo, rinse and know that you did something good to help restore the health of your crowning glory.

Restore Bounce and Highlights

Add 1 teaspoon of champagne to 2 tablespoons of your regular amount of shampoo. Work it into your hair, washing and rinsing as usual. (You can also rinse with a bit of champagne after shampooing.)

The bubbly should help give your hair body and bounce, and the tartaric acid in champagne will bring out your hair's natural highlights—especially if you are blonde.

An End to Split Ends

Before going to bed, apply a coat of olive oil to the bottom 2" to 3" of your hair, and put on a shower cap. Leave it on overnight and shampoo as usual the next morning. Then say "Arrivederci!" to dry, brittle ends!

If sleeping with a shower cap is not for you, then apply the olive oil and shower cap first thing in the morning on a day when you don't have to go out. Wait 8 hours before shampooing.

All-Natural Styling Gel

Store-bought styling gels tend to be sticky and some make hair look as though it needs to be washed. Aloe vera gel (available at health-food stores and many drugstores) is a less sticky, chemical-free, effective alternative.

Get Big Bouncy Curls

Hooray—here's a lovely use for those empty cardboard toilet paper tubes. Wrap a section of damp hair around a tube (you may want to cut the rolls in half, depending on the length and thickness of your hair), and keep them in place with bobby pins or hair clips. When your hair (and the paper tubes) is dry, take out the tubes and unfurl your curls.

Avoid Too-Short Bangs

If you want to avoid too-short-bangs, keep a serious face when you're in the beautician's chair. A big smile raises your forehead, which may lead the stylist to lop off an extra ½".

Hairspray

◆ If you don't want your walls, fixtures and floor or carpet to have sticky hairspray buildup, then step into the shower to spray your hair.

157

Chances are your shower is used daily and the spray residue will be easily rinsed away.

If you need to see your handiwork, attach a small hand mirror to a shower wall with tile adhesive.

Breathe Easier

Hairspray usually contains a small amount of toxic chemicals and inhalants. Hold your breath when you use it, and your lungs will thank you.

◆ To unclog a sticky hairspray nozzle, dunk the clogged nozzle in rubbing alcohol and let it soak for 2 minutes. Rinse it under hot water and dry it, then you should be ready to spray away.

◆ Researchers at Purdue University in West Lafayette, Indiana, suggest this recipe for homemade hairspray—chop 1 lemon (for dry hair, use 1 orange). Place the chopped fruit in a pot with 2 cups of water. Boil the brew until half of the initial amount remains. Let it cool, then strain out the fruit…and pour the remaining liquid into a spray bottle (if it is too sticky, add more water). Store the bottle in the refrigerator until you need to give your hair a sticky spritz.

NOTE: Refrigerated, this homemade mixture will be good for about 1 week.

If you don't want to refrigerate the spray, you can add 1 ounce of rubbing alcohol as a preservative, and the mixture will keep for up to 2 weeks.

Get Rid of Sticky Buildup

Pour 6 tablespoons of flat beer in 1 cup of warm water. Get in the shower and pour the mixture through your hair. It should rinse away buildup from hair gel, mousse, spray and any other commercial product. Then rinse and shampoo as usual.

Removing Gum

◆ Ask someone how to get gum out of hair, and the answer is usually "peanut butter." Yes, it works, but it's still peanut butter that you're using. The truth is, almost any oil-based product—baby oil, cooking spray, petroleum jelly, etc.—will work just as well and may be easier to shampoo out.

◆ Make a paste with baking soda and water—start with 1 teaspoon of baking soda and add ¼ teaspoon of water…more water if you need it. It should be the consistency of runny oatmeal.

Work the paste into the gummed hair, and keep at it until all of the gum is removed. Once the gum is gone, shampoo as usual.

Tear-free Tots

Put a pair of swim goggles on your child and have a "Finding Nemo" or "Little Mermaid" adventure. The eyes will stay soap- and sting-free, and the experience will be more fun for both of you. Bath time will change from teary eyes to cheery eyes!

Hairbrush and Comb Cleaner

Put a leg from a pair of old pantyhose over the hairbrush's head, pushing it down so that all the bristles poke through the hose. Then yank off the hose, taking with it the clinging hair and dust from the brush. *Now you're ready for the second cleaning procedure…*

Fill a basin with warm water and add 4 tablespoons (¼ cup) of borax powder (available at supermarkets and drugstores), and 1 tablespoon of liquid dish detergent. Let your brush and comb soak in the solution for about 15 minutes, then rinse and dry the comb...let the brush air-dry.

Prevent Blow-dryer Burnout

Moisten a cotton swab with rubbing alcohol and use it to wipe the blow-dryer's vents (make sure the dryer is unplugged first!).

Remove dust this way once a month to keep your dryer performing at its peak. It will also keep your hair dust-free.

Improvised Diffuser

When you don't want your blow-dryer spewing out blasts of air at your hair, but you don't have a diffuser attachment, put a sock on it. A clean sock put over the end of the dryer for a few minutes will let heat through gently...which will allow you to create a variety of hairstyles.

Curling Iron Cleaner

Styling products often build up on a metal curling iron, which makes its curling power less effective. When the iron is cool and unplugged, clean it with a paste made from baking soda and water—start with 1 tablespoon of baking soda and 1 teaspoon of water. Wipe it off with a damp cloth, then dry with a soft, clean cloth.

TEETH

Children have 20 first teeth. Adults have 32 teeth. Just like fingerprints, everyone's set of teeth is unique, even those of identical twins. In this section, we offer all kinds of helpful suggestions to take care of your extra-special set of choppers.

Remove Stains Between the Teeth

Dip a strand of unwaxed dental floss in 3% hydrogen peroxide for about 30 seconds, then floss with it. (However, if you've smoked for 20 years and have nicotine buildup, please don't expect this to make much of a difference.)

Prevent Teeth Stains

It is said that many celebrities keep their teeth white and stain-free by drinking coffee, tea and red wine through a straw. Although it might raise eyebrows at the dinner table, it really *does* help prevent stained teeth.

Good to the Last Drop

If you think you've squeezed every last bit of toothpaste out of the tube—think again. Place the tube in a glass of hot water for 1 or 2 minutes. As the heat makes the tube expand, it will release any paste stuck on the sides, and you should be able to get 2 or 3 more squishes out of it.

Quick Toothpaste Substitute

When you run out of your regular toothpaste, make a paste with baking soda and water— use about 1 teaspoon of baking soda and ¼ teaspoon of water.

Brush extra gently at the gum line because the baking soda can be irritating. And don't forget to stop at the store to buy more toothpaste.

Simple Cleaners for Dentures Or a Retainer

◆ Mix equal amounts of distilled white vinegar and filtered or spring water (you don't want your dentures turning green from the chlorine in regular tap water), and put the solution in a clean cup. Soak your dentures or a retainer overnight, and get ready for some clean choppers!

◆ Dissolve 2 teaspoons of baking soda in 1 pint of filtered or spring water. Then drench a clean washcloth and wipe the dentures or the retainer. Rinse and wear.

BAD BREATH

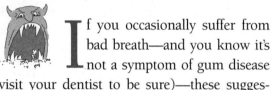 **I**f you occasionally suffer from bad breath—and you know it's not a symptom of gum disease (visit your dentist to be sure)—these suggestions may help you make your mouth fresh and sweet-smelling…

Homemade Mouthwash

Cinnamic aldehyde—the naturally occurring chemical compound in cinnamon that's responsible for its wonderful smell—also helps eliminate odor-causing bacteria in the mouth.

Boil 2 cups of water, then add 5 or 6 pieces of cinnamon stick (available at supermarkets) and let it simmer for 5 minutes.

Once it's cool, strain out the sticks and pour the liquid into an empty bottle. Use it as you would use any commercial mouthwash.

Tea for Sweet Breath

Make your after-dinner drink black tea (such as Pekoe). Researchers at the University of Illinois at Chicago reported that the plant chemicals *catechins* and *theaflavin* are released from black tea leaves during the brewing process. These compounds help shut down the digestive enzymes that trigger odor-producing bacteria in the mouth.

Odor Buster

After eating onion, garlic or anything else that stays on your breath, dip your toothbrush in a small amount of distilled white vinegar and brush your teeth as well as your tongue. This should help clean your breath and may even help whiten your teeth.

HANDS

Without thinking twice, draw a circle in the air with your left hand. If you drew the circle clockwise, chances are you're left-handed. More men are left-handed (12.6% of the male population) than women (9.9% of the female population).

But no matter which handedness you are, both hands should be cared for. *Here are some great ways to do that…*

Reverse Roughness and Dryness

Olive oil is an effective moisturizer. Massage some into your hands and give it time to sink in. (You may also want to put on a pair of rubber or latex gloves to avoid getting oil stains on whatever you touch.) After about 30 minutes, take off the gloves and wipe the oil off your soft, moisturized hands with a dry paper towel.

Soften and Exfoliate

Add 1 teaspoon of sugar to a dollop of baby lotion and rub it over your hands. The lotion softens and moisturizes, while the abrasive sugar exfoliates. This is an effective combination that will leave your hands looking and feeling good.

Cracked Skin Healer

Puncture a vitamin E gel capsule, squish out the oil and rub it on your hands. Do this twice a day—especially in cold weather when the hands tend to be dry and get painful cracks.

Pain-Easing Solution

If your hands are feeling achy, try this solution. In a bowl, combine 3 cups of hot water, 3 tablespoons of witch hazel and ½ cup of Epsom salt (available at supermarkets). Dip your hands in the solution for about 5 minutes...enough time for the magnesium sulfate in the mixture to penetrate and ease the pain in your joints.

Cleaning Grimy Hands

◆ Clean grease, grime or any other dirt from your hands by rubbing on a bit of solid vegetable shortening (such as Crisco) or margarine. Wash with soap and water to clean off the shortening or margarine.

◆ You can also knead some Play-Doh in order to de-grime your hands.

Odor Remover

If your hands have an unpleasant, lingering smell from bleach or any other strong, chemical cleaner, wash them with lukewarm water and some non-gel toothpaste. The mildly abrasive consistency of the paste will scrub off the nasty scent molecules from your skin's surface.

NAILS

If you've ever gotten a black-and-blue nail, you may have wondered how long it would take to grow out. Generally, fingernails grow from the root to the tip in about 6 months. Toenails take 2 to 3 times as long.

The medical community regards fingernails as a mirror of a person's general health. Doctors and nurses can see clues to conditions like asthma, improper nutrition and stress—just by looking at a patient's fingernails. So it's important to skip the polish and faux tips when you go for a medical examination.

If you look at your nails and are not happy with what you see, the following remedies are right at your fingertips...

Speedy Grower and Strengthener

Studies show that women who drink 8 ounces of soy milk daily have longer and stronger nails after 1 week.

In addition to soy milk—or instead of it—consider rubbing a tiny dab of non-gel fluoride toothpaste on each fingernail at bedtime. *Fluoride* is said to help nails grow faster and stronger. (You may want to use this fluoride treatment on the nails of just 1 hand first, to see if it really works for you.)

Brighten and Strengthen

Ginger ale contains *monopotassium phosphate*, a natural bleach and strengthening agent. Soak your nails in a glass of ginger ale for 10 minutes, and then rinse. Do this daily for at least a week, or until your nails look nice and bright.

Yellow Stain Remover

◆ The same abrasive and bleaching properties in tooth-whitening toothpaste can also work on nails. Squeeze out a portion of the paste on an old toothbrush and scrub your fingernails with it. Then wash it off and marvel at the difference.

◆ Soak nails for 15 minutes in a combination of ¼ cup lemon or lime juice and ½ cup water. The citric acid in the lemon/lime juice is a mild bleaching agent that will lift out the yellow stains, especially after you've taken off dark nail polish.

◆ Mix 3 tablespoons of baking soda with 1 tablespoon of 3% hydrogen peroxide. Use a cotton swab to wipe the mixture on top as well as underneath each nail. Wait about 5 minutes, then rinse your stain-free fingernails with warm water.

Shine Up Those Nails

Massage a few drops of olive oil into your nails, then use a tissue to buff them until they're oil-free and shining.

Ridge Remover

In a microwave-safe bowl, combine 2 parts of olive oil to 1 part lemon juice. Zap it for about 20 seconds—just until it's warm, not hot. Work the solution into the bottom part of each nail (where the nail meets the cuticle).

Spend 1 minute on each fingernail every day. You can refrigerate leftover solution, and microwave it again the next day.

Massaging the oil into the fibrous material that runs across the nail will help smooth the ridges and strengthen the nails. Give it a chance…be consistent…and do it daily.

Nail Polish and Manicures

It is said that nail polish was invented in China about 5,000 years ago, during the Ming Dynasty. The most popular colors at that time were red and black.

The Chinese polish was made from a combination of beeswax, egg whites, gelatin, vegetable dyes and Arabic gum. The modern-day form of nail polish is made from a refined version of automobile paint. *Here are some suggestions that will help you get the most out of your manicure and/or pedicure…*

Nonstick Nail Polish Cap

When you open a new bottle of nail polish, put a thin coat of petroleum jelly around the bottle's neck to prevent it from sticking all the other times you're going to use that polish.

Yellowing Prevention

Before you go out in the sun, apply a thin layer of lip balm—the kind that contains sunscreen—to your nails. It will block the sun's rays from yellowing your polish.

And while you're at it, put some balm on your lips, too!

Revive Old Nail Polish

If your nail polish has gotten thick and gloppy, let the bottle sit in hot water for about 5 minutes, and it should be good as new.

Fizz Away Your Polish

When your regular nail polish remover doesn't do a perfect job and there are traces of color left, try this—fill a cup with plain water and drop in 1 denture-cleaning tablet. Once the tablet dissolves, soak your nails in the solution for about 10 minutes.

The tablet's bleaching agents should leave your nails looking like a clean canvas, ready for the artist's brush and paint.

Get a Neater Manicure

Before you polish your nails, use a cotton swab to apply a thin layer of petroleum jelly to the skin around your nails. That way, you won't have to bother taking off the nail polish that dried on your skin while you were giving yourself a manicure.

 Secret to Slimmer Fingers

When you polish your nails, leave a thin unpolished line of space on each side of your nail. By applying polish just down the center of your nails, the illusion of narrower nails is created—which, in turn, makes your fingers look longer and slimmer.

Longer-Lasting Manicure

A clean, oil-free nail surface will help polish stay on longer. Try this—wipe your nails with a cotton ball or pad soaked with witch hazel. Witch hazel (available at health-food stores) is an astringent cleanser, and its salicylic acid helps to remove oils.

Prevent Chips

Every couple of days, polish *underneath* the edges of your nails to strengthen the tips—which are extremely vulnerable to chipping and breaking.

Emergency Nail File Substitutes

◆ If you're away from home and really need a nail file, desperate times call for desperate

measures—go to the nearest bathroom and file your snagged fingernail on the grout (that's the usually rough mortar or plaster used between sections of ceramic tile).

◆ If grout is out, then look around for a book of matches. You can file your nail on the abrasive emery-board-like panel on the back (where you strike the match).

FEET

There are 52 bones in your feet, which is ¼ of all the bones in your body. The average person uses those foot-bones to take about 6,000 steps a day. It's time to step up to the task of taking good care of your feet. *These suggestions can help...*

Eliminate Foot Odor

Boil 2 quarts of water, then steep 5 bags of black tea in it until the tea is cool enough to transfer to a basin (you can also divide the tea between 2 plastic shoe boxes). Soak your feet in the liquid for 10 minutes, then rinse and dry thoroughly.

Tannic acid, the natural astringent found in black tea, neutralizes and absorbs sweat, destroying the moist breeding ground for odor-causing bacteria.

 Socks and Soda Solution

Before putting on socks, apply a thin coat of baking soda on your feet to keep them dry. This will also keep them smelling fresh.

Fix Up Your Hot, Tired Feet

◆ Boil 2 quarts of water and add ¼ cup of baking soda. When it's cool, pour the liquid into a basin (or divide it between 2 plastic shoe boxes). Then soak your feet for about 10 minutes. Rinse and dry thoroughly.

◆ Mix 4 tablespoons of mustard seed into 2 quarts of just-boiled water. When it's cool, pour the mixture into a basin (or divide it between 2 plastic shoe boxes).

Soak your feet for about 10 minutes, enough time for the *sinigrin,* an important compound in mustard, to stimulate blood flow in your tired tootsies. Then rinse and dry thoroughly.

Flaky Skin Scrub

Strawberries, with a little help from oil and salt, work wonders to slough off dead skin cells, so you can say good-bye to dry, flaky feet.

In a blender, combine 1 cup of sliced strawberries, 2 tablespoons of olive oil and 2 teaspoon of coarse (kosher) salt. Pulse the mix until it has a pulpy consistency. Then gently massage it into your feet, especially on the heels where skin is usually the flakiest. Let it stay on for about 2 minutes, then rinse with warm water and dry thoroughly.

Treating Blisters

Dip a cotton swab in 3% hydrogen peroxide and dab it on the broken blister. The antiseptic properties of the peroxide help heal the blister quickly while preventing infection.

Minty-Fresh Feet

If you don't have 3% hydrogen peroxide on hand to treat a blister on your foot, use antiseptic mouthwash.

Blister Prevention

When you get a new pair of shoes that you plan to wear without socks or pantyhose, swipe the inside of the shoes' heels with a stick of clear underarm antiperspirant/deodorant. The waxy silicone in the deodorant creates a barrier that stops the blister-causing friction.

The woman who told us about this remedy claims she has no blisters, no pain and odor-free feet. Sounds good to us, but you be the judge.

SHAVING

If you've ever wondered when and why women started shaving under their arms, we have the answer—the May 1915 issue of *Harper's Bazaar* magazine featured a model wearing a sleeveless evening gown. For the first time in fashion, a woman's bare shoulders and hair-free armpits were exposed.

Along with the start of media advertisements, a savvy executive at the Wilkinson Sword Company (which makes razors and razor blades) mounted a campaign to convince women that their underarm hair was unhygienic and unfeminine...and most women have been shaving their armpits ever since.

If you are intrigued by shaving apparatus and barbershops from bygone eras, consider a trip to The Ed Jeffers Barber Museum in Canal Winchester, Ohio. It's the only museum of its kind in the world, and it's free to the public (by appointment only). For more information, call Zeke's Barber Shop at 614-837-5311 or visit *www.edjeffersbarbermuseum.com.*

If you'd rather skip the museum and move on to super shaving tips, keep reading...

Shaving Cream Substitutes

These suggestions work for both face and legs…

- Shave in the shower and use a thin layer of hair conditioner (or shampoo that has conditioner in it) instead of shaving cream.

    Let it soak in for a couple of minutes, enough time for the steam of the warm shower and the ingredients in the conditioner to soften the hair and moisturize your skin, resulting in a close shave and no razor burn.

- You can also use hand or body lotion as a substitute for shaving cream. And you may like the results well enough to stick with it from now on!

Aftershave Substitutes

- If you're traveling and you forgot to pack your aftershave lotion, check to see if your hotel room has a mini-bar. If you're willing to pay for great skin, open a bottle of vodka and splash it on. It will be a refreshing aftershave, and an interesting anecdote to tell people when you describe your trip and the expensive aftershave you used.

- If you're at home and you run out of aftershave, you could, of course, use vodka—but perhaps you'd rather save that for company. Instead, mix equal parts of apple cider vinegar and witch hazel (both available at supermarkets and health-food stores).

    The concoction should do wonderful things for your complexion, and you may not want to go back to using a commercial aftershave product.

Shave Legs Less Often

Studies show that the *serine protease inhibitors* in soy milk decrease the size of the hair shaft and reduce the rate of hair growth.

Right after shaving and drying your legs, drench a washcloth with soy milk and wipe your legs. Do not rinse it off. Just let your legs air dry.

If researchers are right, not only should you have to shave less often, but the hair growth itself may be less dense. (Of course, if you notice your leg hair getting thicker, stop using the soy milk right away.)

✳ Cutting It Closer

To get a really close shave, shave your legs first thing in the morning. At the end of the day, legs are slightly swollen from being up and around, making it hard for the razor to cut hair as short as in the morning.

Prevent Razor Rust

Put some vodka in a cup and soak your safety-razor blade in it after shaving. The vodka will disinfect the blade and prevent it from rusting.

Prevent After-Waxing Redness

After you have your eyebrows, upper lip or bikini area waxed, dab the area with some eyedrop solution. Eyedrops contain a capillary constrictor, *tetrahydrozoline*, which makes redness disappear.

If you have the waxing done at a salon, you'll be ready to leave there and greet the world without anyone knowing that you were just waxed.

PERFUME & COLOGNE

The comedian Rita Rudner once said—"To attract men, I wear a perfume called New Car Interior." Hey, whatever works! *And whichever perfume you choose to wear, here's how to make the best of it…*

Shelf Life of Scents

The shelf life of perfume is about 12 to 14 months…and the shelf life of cologne is only about 6 months. So don't save your scents for special occasions. You deserve to make every day a special occasion by indulging yourself. You're worth it!

Is It for You?

◆ If you're looking to buy perfume, the best way to tell how a scent will react on your skin is to spray it on the inside of your wrist. Then shop around for a while. About 20 minutes later, take a whiff of the fragrance on your wrist to decide whether or not you like it. Yes? Go back and buy it.

◆ If you can't wait around for 20 minutes, take a few sample cards of the scents you think you'll like—the cards are usually on the fragrance counter, or ask a salesperson to get you some.

Once you're home, brew some non-flavored, regular or decaf coffee. In between sniffs of each fragrance, cleanse your nose's palate by smelling the used coffee grounds. That way, you'll be able judge each perfume sample on its own merit without the scents blending together.

Increase Staying Power

There's no need to keep reapplying fragrance throughout the day and night—just put a light layer of petroleum jelly on your pulse points (wrists, back of knees, behind the ears, etc.), and then apply your perfume or cologne over it.

The stickiness of the jelly will attract fragrance molecules and lock them in. Just be sure you want the scent with you around the clock.

Tone Down Fragrance

You can tone down a too-strong perfume or cologne by adding some vodka—just dab a little at a time to your pulse points until the fragrance is as mild as you want it to be.

Ⓢ Recycling Bottles

Put open, empty perfume or cologne bottles (or the fragrance cards from magazines) in your underwear drawer or linen closet. The aroma will gently infuse your things.

JEWELRY

 Most people know their birthstone…and many women own a piece of jewelry with their special stone. *Here's a list to check to make sure you're right…*

January: Garnet
February: Amethyst
March: Aquamarine and bloodstone
April: Diamond
May: Emerald
June: Pearl, moonstone and alexandrite
July: Ruby
August: Peridot and sardonyx
September: Sapphire
October: Opal and pink tourmaline
November: Citrine and yellow topaz
December: Blue topaz and turquoise

For more information—such as descriptions, legends, symbols and more—about each birthstone, visit *www.about-birthstones.com* And *for more information about caring for your jewelry, simply keep reading…*

Watch Scratch Remover

If your watch has a scratched plastic (not glass) face that's covering the dial, dip a cotton swab in some nail polish remover and rub it over and over and over the face. Keep rubbing until the scratches are gone.

Safe Way to Clean Pearls

Pearls are said to be "the queen of gems and the gem of queens." With that in mind, you should treat them royally.

Never use an ultrasonic cleaner, ammonia, harsh detergents, an abrasive cleaner or an abrasive cloth on pearl jewelry—you may end up with just a strand of beads. The pearl's outer coating (called the *nacre*) is extremely delicate and can wear away. The calcium carbonate in pearls can dissolve from body heat or the skin's oil. To keep your pearls intact, use a soft, lint-free cloth to wipe them as soon as you take them off.

If you need to wash the pearls, use a solution made from mild soap (such as Ivory Snow) and plain water. A spokesperson for the Cultured Pearl Information Center (*www.pearlinfo.com*) suggests rinsing the pearls 3 times more than you think you have to, just to be sure that all of the soap is removed from the drill holes. Be sure to let the pearls air-dry before putting them away.

Use Caution with Pearls

◆ Hairspray and perfume both contain alcohol, which can damage pearls. Spray your hair and apply perfume at least 5 minutes before you put on your pearl earrings, necklace, bracelet, brooch or ring.

◆ The same goes for hand cream, body lotion and makeup. Wait until they're completely absorbed and/or dry before putting on your pearl jewelry.

◆ Exposure to direct sunlight for a long period of time will cause the protein in pearls to turn yellow. Be sure to keep them in a cool, dark, SAFE place.

◆ It's best to keep pearls in a box or pouch. They can get scratched if they rub up against other jewelry.

Keep Pearls Around

The silk or nylon cord that holds your strand of pearls can wear out. The Cultured Pearl Information Center recommends a fine pearl necklace that is worn a few times each week should be restrung every 6 months...pearls worn a couple of times each month should be restrung once every year.

Pearls of Wisdom

You may have heard that the more often you wear your pearls, the better they will look. Although it's a lovely thought, it's a fact that body oils are not the best thing for maintaining—nor improving—the natural luster of pearls.

Many years ago (before cultured pearls came into existence), only super-rich aristocrats could afford strands of rare and prized natural pearls. Believing the myth that wearing pearls enhanced their patina, these wealthy matrons would have their maids sit for hours at a time, several times a week, wearing the pearls. (All that money, and what they really needed was a copy of this book to set them straight!)

Safe Way to Clean Diamonds

Soak diamond jewelry in a small bowl filled with warm sudsy water, or equal parts of distilled white vinegar and warm water.

While the jewelry is soaking, brush each piece with a soft toothbrush. Rinse the jewelry under warm running water. Then pat it dry with a soft lint-free cloth.

Diamonds Are Forever

◆ A diamond is the hardest natural substance in the world, and it will last forever...give or take a few years.

◆ The word *diamond* comes from the ancient Greek word *adamas*, which means *unconquerable*. The Greeks thought of diamonds as the "tears of the gods."

◆ The tradition of wearing a diamond engagement ring on the fourth finger of the left hand dates back to ancient Egypt. It was believed that the vein of love ran from that finger directly to the heart.

 CAUTION: If your jewelry has emeralds, opals, turquoise or pearls in addition to diamonds—*do not* use vinegar!

Opals and turquoise are both porous stones. Just wipe them with a chamois cloth. Emeralds chip easily. They should be cleaned only by a professional jeweler.

In addition, it's not a good idea to wear gold jewelry when swimming in chlorinated water. The gold may react with the chlorine, causing the jewelry to become brittle and break. Think twice before wearing your beautiful gold chain when you're going in the pool.

Remove a Ring Without the Sting

◆ If your finger has become swollen and you can't take off your ring, wet your finger and put 1 or 2 drops of liquid dish detergent (or soapy water) above and below the ring. It will lubricate your finger so the ring can slide off easily.

◆ Soak your hand in a bowl of ice water. Doing this will shrink your swollen finger enough to allow you to remove your ring.

◆ Coat your finger with mayonnaise, olive oil or butter and slip off the ring.

Untangling a Chain

Put the knotted chain on a piece of waxed paper. Sprinkle some talcum powder on the tangle. Then, with a needle or straight pin in each hand, work at untangling the knot(s).

Storing Jewelry

◆ Take a wooden hanger and screw in hooks (the kind used to hang drinking cups) along the width, about 1" apart. This will keep your necklaces tangle-free and easy to see.

◆ You can also use a tie rack as a neat way to store your necklaces.

◆ Keep your earrings paired up and organized in empty ice cube trays or egg cartons.

◆ Keep pierced earrings together by sticking the posts through the holes of a button.

◆ Store and display your bracelets and watches on the branches of a coffee-cup tree.

◆ With a tie knot, tie an unused necktie on your closet rod, and use the tie to hold pins and tacks. You can even push through pierced earring posts. It's a neat way to hold the jewelry and to see things at a glance.

Easy Bracelet Fastening

Instead of going around in circles trying to fasten your bracelet, tape 1 end of the bracelet to your wrist, then simply fasten the clasp. It's so easy when you know how. (Of course, don't forget to remove the piece of tape once the bracelet is fastened!)

Temporary Replacement for Pierced Earrings

Most pierced earrings are made up of the ornament, the post and the *friction nut* (the back part that holds the post to the earlobe). If you lose the friction nut, then you have to take off the earring or, chances are, you'll lose the ornament and post.

If you want to continue wearing the earring, find a pencil with an eraser at the end. Break off a small piece of the eraser, and use the post to make a hole in the middle of the eraser piece. Put the earring post back in your lobe, and attach the eraser as the new, temporary nut. Once you get home, replace the eraser with a real friction nut (available at jewelry stores).

Costume Jewelry

Does your neck or wrist or earlobes or finger change color every time you wear a certain piece of costume jewelry? The solution is to paint colorless nail polish on the jewelry—wherever it touches your skin.

If you are sensitive to regular nail polish, use a hypo-allergenic brand of clear polish.

Cleaning Costume Jewelry

Mix 1 teaspoon of baking soda with 1 cup of warm water, dip a soft cloth in the solution and gently clean the jewelry.

 CAUTION: When cleaning costume jewelry, do not use distilled white vinegar or any other cleanser that might undo the glue bonds.

EYEGLASSES

Many historians believe that the first eyeglasses were invented in Italy around 1284. Throughout the 1300s, eyeglasses became a symbol of wealth and power, since only the rich could afford this luxury.

In 1456, Gutenberg invented the printing press, which made books available...and which created a market for reading glasses. Gradually, eyeglasses became an important part of everyday life for even the most common people.

If spectacles are part of your daily life, here are ways to care for them...

Cheers to Your Specs!

If you're at a bar and you want to see who's paying for your drink, clean your eyeglasses with a little vodka on a soft cloth.

Fog Prevention

Smear a tiny dollop of foam shaving cream or a drop of liquid dish detergent or non-gel toothpaste on both sides of your eyeglasses, and wipe it off with a soft cloth (or you can just spit on them, the way scuba divers do).

Doing this leaves a very thin, invisible coating on the lenses...which will help fend off moisture...which will prevent the glasses from fogging up each time you come out of the cold or while cooking.

Fast Fix for Scratches

If your glasses' plastic lenses are scratched, spray Pledge furniture polish on both sides of the lenses. Rub the polish in, then wipe it off with a soft cloth.

Temporary Screw Replacement

- If you lose 1 of those tiny screws that hold your glasses together, you can fix it temporarily. Here's what to do—thread a piece of dental floss through the holes that the screw goes through. Then knot the floss and cut off the excess. Dental floss is strong and should hold your glasses together until you can replace the screw.

- If you don't have dental floss, take a twist tie (like you use to close garbage bags), and peel off the outer paper or plastic. Thread the thin little wire through the screw holes of the eyeglasses, and twist it closed.

     Cut off any excess wire so that it will be safe to wear the glasses until you can replace the screw.

- Of course, you can always use a nerdy-looking small safety pin (or a toothpick...or a wooden match) to keep your glasses together until you can replace the screw.

Loose Screws Sink Ships

- If you can do delicate work with a tiny screwdriver, then unscrew the screws on each side of the glasses ¾ of the way. Apply a coat of colorless nail polish to the threads of each screw, and then tighten them. This procedure will prevent the screws from getting loose again.

- If the screws are popping out and you don't have a tiny screwdriver, press a pencil eraser against each screw and turn the pencil (remember—lefty-loosey, righty-tighty). The eraser is non-slippery, so it will provide enough traction to get the screws out. Apply clear nail polish to the heads of the little screws and then tighten the screws back into place with the pencil.

Do-It-Yourself Magnifier

- When you want to read a price...or look up a phone number...or see what time it is on your watch, but the type is too small to see without your glasses, try this—make a fist, leaving a small hole between your palm and pinky. Bring your fist up to your eye, look through that small hole and focus on the number you want to read. For some unknown reason, the small channel of light entering your eye clears the vision.

- You can also puncture a small hole in a piece of paper with a pen point. Hold the paper hole to your eye, focus on the number and see it come into view—large and sharp.

CLOTHING

Whether you're a slave to fashion...or you base your fashion taste simply on what doesn't itch, there are ways you can wear clothes easier and have them look better. *Check out these hip suggestions...*

Clothing Storage

- If your closet space and storage space are both limited, store out-of-season clothes in empty suitcases.

NOTE: No matter where you store your out-of-season clothes, if they are machine washable, wash them before packing them away. It will help prevent a moth infestation.

- Clothing fibers need to breathe, so do not hang them in plastic bags, especially those you get from the dry cleaner's. If you want to cover any of your garments, use old, clean pillowcases. Just cut a hole in the top to accommodate the hanger.

◆ Shoeboxes—either cardboard or plastic—that are lined up side by side in your dresser drawers will help keep underwear, socks or pantyhose reasonably neat, and make specific items easy to find.

 Fragrant Mothball Substitute

To repel moths when storing clothes, use whole cloves (the kind used when making a citrus pomade or preparing ham). Wrap a handful of cloves in a piece of old pantyhose, and tuck them in with your winter woolens. They will serve the same repellent purpose as efficiently as mothballs, but they smell much better.

If you're feeling particularly protective of your special cashmere sweaters or other woolen garments, store the cloves with the sweaters in large glass jars.

Hide Cellulite

If your thighs and tush have cellulite, stay away from clingy, too-tight clothes. In other words, let your clothes stay away from you. Rub a fabric softener sheet over your dimpled flesh and inside the clothing that will touch it. No cling...no cellulite show-through.

Swimsuit Shopping Made Kinder

Shopping for a swimsuit is an ordeal for most women. Before you head for the mall, put on a pair of pantyhose that are a couple of shades darker than your skin tone. You'll boost your self-esteem with your legs looking their sun-tanned best when you're in the changing room.

Zippers

◆ If the teeth are properly aligned, but the zipper doesn't go up and down smoothly, rub the teeth with a bar of soap or a candle. It should make a difference.

◆ Also, you can try rubbing the teeth with a pencil. The graphite should help the zipper glide more easily.

 NOTE: It's best to use the pencil only on dark-colored clothes. You may not want to take the chance of graphite smudging on light-colored garments.

◆ If your skirt or dress zipper unzips when it shouldn't, coat the teeth with a little spritz of hairspray once it's in place. The stickiness of the spray should keep the zipper zipped—until you're ready to unzip it.

Pantyhose

◆ Consider buying pantyhose 1 size larger than usual. The less stress put on the hose, the longer they will last.

◆ Got a run in your pantyhose? When you take them off, put a dot of red nail polish on the waistband. From then on, you'll see at a glance that this pair of pantyhose should only be worn under slacks, where the run will not show.

Lingerie Camouflage

If you don't want your underwear to show through the white shirt or pants you're wearing, put on a bra, slip or panties that matches your skin color.

Create Cleavage

◆ *If you wear a B-cup bra...*loosen the straps on your bra until they can't be any looser. Then, while wearing the bra, bring the straps together at the nape of your neck and pin them with a safety pin. If this trick created the cleavage you were hoping for, take off the bra, sew the straps together securely and remove the safety pin.

◆ *If you wear a C-cup (or larger) bra...*for an uplifting experience, attach a wide barrette to your bra straps—it should be in the middle of your back. This will improve your posture and your bustline without the reminder to keep your chest out and shoulders back.

FOOTWEAR

Y ou think you have a lot of shoes? Imelda Marcos, wife of deposed Philippine president Ferdinand Marcos, once had 1,500 pairs of shoes in her shoe room. Yes, she had a *shoe room!* And if you feel guilty about splurging on a recently purchased pair of shoes, just think about the $665,000 that was paid at auction for 1 of the 8 pairs of ruby slippers made for Judy Garland to wear in *The Wizard of Oz.*

Now that your shoe collection is in its proper prospective, here are some ideas on how to wear them more comfortably.

Keep Shoes On

If your slingbacks aren't adjustable and they keep slipping off, find a shoemaker and have him/her put a half-pad beneath the shoe's inner-sole liner. That half-pad will make the whole difference. It will push the front of your foot backward, tightening the slingback strap enough to keep it from slipping off your heel.

Put on Boots

If your boots don't have zippers, a plastic bag can help you get them on easily. Place a closed plastic bag into the boot, with the bottom of the bag reaching into the boot's foot area and the top of the bag hanging out over the top.

Hold the top of the bag and the top of the boot with both hands, then slide your foot along the plastic and into the boot. Once your foot is in the boot, pull out the bag.

✳ Easy Way to Slip on Shoes

If you don't have a shoe horn, use a large spoon or a narrow, thin spatula. (Run it through the dishwasher after you get your shoes on!)

Foot Note

I f you're *really* head-over-heels about footwear... over 10,000 shoes are housed at the Bata Shoe Museum in Toronto. This unique museum celebrates the style and function of footwear. Exhibited artifacts range from Chinese bound-foot shoes and ancient Egyptian sandals to chestnut-crushing clogs and a collection of celebrity shoes.

For more information, call 416-979-7799 or visit *www.batashoemuseum.com.*

HANDBAGS

W e know that the first handbag dates back to ancient Egypt—hieroglyphics depict purses attached to "girdles" and fastened at the waist. Jewels and embroidery usually embellished the bag, and these decorative touches indicated social status—the richer the person, the more complex the bag.

Times may have changed, but you can still tell a lot about a woman from the handbag she carries. *For example...*

◆ Bulky, oversized bags tend to be used by down-to-earth, low-maintenance women.

◆ Designer handbags, which often cost more money, are often associated with high-maintenance, confident women.

◆ Cigar-box purses are for women who like to stand out in a crowd. They tend to be comfortable with themselves and very independent—don't try to tell them what to do!

◆ Leather bags with buckles and zippers signify a "bad girl" image—these women are unleashing their wild side. They tend to act before they think and are always up for a good time.

◆ Bright-colored handbags in pink, purple and bright green indicate women who are fun, friendly and easy to approach. They can start a conversation with complete strangers.

◆ Black and brown handbags may represent women who are more reserved. They can be shy at first, but open up after a while.

The purses we carry often become an extension of ourselves—and sometimes an extension of our home office. Writer Anita Daniel once said, "Every woman's handbag is a lost-and-found department in itself." With that in mind, we hope you'll *find* these handbag hints helpful. Hmmm...now where did I put my keys?

Perk Up a Straw Bag

Bring last year's straw bag back to life by dusting it off and then coating it with hairspray (do this outdoors or in a well-ventilated room).

Your bag will take on a whole new shine. This trick also works on straw hats!

Nonslip Shoulder Strap Solution

It's so annoying to carry a purse with a shoulder strap that keeps slipping off your shoulder. Try this—sew a BIG button on your jacket or coat...under the collar...on the side you usually carry your bag. Use the button as a hook to keep the slippery strap in place.

> **NOTE:** For this solution, try to find a button that matches the color of your jacket, so that it will blend in.

Pen Holder for Your Purse

You should always carry around something to write with (what would happen if the battery ran down on your Palm Pilot or your BlackBerry?). But instead of having pens or pencils floating around loose inside your purse, put them in a plastic toothbrush holder.

The holder is easy to find in a crowded bag, and it will also prevent a pen from accidentally losing its cap and making marks inside the bag's lining. (If you already carry a toothbrush in a holder in your purse, be sure to label the containers accordingly.) ■

■ Products ■

E-Pen™ Electrolysis System

With patience and persistence, this system will remove hair safely and permanently. And it's a lot less expensive than going to an electrologist. Unlike the needle system of electrolysis, this unit treats many hairs simultaneously. Most important, there is no pain, scarring or pitting.

It comes with simple, detailed instructions and includes everything you need to customize the treatment. It also has a soft carrying case.

Source: The Sharper Image, 800-344-4444, *www.sharperimage.com.*

T3 Tourmaline Featherweight Ionic Hair Dryer

The T3 is a bit of a splurge, but it can save you time and money at the hair salon. Tourmaline, a semi-precious gemstone, is said to produce more negative ions than any other substance. The ions make water evaporate more quickly.

We don't really know about negative ions, but we do know that the T3 leaves our hair smooth, shiny, frizz-free and damage-free.

Source: T3 Micro, Inc., 866-376-8880, *www.t3tourmaline.com.*

Lite-E-Nuff Key Light

Be safe and stop scratching the keyhole of your door. This small key-ring accessory fits over any key and aims a small, powerful beam of light wherever your key points. It also helps you open your car or house door quickly instead of fumbling in the dark.

Magnetic Clasp

If you've ever struggled to clasp a favorite necklace, this clever item makes it easy to be self-sufficient. In a few seconds, you can convert your hard-to-hook necklace or chain into a simple, secure, no-problem-to-put-on-and-take-off magnetic clasp. The 2 brass magnetic clasps come with gold or silver plating.

It works for bracelets, too.

Jewelry Clasp

When you're tired of chasing your slippery bracelet around your wrist, trying to clasp it, this 6" clip—which is as simple as it is helpful—will hold the fastening ring in place while you close the clasp.

Source: Miles Kimball, 800-546-2255, *www.mileskimball.com.*

Index

A

Acne, remedies for, 108
Acupressure
    for back pain, 110
    for brain function, 113
    for stress, 137–138
Age spots, remedies for, 152
Alcohol
    fertility, effect on, 125
    for parties, 84–88
Allergies
    to costume jewelry, 169
    to insect bites/stings, 130
    to poison ivy/oak/sumac, 136
    remedies for, 108
Almond Crisped Rice Treats, 76
Aluminum pots
    caring for, 12, 13
    and spinach, 62
    and turnip greens, 66
Ammonia and vinegar, 2
Anemia, pernicious, B-12 for, 113
Anxiety and stress, 137–139
Apple cider, 25
Apples, 25–26
Appliances, cleaning, 4–12
Aromatherapy for stress relief, 138
Arthritis, remedies for, 108–109, 161
Asparagus, 26
Aspirin and gout, 127

Asthma, remedies for, 109–110
Atopic dermatitis (eczema), 122–123
Automatic Blood Pressure Monitor with Comfit Cuff, 147
Avocados, 26
    Avocado & Banana Ice Cream, 77
    Avocado Cake, 71

B

Back pain, remedies for, 110
Bacon, 26–27
Bacon Sticks, 26
Bacteria. *See also E. coli; Listeria; Salmonella*
    in pies, 56
    in stuffing, 62
Bad breath, remedies for, 110–111, 160
Bad hair day and depression, 121
Baked Beans in Tomato Sauce Cake, 71
Baking soda
    freshness test for, 4
Baking tips, 70
Bananas, 27
Barbecuing
    condiments, serving, 37
    grill cleaning, 8
Barber Museum, Ed Jeffers, 164
Bata Shoe Museum, 172

Bay leaves, 27
Beans, 27–28
    to keep kosher salt clump-free, 60
Beef, 28–29
    alternatives, 29
    cooking temperatures, 64
Beer, 88
Bee stings, 130
Berries, 30
Biscuits, 30
Bladder infection. *See* Urinary problems
Bleach and vinegar, 2
Blender, cleaning, 5
Blisters, remedies for, 111, 164
Blood cleanser, 112
Blueberries
    for bladder infections, 111
    for memory retention, 114
Book or DVD club, starting, 89
Brain boosters, 112–115
Bread and biscuits, 30
    napkin rings, bread, 81
Bread crumbs, 30
Breakfast and brain function, 112–113
Breast-feeding, benefits of, 115
Breathing
    exercise for hypertension, 129
    for stress relief, 138
Bronchitis, 115–116

Brown sugar. *See* Sugar
Bruises, 116
Butcher's block, caring for, 20
Butter, 31
    substitute for, 117
Buttermilk, substitutes for, 31

C

Cabbage, 31
Cake, 29–30. *See also* Recipes
    egg substitute, 41
    frosting, 32, 36
    recipes, 71–75
Candles
    meaning of Kwanzaa, 104
    for parties, 83–84
Candy, 32
Can opener, cleaning, 4–5
Cans, disinfecting tops of, 32
Carbon-steel knives and spinach, 62
Carpal tunnel syndrome, 116
Carrots, 32
Cast-iron cookware, caring for, 12, 13–14
Catsup. *See* Ketchup
Cauliflower, 33
Caviar, 33
Celebrations—The Jewish Museum Design Shop, 106
Celery, 33–34
Cellulite, hiding, 171
Chain necklace, untangling, 168
Champagne for parties, 85–86
Chanukah, 99–101
Cheesecake, 35. *See also* Recipes
Cherry Cola–Chocolate–Mayonnaise–Sauerkraut Bundt Cake, 72
Chewing gum, removing from hair, 158
Chicken, 35
    cooking temperatures, 64
Chiffon Cake, 72
Children, shampooing hair and, 158
Chili, 35

China
    caring for, 16
    cracks in, 16
Chlorine-damaged hair, 155
Chocolate, 36
    Chocolate Fudge Frosting, 78
    Chocolate Potato-Flake Cake, 73
    dark, to lower cholesterol, 117
    making shavings, 35
    melting, 70
    for tongue burn, 140–141
Chocolove, 106
Cholesterol, 117–118
    Cholesterol Monitor, 148
Chopsticks, 36
Christmas, 101–103
Clay cookware, caring for, 14
Cleaning products, make-it-yourself substitutes for, 3
Cleavage, creating, 171–172
Clogged drains, 17
Clothing, 170–172
Coconut
    oil for hair care, 155–156
    oil for stretch marks, 139
    oil for urinary tract infections, 141
    opening a, 36
Coffee, 36–37
    mochaccino substitute, 142
    for tension headaches, 128
Coffee grinder, cleaning, 5
Coffee maker, cleaning, 5
Cognitive function, boosting, 112–115
Colds and flu, remedies for, 118
Cold sores, remedies for, 118
Colic, remedies for, 119
Colors
    pink to lift depression, 121
    purple for alertness, 114
Conception, 125
Condiments, serving, 37, 48
Confetti Salad, 104
Conscious eating, 143
Constipation, remedies for, 119
Contact lenses, 119

Cookies, 37
    cookie sheet, 37
    Crispy Potato Chip Cookies, 75–76
    Overnight-Delight Cookies, 76
Cooking answers from USDA, 65
Cooking spray, 37
Cooking temperatures of meats, 64
Cookware. *See* Pots and pans
Cooper Shop, The, at The Jewish Museum, 106
Corn, 37–38
CorningWare, caring for, 16–17
Cornstarch
    to keep salt clump-free, 60
    substitute for, 38
Cornucopia centerpiece, 96–97
Costumes, Halloween, 95–96
Cough, 119–120
Countertops, caring for, 21
Crackers, soggy, 38
Cramps, menstrual, 134
Cranberries, 38
    for urinary infections, 111, 141
Cream
    sweet, 64
    whipped, 66
Cream Cheese Frosting, 71
Creamy Coffee Cheesecake, 73–74
Crispy Potato Chip Cookies, 75–76
Crumbs, making, 38
Crystal
    caring for, 14–15
    vases, cleaning, 15
Cucumbers, storing, 38
Cupcakes, 38
Cutting board, caring for, 20

D

Dandruff, remedies for, 120, 156
Decorations. *See also* Holidays
    for Christmas, 102–103
    for Kwanzaa, 105
    table, 81–82
Deep vein thrombosis (DVT), 124

Dental problems. *See* Teeth
Dental floss
    to cut cheesecake, 35
    to fix eyeglasses, 170
Denture cleanser, 159–160
Deodorant, natural, 150
Depression, 120–121
    B vitamins for, 113
Diamonds, cleaning, 167
Diarrhea, remedies for, 122
Dish detergent, make-it-yourself, 3
Dishwasher, cleaning, 11
Disinfecting
    butcher's block, 20
    can tops, 32
    sponges, 3
Dog
    petting, to lift depression, 121
    walking, to lose weight, 144
Drains, unclogging, 17
Drugs, compounding
    pharmacies, 145
Dry eye syndrome, 122
DVD or book club, starting, 89
Dye, hair, 154
Dysmenorrhea (menstrual
    cramps), 134

E

Easter, 93–94
E. coli, 25, 126
Eczema (atopic dermatitis),
    122–123
Edema, 123
Ed Jeffers Barber Museum, 164
Eggplant, 39
    Eggplant Pudding Cake, 74
Eggs, 39–42
Elbows, dry, 144–145
Energy boosters, 123–124
Enova oil, 143
E-Pen Electrolysis System, 174
Epsom salt
    as hair volumizer, 155
    for muscle and joint pain,
        134, 161
    for oily hair, 156
Equivalents for measuring, 51

Erectile dysfunction, 124–125
Essential oil for nosebleed, 135
Exercise
    for depression, 120
    and music, 114–115
    for weight loss, 144–145
Extracts in baking, 42
Eyeglass care, 169–170
Eyes. *See also* Eyeglass care
    eye makeup, 153
    magnifier, do-it-yourself, 170
    sties, remedies for, 139–140

F

Face care, 150–152. *See also* Skin
    care
Fan filter, oven, cleaning, 7
Fat, removing
    from gravy, 46
    from soup, 61
Fatigue. *See* Energy boosters
Fat substitutes
    for beef, 29
    for butter, 31
    for cake, 31, 32
    for cream cheese, 34–35
    for egg yolks when baking, 42
    for oil in baking, 53
    for shortening, 60
Feng shui, 92
Fertility, 125
Fever, 125–126
Fish. *See* Seafood
Flag etiquette, 94
Flour, 43–44
Flu, remedies for, 118
Food. *See also* Holidays; Parties;
    Recipes; *individual food listings*
    bacteria in, 56 See also *E. coli;*
        Listeria; Salmonella
        burned-on, removing,
            12–13
        cholesterol-lowering,
            117–118
        constipation-preventing,
            119
        foodborne illnesses,
            preventing, 42

    freezing, 10–11, 30, 47
    gout triggers, 126
    hand-washing and
        handling, 2
    leftovers, 49
    scale, accuracy of, 17
    scraps, garbage bowl for,
        46
    smell of, and weight loss,
        144
    storage and power outage,
        10
    storage times, 66
    temperatures, cooking, 64
    weight control with,
        142–146
Food poisoning, 126
Food processor, cleaning, 6
Food Safety and Inspection
    Service Web site (USDA), 66
Foot care, 163–164. *See also* Hand
    care; Skin care
Footwear, 172
4th of July, 94–95
Freckles, remedies for, 152
Freezer
    cleaning and defrosting, 10
    efficiency, optimizing, 10–11
Freezing food. *See* Food and
    individual food listings
Frosting
    for cake, 32
    chocolate design, 36
    Chocolate Fudge Frosting, 78
    Cream Cheese Frosting, 71
    for cupcakes, 38
    Glaze Frosting, 72
    Lemon Sauce, 78
    Peanut Butter Frosting
        (Broiled), 78
    Quick-and-Easy Tropical
        Frosting, 78
Fruit, 44
    in baking, 70
Fungal infections, 134–135

G

Games, Thanksgiving, 98–99
Garbage bowl for food scraps, 46

Garbage can, cleaning, 19

Garbage disposal, cleaning, 12

Garlic, 45

Gas, intestinal, from beans, preventing, 27

Gelatin, 45

Genital warts, 142

Ginger, 46

Glass and crystal
    broken glass, cleaning up, 14, 46
    caring for, 14–15
    unsticking drinking glasses, 14

Gloves, rubber, tips for using, 4

Gold jewelry and chlorinated water, 168

Gout, 126–127

Grapes, 46

Grater, 46
    cleaning, 21

Gravy, 46–47

Grease, removing from hands, 161

Greens. *See* Salad greens

Grill rack, cleaning, 8

Guacamole, keeping fresh, 26

Guest treatment at parties, 90

Gum, removing, from hair, 158

Gum disease, remedies for, 110–111

H

Hair
    bad hair day and depression, 121
    care, 154–159
    shampoo, nourishing, 127

Hair dryer in kitchen, 47

Halloween, 95–96

Ham, 47

Hamburgers, cooking temperatures of, 64

Handbags, 172–173

Hand care, 160–161. *See also* Foot care; Skin care

Headache, 127–128

Herbs, 47

Herpes simplex virus (cold sores), 118

Hiccups, 126

High blood pressure. *See* Hypertension

Highchair tray, cleaning, 22

Holidays
    Chanukah, 99–101
    Christmas, 101–103
    Easter, 93–94
    Halloween, 95–96
    Independence Day, 94–95
    Kwanzaa, 103–105
    New Year's, 91–92
    St. Valentine's Day, 92–93
    Thanksgiving Day, 95–99

Honey, 47

Hypertension, 129
    Automatic Blood Pressure Monitor with Comfit Cuff, 147
    RESPeRATE, 147

I

Ice cubes, 86–88

Icing, cake. *See* Frosting

Independence Day, 94–95

Indigestion, 129–130

Innerscan Body Composition Monitor, 147

Insect bites/stings, 130

Insects in vegetables, washing away, 31, 33

Insomnia, 130–131

Intestinal parasites, 131

Invitations, 79

Itchy skin, 132. *See also* Eczema

J

Jars
    labels, removing, 18
    opening, 18
    rinsing, 18

Jellyfish sting, 132–133

Jelly/jam, 48

Jewelry, 166–169

Jewelry Clasp, 174

Jewish Museum, The, 106

Joint pain, remedies for, 109, 134, 161

Juice boxes, 48

K

Ketchup, 48

Kitchen fires, 1–2

Kiwi, 48

Knives, kitchen
    care of, 19–20
    and spinach, 62
    for squash, 62

Kosher salt, 60

Kwanzaa, 103–105

L

Labels on jars, removing, 18

Lasagna, 48

Laughter, for weight loss, 144

Laxatives, natural, 119

Leftovers, 49

Lemons and limes, 49
    zest conversion, 46

Lemon Sauce, 78

Lentils, 49

Lettuce. *See* Salad greens

Lilly's Luscious Latkes, 99

Lingerie camouflage, 171

Lips
    chapped, remedies for, 152
    lipstick and gloss, 152

Listeria, 25

Lite-E-Nuff Key Light, 174

Liver cleansers, 133

M

Magnetic Clasp, 174

Makeup, 152–153

Make-Your-Own Pita Chips, 57

Marshmallows, 50
    to keep brown sugar clump-free, 63

Masks, facial, 151

Measurements, common kitchen, 51
    champagne equivalents, 86

Measuring spoons/cups, 50, 60

Meat. *See* Beef; Cooking temperatures of meat
Meat & Poultry Hotline (USDA), 66
Meatloaf tips, 29
Medications, compounding pharmacies, 145
Meditation or prayer, for weight loss, 145–146
Melatonin
    for insomnia, 131
    for migraines, 128
Memory, increasing, 112–115
Men
    prostate, enlarged, urinary problems with, 141
    walking barefoot for stress relief, 138–139
Menopause, 133
Menstrual cramps (dysmenorrhea), 134
Mercury in fish, 114
Microwave oven
    cleaning, 6
    plastic wrap in, 2
Migraine headaches, 128
Milk, 50–51
Mindful eating, 143
Mixer, hand or electric, cleaning, 6
Mi-Yuk Gook (Korean seaweed soup), 112
Mold on cheese, 34
Monosodium glutamate, 29
Mothball substitute, 171
Muffins, 51–52
    muffin-tin tips, 51
    Orange Bran Flax Muffin Magic, 77
Mushrooms, 52
Music. *See also* Singing
    and exercise, 114–115
    to lift depression, 121
Mustard for insect bites/stings, 130

N
Nail care, 161–163
    fungus, 134–135

Napkins and napkins rings, 81
Nausea, 135
New Year's, 91–92
Nosebleed, 135
Nuts, 52
    in baking, 70
    toasting, 53

O
Oatmeal and brain function, 112–113
Obesity
    and arthritis, 109
    weight-control strategies, 142–146
Odors, eliminating. *See also* Smell
    body, 150
    of cabbage cooking, 31
    of chlorine in water, 66
    on cutting boards, 20
    from feet, 163
    of fish, 43
    from hands, 161
    in garbage can, 19
    in garbage disposal, 12
    of garlic, 45
    in kitchen, 39, 61
    in lunchbox, 22
    in microwave oven, 6
    of onion on hands, 53
    in plastic containers, 22
    in refrigerator, 9
    of turnip cooking, 66
Oil, 53. *Also see* Essential oils
    cooking spray, 37
    olive, for dry hands, 160
    olive, for nail care, 162
    shortening, 60
Onions, 53–54
Orange Bran Flax Muffin Magic, 77
Osteoarthritis. *See* Arthritis, remedies for
Osteoporosis, breast-feeding and, 115
Oven, cleaning, 7
Overnight-Delight Cookies, 76
Ovulation, 125

P
Pancakes, 54–55
Pantyhose, 171
Papain, 29
Paper towel alternative, 55
Parasites, internal, 131
Parchment paper for cookie sheet, 37
Parsley, 55
Parties
    alcohol and other beverages, 84–88
    candles, 83–84
    guest treatment, 90
    invitations, 79
    napkins and napkin rings, 81
    photographing at, 90–91
    picnics, 89
    place cards, 80
    table decorations, 81–82
    themes, 89
Pasta, 55
Peanut Butter Frosting (Broiled), 78
Peanut butter, natural, 55–56
    for weight loss, 142
Pearls, cleaning, 167
Pen holder for purse, 173
Peppers, bell, 56
Pepper shaker, 56
Perfume and cologne, 165–166
Pernicious anemia, B-12 for, 113
Pesticides, removing, from produce, 44
Pharmacies, compounding, 145
Phenylethylamine (PEA), 92
Phone, hands-free, in kitchen, 56
Photographing at parties, 90–91
Picnics, 89
Pies and piecrust, 56
Pimples, remedies for, 108, 151–152
Pineapple, 56
Pita, 56
    Make-Your-Own Pita Chips, 57
Place cards, 80
    for Easter, 94

for Thanksgiving, 98
Plantar warts, 141–142
Plastic wrap
    cleaning off toaster, 5
    in microwave, 2
    to prevent odors, 22
    tips for using, 4
    for top of refrigerator, 9
Pocketbooks (purses), 172–173
Poison ivy/oak/sumac, 136
Popcorn, 57
    Popcorn Cake, 74
Porcelain
    caring for, 16
    sink, cleaning, 17
Pork, cooking temperatures of,
    64
Positive affirmations, 121
Potatoes, 57–58
Pots and pans
    care of, 12–14
    stacking, 19
Power outage and food storage,
    10
Prayer or meditation for weight
    loss, 145–146
Prescription drugs, compounding
    pharmacies, 145
Produce. *See* Fruit; Salad greens
Products
    Automatic Blood Pressure
        Monitor with Comfit Cuff,
        147
    Celebrations—The Jewish
        Museum Design Shop, 106
    Cholesterol Monitor, 148
    Cooper Shop, The, at The
        Jewish Museum, 106
    E-Pen Electrolysis System, 174
    Innerscan Body Composition
        Monitor, 147
    Jewelry Clasp, 174
    Lite-E-Nuff Key Light, 174
    Magnetic Clasp, 174
    Purebrush Antibacterial
        Toothbrush Purifier, 147
    RESPeRATE, 147
    Talking Timer, 23

T3 Tourmaline Featherweight
    Ionic Hair Dryer, 174
    Touchless Trashcan, 23
Prostate, enlarged, urinary
    problems with, 141
Pumpkin pie topping, 50
Purebrush Antibacterial
    Toothbrush Purifier, 147
Purses, 172–173
Pyrex, 16

Q

Qigong to lift depression, 121
Quick-and-Easy Tropical Frosting,
    78

R

Range, electric, cleaning, 7
Rapid Ice Cooler for Wine, 106
Recipe holder, 59
Recipes
    Almond Crisped Rice Treats, 76
    Avocado & Banana Ice
        Cream, 77
    Avocado Cake, 71
    Bacon Sticks, 26
    Baked Beans in Tomato Sauce
        Cake, 71
    Cherry Cola–Chocolate–
        Mayonnaise–Sauerkraut
        Bundt Cake, 72
    Chiffon Cake, 72
    Chocolate Potato-Flake Cake,
        73
    Confetti Salad, 104
    Cornucopia Centerpiece, 97
    Creamy Coffee Cheesecake,
        73–74
    Crispy Potato Chip Cookies,
        75–76
    Eggplant, 74
    Lilly's Luscious Latkes, 99
    Make-Your-Own Pita Chips,
        57
    Mi-Yuk Gook (Korean
        seaweed soup), 112
    Orange Bran Flax Muffin
        Magic, 77
    Popcorn Cake, 74
    Singing Cake, 75

Yogurt Dessert, 67
Reflexology
    for alertness, 113
    for stress relief, 138
Refrigerator
    cleaning, 8–9
    deodorizers, 9
    efficiency, optimizing, 9–10
RESPeRATE, 147
Rice, 58
Ring, removing, from swollen
    finger, 168
Rolls, 58–59
Rosemary for menopausal
    symptoms, 133
Roundworms, 131
Rubber gloves, tips for using, 4
Rust rings, preventing, 18

S

Safety. *See also* Disinfecting
    of apple cider, 25
    in bathtub, 132
    fire in kitchen, 1–2
    fireproofing Christmas tree,
        101
    plastic wrap and microwave,
        2
    vinegar, cautions with, 2
Saint Valentine's Day, 92–93
Salad bowls, wood, washing, 19
Salad greens, 47, 49–50, 59, 66
Salmonella, 25, 40
Salsa, 59
Salt, 59–60
    to chill wine, 84
    for oily hair, 156
Sandwiches, 60
Sanitizing. *See* Disinfecting
Sausage, 60
Scale, food, accuracy of, 17
Scissors, care of, 20
Scouring powder, make-it-your-
    self, 3
Seafood, 43, 60
    to increase brain function, 114
    and mercury contamination,
        114

Seaweed soup
as blood cleanser, 112
for breast-milk production, 115
Selenium, food sources of, 123
Serving sizes of food, 143
Sex, to prevent gout, 127
Shampoo as dish detergent, 3. *See also* Hair
Shaving, 164–165
Shoe Museum, Bata, 172
Shoes and boots, 172
Shortening, 60
Shrimp. *See* Seafood
Singing. *See also* Music
as energy booster, 124
to lift depression, 121
for stress relief, 139
Singing Cake, 75
Sinus problems, 136–137
Skin care. *See also* Face care; Foot care; Hand care
blemishes/stretch marks, 139
bumps remover, 149
elbows, dry, 149–150
sun damage, 140
Sleep. *See also* Insomnia
Smell, of food, effects of, 144. *See also* Odors, eliminating
Smoke alarms, in kitchen, 1–2
Smoking, and erectile dysfunction, 124
Sore throat, 137
Soup, 61
Sour cream, 61
Soy milk
to reduce hair growth on legs, 165
for strong nails, 161
Spaghetti, uncooked, as cake tester, 70
Spices, 61–62
Spinach, 62
Sponges, disinfecting, 3
Spray bottles, 62
Squash, 62
Stainless-steel
knives and spinach, 62
pot for cooking turnip, 66

pots, caring for, 12, 13
silverware and salad greens, 47
Stains
on china, 16
on countertops, 21
grease, on potholders and oven mitts, 19
on plastic containers, 22
Staph aureus, 126
Steak, cooking temperatures of, 64
Steel wool, tips for, 3
Sties, remedies for, 139–140
Stomachache (indigestion), 129–130, 135
Storage times for vegetables, 66
Stove or range, cleaning, 7
Strawberries, 62
Stress and anxiety, 137–139
Stuffing, 63
Substitutes. *See also* Fat substitutes
for aftershave, 165
for brown sugar, 63
for coffee (mochaccino), 142
for confectioners' sugar, 63
for cornstarch, 38
for deodorant, 150
for eggs, 42
for flour in baking, 43–44
homemade hairspray, 158
for lemon juice, 49
make-it-yourself cleaning products, 3
for measuring cup, 50
for milk, 51
for mothballs, 171
for nail file, 163
for oil in baked goods, 53
for onions, 54
for paper towels, 55
for shaving cream, 165
for shoe horn, 172
for shortening, 61
for soup thickeners, 61
for sour cream, 61
for toothpaste, 159–160

Sunscreen, 140
as hair moisturizer, 156
Supplements. *See also specific diseases or conditions*
B-complex, 113
magnesium for stress, 137
quercetin, 127
vitamin C for bruises, 116
vitamin E for cold sores, 118
vitamin E for cracked skin, 161
Sweet cream, 64
Swimsuit shopping, 171

T

Table decorations, 81–82. *See also* Holidays
Tacos, 64
Talking Timer, 23
Tapeworms, 131
Tea, 64
for bad breath, 160
cornsilk, to prevent impotence, 125
for gout, 126–127
green, for weight loss, 143
for migraines, 128
oolong, for eczema, 122
Teeth
bad breath, gum disease, toothache, 110–111
care of, 159–160
Purebrush Antibacterial Toothbrush Purifier, 147
vinegar on, 2
Temperatures, cooking, 64
Tension headaches. *See* Headache
Textured vegetable protein (TVP), 29
Thanksgiving Day, 96–99
Themes for parties, 89
Thermometers/cooking temperatures, 64
Thermos, cleaning, 21
Thickeners for soup, 61
Toaster, cleaning, 5
Tomatoes, 65
tomato sauce/paste, 65

Tongue burn, 140–141
Toothaches. *See* Teeth
Touchless Trashcan, 23
Travel, water when abroad, 131
T3 Tourmaline Featherweight
    Ionic Hair Dryer, 174
Tuna salad, 65
Turkey, 65–66
    cooking temperatures of,
      64–65
Turmeric
    for carpal tunnel syndrome,
      116
    for joint pain, 109
Turnips/turnip greens, 66

U

United States Department of
    Agriculture (USDA), 66
Urinary problems, 141
    bladder infection, remedies
      for, 111

V

Vacuum Wine Saver, 106
Valentine's Day, St., 92–93
Varicose vein treatment, 150
Vases, cleaning crystal, 15

Vegetables, storage times for, 66
Vinegar, apple cider
    as aftershave substitute, 165
    as deodorant substitute, 150
    for diarrhea, 122
    as hair thickener, 155
    for insomnia, 131
    for migraines, 128
    for oily hair, 156
    for pimples, 151–152
Vinegar, distilled white
    for bad breath, 160
    cautions about, 2
    for jellyfish stings, 132
    and painted plates, 66
Vitamins. *See* Supplements
Vodka, 88

W

Waffle iron, cleaning, 6
Walking for weight loss, 144
Walnuts, to lower cholesterol,
    118
Warts, 141–142
Watch scratch remover, 166–167
Water, 66
    for weight loss, 143

Watermelon, 66–67
Waxing, preventing redness after,
    165
Weight control, 142–146
    Innerscan Body Composition
      Monitor, 147
Whipped cream, 66
Wine, for parties, 84–86
Wine Server Crystal, 106
Witch hazel
    as aftershave substitute, 165
    for joint pain, 161
    for manicure, 163
    for varicose veins, 150
Women, reflexology for stress
    relief, 138
Wood salad bowls, washing, 19

Y

Yin and yang, 92
Yogurt, 34, 67
    as substitute for cream
      cheese, 34–35

Z

Zippers, 171
Zucchini, 67